PRAISE FOR *BLISS*

"Ashley's blog, Blissful Basil, won over both my heart and [...] done the same. As always, her recipes are filled with mouthwate[...] ingredients. But above all, they're infused with love and her firm belief in the power of wholesome, plant-based foods to promote happiness and well-being. With its stunning photography and enticing collection of recipes—ranging from online classics like the Spicy Cauliflower Rice, Roasted Sweet Potatoes + Avocado Mash power bowl to the all-new Cosmically Fudgy Cacao-Tahini Brownies—the *Blissful Basil* cookbook is bound to become a household staple for seasoned vegans, 'new' vegans, and non-vegans alike."

—Angela Liddon, *New York Times* bestselling author of *The Oh She Glows Cookbook*

"Ashley Melillo's *Blissful Basil* has it all: sumptuous, creative recipes; bold and beautiful photography; and plenty of user-friendly tips on how to easily transition into plant-centric cooking. What's most special about this collection, though, is the power of Ashley's personal narrative of healing through colorful, nourishing, and wholesome meals. These are the recipes that transformed Ashley's life, and her passion and gratitude shines through each and every bite."

—Gena Hamshaw, author of *Food52 Vegan* and *Choosing Raw*

"This is way more than a cookbook. It's a coming-of-age story . . . that happens to have really incredible recipes and beautiful food. Ashley is a true inspiration and her encouraging, nonjudgmental, and nurturing wisdom makes you feel like anything is possible."

—Jessica Murnane, author of *One Part Plant* and host of the One Part Podcast

"Ashley's *Blissful Basil* cookbook is beyond beautiful! Ashley is one of my all-time favorite bloggers and now authors because her recipes are always colorful, nourishing, and inspiring. I love that Ashley's cookbook contains loads of comfort food favorites like nachos and creamy soups, as well as creative plant-based classics like morning smoothies and chia bowls, beet balls, dairy-free cheese, and more. Along with her delicious recipes, she adds a beautiful piece of her soul to each project."

—Kathy Patalsky, blogger at HealthyHappyLife.com and cookbook author

"Ashley's photos are stunning and do an amazing job of showing off how gorgeous fresh plants are in their natural form. She brings life to food in a delicious and wholesome way. I'm pretty sure my life will be 200 percent improved once I make the Sweet Potato Cinnamon Rolls with Maple Glaze. This book is full of practical information about ingredients, techniques, and new ways of thinking about how and what we eat. It's a must for anyone looking to get more thoughtful with what's on their plate."

—Emily von Euw, creator of the food blog This Rawsome Vegan Life and bestselling author of *Rawsome Vegan Baking*

BLISSFUL BASIL

OVER 100 PLANT-POWERED RECIPES TO
UNEARTH VIBRANCY, HEALTH & HAPPINESS

ASHLEY MELILLO

BenBella Books, Inc.
Dallas, TX

BenBella

BenBella Books, Inc.
10440 N Central Expy Ste 800
Dallas, TX 75231
www.benbellabooks.com
Send feedback to feedback@benbellabooks.com

Printed in the United States of America
10 9 8 7 6 5 4 3 2 1

Library of Congress Cataloging-in-Publication Data
Names: Melillo, Ashley.
Title: Blissful basil : over 100 plant-powered recipes to unearth vibrancy,
    health, and happiness / Ashley Melillo.
Description: Dallas, TX : BenBella Books, Inc., [2016] | Includes
    bibliographical references and index.
Identifiers: LCCN 2016019973 (print) | LCCN 2016024549 (ebook) | ISBN
    9781942952459 (paperback) | ISBN 9781942952466 (electronic)
Subjects: LCSH: Vegan cooking. | Cooking (Vegetables) | BISAC: COOKING /
    Vegetarian & Vegan. | LCGFT: Cookbooks.
Classification: LCC TX837 .M516 2016 (print) | LCC TX837 (ebook) | DDC
    641.5/636—dc23
LC record available at https://lccn.loc.gov/2016019973

Editing by Maria Hart
Copyediting by Karen Levy
Proofreading by Brittney Martinez and Laura Cherkas
Indexing by WordCo Indexing Services, Inc.
Text design and composition by Aaron Edmiston
Cover design by Sarah Dombrowsky

Logo artwork by Leslie Vega Design, LLC
Food photography by Ashley Melillo
Lifestyle photography on back cover and pages 2, 8, and
    16 by Sprung Photo
Printed by Versa Press

Distributed by Perseus Distribution
www.perseusdistribution.com

To place orders through Perseus Distribution:
Tel: (800) 343-4499
Fax: (800) 351-5073
E-mail: orderentry@perseusbooks.com

Special discounts for bulk sales (minimum of 25 copies) are available.
Please contact Aida Herrera at aida@benbellabooks.com.

This book is for everyone.
But naming every person would be quite the task,
so I'll name just one…

DAN

Thank you for reminding me to be brave,
opening my heart to the adventures I was once afraid of,
and unconditionally sharing your optimistic warmth.
You are my love, my teacher, and my daily source of laughter.
Olive juice.

CONTENTS

INTRODUCTION
Rooted Habits

One humid summer evening in 2010, I started a food blog on a whim. I was in graduate school at the time and figured it would be a fun hobby during a leisurely summer semester. Well, it's been six years since I shared that first post, and I think it's safe to say that blogging turned out to be much more than a steamy summer fling. It has been one of the most joyful, worthwhile, and transformative endeavors of my life.

Over the years, Blissful Basil has been a place for me to share not only recipes, but also life stories. And I've shared lots of them. Some of the stories have been happy, some have been sad, and some have even been funny—like the time I lost a shoe during a job interview. But there's a story I haven't shared, and it's probably the most important one to tell because it's shaped everything from the way I think to the foods I eat. It wasn't always peace, self-love, and kale salads up in here.

THE UNTOLD STORY

To build a sturdy, unshakable house, you must first build a sturdy, unshakable foundation. That concrete foundation might not be the most glamorous or appealing part of the house, or the part you want to show off at a dinner party, but without it, every other part would eventually crumble. You could create a facade of beauty and strength by bracing the house's roof with steel beams, lining its walls with slabs of stone and its floors with polished marble, and filling its rooms with high-tech gadgets, but it would always be weakened by the instability of the ground beneath it.

In my late teens and early twenties, I gave great care and attention tending to my facade. I honestly and wholeheartedly believed I could guarantee my happiness by looking a certain way, studying my way to a well-respected career as a psychologist, and presenting myself as someone who had it all together. I took so much care in hiding my insecurities from others that I managed to hide them from myself, too. As someone who is a rule-follower to a fault, I was careful not to look too deeply into myself for fear that I would then be obligated to see my truth: I was anxiety-ridden and cared more about what other people thought of me than I cared about myself.

These internal battles weren't newly formed—I had encountered them time and time again as a child—but over the years, I learned how to avoid them. When our paths crossed in everyday life, I turned the other direction and ran as fast as I could, or I strutted right past them, hands shielding my eyes, as if they didn't exist.

I would probably still be running today if my anxiety hadn't been such a relentless jerk during my early twenties. It was a shape-shifter of sorts—changing forms and disguising itself under a variety of pseudonyms and maladies, yet always presenting with the same all-consuming, life-swallowing quality. By the time I was twenty-one, anxiety gave up on casually crossing my path and began jumping out in front of me, chasing me down, and clinging to my back.

Once I could no longer ignore my anxiety, I made the mistake of indulging it by believing its every word, giving it far more power than it should ever be given. If you've experienced debilitating anxiety, then you know that the moment you stop questioning its sanity, it runs frantically through your memories and current experiences posing "what if" questions and hypothetical catastrophes. Innocent moments become stomach-dropping roller coasters and heart-pounding nightmares. And the second you find a glimmer of peace within the welcoming arms of a distraction, anxiety pops in to scream hello, violently gathering your hair within its viselike grip to drag you back.

I had found coping methods (read: distractions) to coexist with a moderate amount of anxiety; however, during the winter of my senior year of college, when the days grew shorter, my anxiety multiplied tenfold (hellooo, seasonal affective disorder). As the hours of sunlight dwindled, anxiety swept in and held its longest and darkest reign over me. I gave up on my applications for graduate school, because I had neither the energy nor the motivation to complete them. To be honest, I stopped caring about the idea altogether. My mind was so consumed with worry that there was little room for anything else.

I worried tirelessly about my health and the health of loved ones and literally spent *hours* each day conducting Internet research on behalf of my fears. Perhaps my relentless foe, Anxiety, thought she needed to write a senior thesis paper to graduate, too. If so, her opening statement was something along the lines of "It's 99.99 percent likely that you will contract every rare, terrifying, and debilitating disease all at once. But don't worry, the Mayan calendar ends in December of 2012, at which time a meteor will probably crash through the sky and squish you before you die from any of these illnesses." Wow! Thanks for that breath of fresh air, Anxiety. I think I'll just curl up in my room and nap the rest of my days away.

I wish I could say that was the experience that pushed me to peel back that facade and look a little deeper, but once my anxiety relented in the spring, I tried my best to pretend those months of merciless worrying never happened. I graduated from college in May of 2006, moved back home, and began interviewing for jobs, knowing that I would eventually find my way to graduate school. In September, I took an administrative position at an investment firm in the financial district of Chicago while continuing to foster my love for psychology through volunteer work at a 24-hour crisis hotline. Everything was falling back into place.

Until November—oh, November—the place where Anxiety awaited my return, ready to ambush me. Like clockwork, anxiety crept in as the daylight dwindled, and I didn't have the strength or the courage to fend it off. So there I went again, trading every present moment I had for worries and perpetual fear about the future.

By this time, my worries were manifesting as somatic symptoms. I had developed sharp, shooting stomach pain that I was certain indicated the presence of a life-threatening disease, and my symptoms were just alarming enough that my doctor referred me for an ultrasound in an effort to rule out anything malicious.

The ultrasound turned out to be jet fuel for my anxiety. It identified something that was either a cyst, a tumor, or a severe case of trapped air (i.e., gas). The logical part of my mind held on to hope that it was the latter of the three. But rest assured, Dr. Anxiety reinterpreted the results for me so that I could clearly comprehend them: "I have good news and I have bad news. The bad news is that you're going to die. The good news is that I'll be right here with you until the very end, and I'll be sure to alert you of any and all potential threats." Great.

To pinpoint which of the three issues it was, my doctor suggested I go through more testing. Well, another ultrasound and a CT scan later, the doctors had concluded that the only malicious thing looming in my intestines was an alarming amount of trapped gas. The treatment? Let it go. Literally. Given the ridiculousness of it all, there was nothing I could do at that point except nervously laugh and feel grateful for my health. As for Anxiety? She must have realized what a fool she made of herself after setting off the alarms over a case of hot air, because she retreated without a moment's notice.

A (SEEMINGLY) FRESH START

The following spring, I moved into a charming apartment in the city of Chicago with my best friend, Sally. It was a fresh and exciting time, and just one month later, two of the most special beings came into my life within five days of one another: my husband, Dan, and our sweet orange tabby cat, Jack. I adopted Jack on May 28, 2007, and I met Dan on June 1. Within just a few months, Dan and I were spending as many moments together as we could (many of them with Jack, too). We traveled back and forth between Milwaukee, where he was living at that time, and Chicago. It was the happiest, most blissful time of my life, and I couldn't imagine anything taking that joy away from me.

Until November. One night as I was riding the bus home from work, a sense of impending doom struck me. It came out of nowhere, and I've never hated anything as much as that feeling because it colored my bright, sunshiny yellow happiness in gloomy gray and blue. Perpetual worry took hold and shaded my weeks in fear. I waited in darkness for the light of those weekends with Dan, because his positive spirit and witty humor lifted the weight off my heart. I hid my anxiety from him and made sure that my happy facade was tightly adhered whenever I was in his presence, never wanting to dampen his bright spirit with my worries.

My memories from November and December of 2007 have a stark contrast to them: those with Dan were happy and bright; those without him were lonely and cast in deeply shadowed anxiety. On the morning of December 8, I hugged him good-bye before he boarded a plane for a two-week trip to Europe. My stomach sank as my happiness walked away from me and anxiety's cold fingers grasped my shoulders once again.

With Dan away, there was nothing to stop Anxiety from staring me straight in the face, and I realized that asking someone else to be my sole source of peace and happiness was far too great a request. I needed to build and sustain my own happiness and peace. Ironically, pushing Anxiety away was exactly what had fueled its power, and by pretending it didn't exist, I had allowed it to become the driving force in my life. It dictated my thoughts, my emotions, my actions, and even the way I felt physically. As terrified as I was to admit it, I knew that the only way around my anxiety was to take it by the hand and walk right through it.

Exactly one week after Dan departed, I tearfully plopped down on the stereotypical couch in my newfound therapist's office and took the first of many steps on my journey to self-acceptance, self-love, and sustainable joy. Looking back, the decision to go to therapy was a life-changing pivot point, because it was the first time I turned to face anxiety head-on. And although the weekly sessions I attended over the next six months offered me a safe space to acquire a few powerful coping strategies, it was actually the small but consistent shifts I made in my everyday habits that led to the real magic.

SHIFTING HABITS: ADOPTING EXERCISE

With hindsight on my side, I recognized a pattern: the longest periods of reprieve from those intense bouts of anxiety coincided with the times in my life when I was regularly exercising. Between small bits of information from undergrad psychology classes and my anxiety-refined Google research skills, I was able to piece together a basic understanding of the relationship between cardiovascular exercise and mental health. What I uncovered was enough to convince me to get moving, and I started exercising four to six days a week to offer my brain a natural boost of mood-balancing neurotransmitters (i.e., serotonin, dopamine, and norepinephrine).

It wasn't easy to muster the motivation to get moving at first, but once I built up a bit of momentum, this newfound habit took hold as a foundational component in my weekly routine. Even better, when November rolled around and Anxiety politely knocked on my door to say hello, I was able to welcome it with patience and understanding while kindly informing it that I would no longer be handing it the master key to my thoughts and emotions.

In the years that immediately followed, regular exercise continued to stave off those massive, debilitating bouts of winter anxiety, but it, alone, wasn't enough to counteract the pesky, doubt-spawning undercurrent of fear I experienced day in and day out. And it became more and more evident that the foundation beneath my feet still needed tending to.

THE SUM OF SMALL CHOICES

I had made good choices when it came to physical activity, but now it was time to enter the next phase of self-care. I started paying even more attention to how the seemingly small choices I made on a regular basis gathered together to form something powerful, either supporting or undermining my ability to thrive physically, cognitively, and emotionally. When I felt emotionally chaotic, physically drained, and cognitively foggy, I made note of the things I'd done that derailed me. When I felt emotionally at peace, physically vibrant, and cognitively sharp, I made note of the choices that kept things on the upswing.

During a two-week trip to Ireland in 2010, I made the decision to go vegetarian after an experience there confirmed that my love for animals had officially reached a point where it far outweighed my desire to eat meat. Although the choice was motivated by compassion, just a few months into the transition I noticed physical and emotional benefits that extended far beyond the sense of peace I felt from an ethical standpoint. Over the next three years, it became more and more apparent that what I ate affected not only how I felt physically but also how I felt emotionally, for better or worse. With meat removed, there was more room to fill my plate with a rainbow of fruits and veggies, greens, legumes, and whole grains. As a self-proclaimed cheese fanatic, I also filled that meatless space with cheese pizza, veggie lasagna, and more. But one thing became clear to me: as my ratio of plant-based foods to animal-based foods increased, that undercurrent of anxiety began to fade.

Like many vegetarians, I consistently sang the I-Could-Never-Go-Vegan song (Because-I-Love-Cheese-Too-Much remix). Cheese had become a staple in my diet, and I couldn't imagine life without it. But in the spring of 2013, I took an interest in making vegan dishes and even shared a few of the recipes on my blog. The strange thing? I didn't really miss the cheese in those meals. I even dropped the naysayer attitude and considered the possibility that maybe, someday, I could and *would* go vegan. From an ethical standpoint, I was drawn to the lifestyle, but I wasn't quite ready to make the jump at that point. I did, however, make a concerted effort to reduce the amount of dairy I was consuming.

About six months later and seemingly out of nowhere, I developed a nagging stomach pain that was keeping me awake at night. At first, I dismissed the pain as a by-product of work-related stress, but after a month of sleepless nights and digestive issues, I realized there was probably more to it. Dan suggested dairy might be the problem (he faced similar issues before finding out he was lactose-intolerant), and by that point, I was willing to consider it. About a week later, I dove straw-first into a three-day juice cleanse in hopes of resetting my system and pinpointing the root of my digestion woes. I slept like a baby all three nights and, aside from a few detox symptoms, felt the best I had in months. I maintained a vegan diet for the week that followed and continued to feel great, but as soon as I reacquainted myself with cheese, my stomach protested. One sleepless night and a teary viewing of the trailer for *Earthlings* later, I vowed to move in the direction of a plant-based lifestyle.

Over the course of the six months that followed, I ate vegan 95 percent of the time. I immediately gave up all dairy and was pleasantly surprised to find gooey, delicious plant-based alternatives. By the time March of 2014 rolled around, the only thing that stood between me and a vegan diet was an egg or two per week (even my blog had gone vegan by that point). And on March 20, 2014, I officially took the plunge.

After making the shift, I expected to feel ethically at peace, and I knew my digestion would thank me, but I didn't anticipate the slew of other emotional, cognitive, and physical benefits that I would experience from following a fully plant-based diet, benefits far greater than the ones I experienced after becoming vegetarian. I learned to differentiate between the foods that allowed me to thrive (i.e., whole, vibrant, minimally processed foods) and the foods that left me feeling less than optimal (i.e., processed meat substitutes, gluten, refined sugar). I ate more of the foods that enhanced my well-being and less of the foods that dissolved it. But I also left plenty of room for the gray in between, because I promised myself I would never strive for pristine perfection or get into the habit of labeling foods as inherently bad or good.

As time unfolded, I discovered that my body didn't just *function* on plants—it *thrived* on plants. My energy and motivation increased, my skin glowed, my hair shined, my thoughts cleared, and my heart opened to possibility. That undercurrent of anxiety softened further, and in its wake, a sense of peace, calm, and hopefulness reverberated within me. And it proved, without question, that the small choices I made day in and day out gathered together over time to affect my entire state of being.

It's taken nearly a decade and more ups and downs than I can summarize within these pages, but I've finally learned to greet anxiety with gratitude, because it is not my enemy but my teacher. And it's taught me one of the greatest lessons of all: When faced with a problem, you can choose to avoid it, you can walk around it, and you can pretend it doesn't exist, but you will repeatedly run into its pain until you open your heart to its purpose.

Before anxiety knocked a bit of wisdom into me, I operated on the premise that it was possible to chase down happiness in external circumstances and outrun fear. But all that chasing and running left me gasping, breathlessly, amid thin air. And then I realized something: Happiness doesn't happen to us. It's not guaranteed simply because our circumstances manifest as we had hoped, and it's not inaccessible when our circumstances fall short. And there isn't a meal, a dessert, a drink, a pill, a diet, a lifestyle, a body, an outfit, a house, a paycheck, a career, or a person that's going to offer it up on an infinity platter.

There wasn't one surefire "cure" to make me happier or less anxious. Rather, the solution has been an ongoing, ever-evolving process. Each of the shifts I've made within my everyday choices and habits—facing my fears; regularly moving my body; swapping meat, dairy, and processed foods for a vibrant rainbow of whole foods—has played an equally important role in fostering my well-being. And it's been the consistency of choosing those things over and over again (even when it's difficult) that's allowed me to maintain it. Do I feel happier now than I did all those years ago? Absolutely. But far more importantly, I feel whole.

The habits that worked for me aren't necessarily the habits that will work for everyone. In fact, forget about what works for me or even for most people; this is about what works for *you*. Identify the things that allow *you* to thrive and honor yourself by choosing those things more consistently.

As Aristotle wrote, "We are what we repeatedly do. Excellence, then, is not an act, but a habit." By consistently choosing the habits that nurture our ability to build a solid foundation from within, we cultivate a sense of wholeness and draw more joyfulness, serenity, and resilience into our state of being. And we position ourselves in such a way that when life *does* shake us to the core, we can step fully into the experience, bearing its weight, without the fear of it crushing us.

THE POWER OF ONE CHOICE

If we view our present experience as the sum of a collection of countless small decisions, it becomes clear that every choice matters and that each passing moment offers us the opportunity to nudge ourselves toward our optimal path. To yield a more peaceful existence, start with just one choice that votes in favor of a vibrant, thriving you. And if you root that choice in healthy soil and water it with consistency, it just might flourish into a life-changing habit.

With this in mind, I invite you to join me, one meal at a time, on this plant-powerful journey. Start small. Use a determined mind to guide your first choice and allow intuition to unfold the path that follows, eating with the rhythm of your body, heart, and mind.

A BLISSFUL KITCHEN
Pantry Roots + Essential Equipment

How does that saying go? Fail to plan, plan to fail. It feels a bit dramatic in this instance, so let's modify it. Plan to prepare, prepare to conquer. As in, "prepare to conquer these recipes."

It took me several months to transform my pantry to align with a plant-based lifestyle; however, once I got a handle on the staples, cooking and shopping became a breeze. I'm not talking about the lightest, airiest, and most wonderful breeze, but a nice breeze nonetheless. My number one tip is to **form habits around grocery shopping**; shop on the same day, around the same time, and at the same store(s) every week.

Prior to developing a few handy habits, I found grocery shopping to be an arduous task. However, about three years ago, I started shopping on my way home from work every Friday afternoon, and over the years, it's become something I look forward to. Undesirable tasks always feel a bit more palatable near the end of the week, don't they? If you can relate, try shopping on Thursday or Friday and see if that end-of-the-week excitement allows you and your cart to sail through those aisles with a smile on your face.

As you flip through the next several pages, you'll find a list of the staples I keep on hand. I've also outlined some nutritional perks as well as tips for finding a few of the more elusive items (see the "Where to Find It" sections below for recommended sources).

GRAINS + GRAINLIKE SEEDS

Raw Buckwheat Groats | Despite the glutenous-sounding name, buckwheat groats don't contain wheat or gluten. In fact, they're technically not even a grain but a seed. Fool me once, shame on you. Fool me twice, shame on me. Unless of course you're buck-wheat, because then you'd be named in a manner that fools time and time again. These heart-shaped, pale green and white seeds belong to a plant in the rhubarb family, and they're nutritionally powerful and versatile. They can be ground into a flour, cooked whole as a base for Buckwheat Breakfast Risotto (page 50), or toasted up alongside oats and other goodies in a batch of SuperSeeded Oatmeal-Raisin Granola Clusters (page 35). Nutritionally, buckwheat is hard to beat. It's considered to be a potent cholesterol-lowering food thanks to its dense phytonutrient content (well, hello there, lignans). It's also been known to lower blood glucose and insulin responses and has even been found to have preventive properties to protect against breast and other hormone-dependent cancers.

Where to Find It | *Raw buckwheat groats are often sold in bulk at specialty markets (e.g., Whole Foods) and can also be found in prepackaged bags (e.g., Bob's Red Mill) at many conventional grocery stores.*

Old-Fashioned Rolled Oats | Affordable and natural, old-fashioned rolled oats are a whole grain to be reckoned with. They make a tasty, fiber-packed base in my Soft + Chewy Trail Mix Cookies (page 101) and a delectable outer crust for my Crispy Cauliflower Tacos (page 175). Oats are naturally gluten-free but are susceptible to cross-contamination during packaging; thus, if you have a gluten allergy, be sure to purchase certified gluten-free oats just to be on the safe side.

Brown Rice | If I had to pick one grain to eat for the rest of my days, it would be brown rice. I love its mild, nutty flavor and the hearty vibe it lends, transforming light dishes into satisfying meals. It offers high levels of manganese, selenium, phosphorous, and magnesium, and unlike white rice, brown rice has intact bran, germ, and aleurone layers. To make white rice, those three layers are stripped and polished, washing away most of the grain's nutrients along with its beige-colored clothes. White rice might look prettier, but it pales in comparison to brown rice's nutty nutri-tional goodness. Give it a whirl in one of my all-time favorites: the Flourishing Fiesta power bowl on page 165.

Black Rice | Black rice has a rich, nutty flavor, and there is something so crazily satisfying about it. It's hailed as a cancer-fighting superfood because of its high anthocyanin antioxidant content, and it's rich in vitamin E and fiber. I prefer the short-grain variety, because it cooks up with a wonderful sticky quality, but feel free to use long-grain if you prefer it. Nestle it into a power bowl alongside the Spicy Chile-Garlic Eggplant on page 163.

Lentils | Give me all the colors and types of lentils—red, green, brown, French green, beluga, Puy, and so many more—I don't discriminate. During my vegetarian days, I often overlooked lentils as round, confetti-like split pea knockoffs. But let me tell you, I certainly don't overlook them now; I love these small, mighty, and protein-packed legumes. If you haven't hopped on the lentil train yet, you'd best jump on now, because good things are happening.

One cup of cooked lentils offers 18 grams of protein, and when you pair that with the fact that they're a good source of cholesterol-lowering, blood-sugar-stabilizing fiber, they become all the more enticing. Lentils are also rich in molybdenum, folate, copper, phosphorus, manganese, iron, vitamin B_1, and vitamin B_6. I'm particularly fond of green lentils, because they are incredibly versatile and can be used in everything from salads to veggie burgers. Give them a try in the Mushroom-Lentil Sliders with Herbed Hemp Aioli on page 183.

Quinoa | Like buckwheat groats, quinoa is a trickster of sorts. It looks like a grain, behaves like a grain, and tastes like a grain; however, it's a seed at heart. Harvested from the goosefoot plant, quinoa is more closely related to spinach and beets than it is to cereals and grains. It has a higher fat content than cereal grains, such as wheat, and offers a boost of heart-healthy monounsaturated fat. Despite its slightly higher fat content, quinoa isn't susceptible to rapid oxidation; thus, boiling, simmering, and steaming won't significantly compromise the quality of its omega-3 fatty acids. Who says omega-3s only come from fish oil? Try this little seed on for size in the Pretty in Pink Quinoa Confetti Salad found on page 145.

Sorghum | Sorghum, one of the oldest of all ancient grains, is a staple in African and Indian cuisines and is considered to be one of the most important cereal grains grown in the world. It's a slightly chewy, mild-flavored, and affordable grain that's gluten-free to boot. Although well known in the Midwest to Southern regions of the United States, sorghum is still gaining its footing in other areas. But I have a sneaking suspicion it will eventually advance to gluten-free grain/seed royalty along with quinoa and brown rice. Sorghum is wonderful in salads, because it doesn't clump together like so many other grains do. Give it a go in the Sorghum + Heirloom Cherry Tomato Salad with Basil Vinaigrette (page 146).

Where to Find It | *Sorghum can be found in prepackaged bags (e.g., Bob's Red Mill) at many specialty markets (e.g., Whole Foods) as well as some conventional grocery stores.*

Millet | Millet looks an awful lot like birdseed, because it *is* birdseed—or at least the primary ingredient in it. But it isn't just for the birds. This smaller version of the illustrious sorghum is a good source of copper, manganese, phosphorus, and magnesium. Magnesium acts as a cofactor for hundreds of enzymes, including those associated with the body's use of glucose and insulin secretion, as well as reducing the risk of heart disease and certain cancers. Research suggests that regular consumption of magnesium-rich foods, such as whole grains like millet, reduces the risk of type 2 diabetes. This naturally gluten-free grain makes a fantastic substitute for couscous, and its mild, nutty flavor is a perfect addition to salads—try it in my Mediterranean Millet with Lemony Hummus power bowl (page 159).

Where to Find It | *Millet can be found in prepackaged bags (e.g., Bob's Red Mill) at many specialty markets (e.g., Whole Foods) as well as some conventional grocery stores.*

ALL THINGS COCONUT

Virgin Coconut Oil | Not all saturated fats are created equal, and the type of saturated fat found in coconuts (i.e., medium-chain triglycerides) moves directly to the liver, where it's converted into fuel (i.e., ketones), making it readily available to our bodies rather than being stored away as fat. Ketones, in particular, have been shown to promote neural connections, enhance memory, and increase cognitive efficiency. While I'm not advocating you heap spoonfuls straight into your mouth, if you're going to incorporate saturated fat into your diet, make it count for something. Just be sure to stick with virgin coconut oil, as some refined varieties contain trans fats. I don't believe in demonizing foods, but I'll bend my beliefs for trans fats.

Coconut Butter | Coconut butter is made by grinding the meat of a coconut into a creamy white butter. At room temperature, it's in a solid state; however, it can be warmed to create a smooth, creamy liquid. Health food stores often carry it, but it can be quite pricey and tricky to locate—I once paid upward of $14 for just 16 ounces. *Yowza.* However, you can save those pretty pennies, because making coconut butter at home is easy and costs just a few dollars. All you need is a bag of unsweetened shredded coconut and a food processor with a bit of endurance. See the recipe for Homemade Coconut Butter on page 299 for tips and tricks.

Full-Fat Coconut Milk | Full-fat coconut milk is typically sold in 14-ounce cans and can be found in most grocery stores. Although many brands offer a "lite" variation, it doesn't firm up or set the way that full-fat coconut milk does, so be sure to double-check your labels and purchase the full-fat variety. Otherwise, your Coconut Whipped Cream (page 308) and other treats will fall flat (quite literally). At room temperature, canned coconut milk is typically in a creamy liquid state; however, with an overnight chill in the refrigerator, the coconut cream and coconut water separate from one another, leaving a thick, scoopable cream at the surface of the can. That's where the magic happens, which is why recipes will typically call for chilling the can before opening.

Raw Cacao Powder | Cacao powder is the raw, unprocessed form of cocoa powder. It has more vitamins, minerals, fiber, and healthy fats than cocoa powder does, and it has a richer, deeper chocolate flavor as well. All that goodness does come at a cost though, and cacao powder usually has a steeper price tag than cocoa powder. However, if you substitute cocoa powder for cacao powder, you'll need twice the amount to achieve the same rich, chocolaty flavor, so the difference in cost is essentially nullified when all is said and done. But the difference in nutrients? Well, cacao powder easily takes the (chocolate) cake.

Where to Find It | *Cacao powder can be found at specialty markets (e.g., Whole Foods) as well as some conventional grocery stores. Larger, 16-ounce packets can also be found online (www.amazon .com) and typically cost even less than an 8-ounce store-bought packet.*

Cacao (or Cocoa) Butter | Cacao butter, also referred to as cocoa butter, is a pure, crushed butter from the cacao (i.e., chocolate) bean. It's a necessary component in both white and dark chocolate as it sets the chocolate and gives it that rich, melt-in-your-mouth texture. Many specialty markets carry it (e.g., Whole Foods), but I prefer to purchase it online because it's typically a fraction of the price. Also, a little goes a long way, so it's a worthy investment if you want some homemade chocolate in your life. However, if this is all feeling a bit fussy, don't sweat it. For most recipes that call for cacao butter, I've included a practical, ready-made alternative.

Where to Find It | *Cacao butter is far more affordable online (www.amazon.com). I typically stock up by purchasing a 16-ounce bag, which lasts me anywhere from six months to a year (depending on how many times I make the* Cosmically Fudgy Cacao-Tahini Brownies *on page 251).*

Cacao Nibs | Cacao nibs are simply raw cacao beans that have been chopped up into bits. Think of them as Mother Nature's chocolate chips. They're unsweetened and free from added fat, so they have a bitter bite to them that's often an acquired taste. Cacao nibs are packed with antioxidants and offer a lovely crunch when sprinkled over Double-Chocolate Cherry Chunk Ice Cream (page 266). They also make an excellent substitute for chocolate chips in the Raw Cannoli Bars on page 257.

GO NUTS + GET SEEDY

Raw Cashews | These subtly sweet, mild-flavored nuts are ***always*** tucked away in my pantry. They can be blended with filtered water to create a plant-based alternative to heavy cream, or processed with Medjool dates and other goodies to form the filling in my Raw Cannoli Bars (page

257). My absolute favorite way to transform cashews is to blend them with a bit of filtered water, nutritional yeast, apple cider vinegar, arrowroot (a thickening agent), and sea salt and heat the mixture until it becomes thick and stretchy Cashew Mozzarella Cheese (page 305). With the addition of a few other ingredients, that gooey mozzarella can be transformed into cheddar and even Swiss cheese. Pretty snazzy, huh? If you're allergic to nuts, don't worry one bit—most recipes that call for cashews can be made with shelled hemp seeds, and I've included substitution notes whenever possible.

Raw Walnuts | Given my background in psychology, I'm a sucker for foods that offer a cognitive boost, and raw walnuts are fantastic brain food thanks to their omega-3 content. Plus, they look like little brains, which makes this nugget of information easy to remember. Walnuts have a hearty, almost meaty texture when chopped or pulsed into bits, making them perfect for meatless remixes of classically meat-heavy dishes such as my Baked Mostaccioli with Walnut Bolognese + Cashew Mozzarella (page 219) and Easy Does It Sunday Evening Chili (page 243).

Raw Almonds, Brazil Nuts, Hazelnuts, Pecans | This nutty quartet contains four more of my favorite nuts. I prefer to purchase raw nuts, because they're more versatile—they can be left raw, roasted, toasted, or soaked to make anything from smoothies to raw desserts. Almonds lend a comforting heartiness to snacks, such as the Cinnamon-Almond Granola Bar(k) on page 94. And if you're looking for a Nutella-like combination, flip to page 80 and whip up my Double-Chocolate Hazelnut Espresso Smoothie!

Shelled Hemp Seeds | Hemp seeds are a fantastic source of protein, containing a digestible balance of essential amino acids. They also have an omega-6 to omega-3 ratio of 3.38:1, which is right in line with what's considered optimal. They can be sprinkled over salads, crisped up in granola, and strewn throughout my Energizing Triple-Seed Morning Pudding with Berry Compote (page 41). My absolute favorite way to enjoy them is in creamy, nutrient-dense sauces and dressings. Be sure to try the Mushroom-Lentil Sliders with Herbed Hemp Aioli on page 183 for a taste of the good stuff.

Where to Find It | *Hemp seeds can be purchased in bulk or prepackaged bags at many specialty stores (e.g., Whole Foods). My absolute favorite are Manitoba Harvest's Organic Hemp Hearts. They blend up super creamy and offer a milder, more appealing flavor than any other brand I've tried.*

Pepitas (Raw Shelled Pumpkin Seeds) | I've been known to sprinkle pepitas on almost anything. From smoothies to chia puddings to salads and back again, there are few dishes a dash of pepitas doesn't do good. They're rich in manganese, phosphorous, and magnesium, and they offer a diverse array of antioxidants. Give them a whirl in the SuperSeed Pesto on page 297.

Raw Shelled Sunflower Seeds | Raw shelled sunflower seeds have become a favorite of mine over the past couple of years. They're one of the most affordable and versatile seeds: you can toss them into salads, add them to Soft + Chewy Trail Mix Cookies (page 101), or grind them into a flour to make Power Biscotti (page 91). Sunflower seeds are rich in vitamin E and copper and have a mild earthiness when enjoyed raw. When roasted, they have a rich nutty flavor that makes them an excellent substitute for peanuts.

Chia Seeds | Chia seeds are great for much more than sprouting "fur" on the backs of terra-cotta animal figurines—Ch-Ch-Ch-Chia! These crunchy little seeds work some detoxifying magic in our digestive tracts. When they come into contact with liquid, chia seeds take on a gelatinous quality that allows them to grab hold of long-forgotten toxins in our intestines and politely escort them out of our bodies. They can be sprinkled over smoothies, tossed into granola, or used to thicken a big batch of Get Glowing Strawberry-Mango Chia Pudding (page 49).

Flaxseeds and Flaxseed Meal | Flaxseeds offer a generous amount of omega-3 fatty acids. Why is this important? Modern diets tend to be devoid of omega-3 and far too rich in omega-6. And why does this matter? Omega-3 and omega-6 battle one another for the same conversion enzymes in our body, and omega-6 is almost always winning because we consume too much of it. Although the optimal ratio of omega-6 to omega-3 consumption is anything under 4:1, most Americans consume a ratio ranging from 25:1–50:1. The problem? Omega-6 is pro-inflammatory, whereas omega-3 is neutral and ultimately helps reduce inflammation in our bodies. When our omega-6–omega-3 ratio is out of whack, our bodies have an increased risk of developing inflammatory diseases like cardiovascular disease, arthritis, asthma, cancer, and even depression. These affordable little seeds can be purchased in whole or ground form. Ground flaxseed (i.e., flaxseed meal) is essential to vegan baking, because it can be mixed with water to create an egg-like binder.

Nut and Seed Butters: Almond Butter, Peanut Butter, Sunflower Butter | These are the three nut and seed butters I use most often in life and in this book. I recommend purchasing natural, unsweetened nut and seed butters because they're less likely to have funny additives or palm oil. If you're feeling extra fancy, make your own by putting a few handfuls of roasted nuts or seeds in your food processor and processing for 4–12 minutes, or until smooth.

Tahini | Tahini, or sesame seed paste, is a savory, subtly sweet, and slightly bitter seed butter that offers a nice boost of calcium. It makes a wonderful base for creamy dressings and can even be used as a substitute for butter or oil in baked goods. You'll notice that certain recipes call for "runny" tahini, and although I wish there were a more technical term to describe it, we're just going to have to make do with "runny." I've found it's important to specify, because the texture of tahini can vary significantly between brands—some are thick and pastelike while others are glossy and pourable. There is a little bit of wiggle room with some recipes (e.g., dressings); however, when "runny tahini" is specified, be sure to use it, or the recipe results will be unpredictable at best. As a general observation, I've noticed that tahini in glass jars tends to be thick, whereas tahini in plastic tubs or containers tends to be runny and glossy. Whole Foods' 365 brand of tahini is a glossy, pourable dream, as is Cedars brand. They're also two of the most affordable options out there, so grab one of those if you can.

SWEETEN IT

Coconut Sugar (or Coconut Palm Sugar) | Coconut sugar, sometimes referred to as coconut palm sugar, is a raw, unprocessed sugar derived from the coconut palm tree. Most sugars have a glycemic index (GI) of over 50; however, coconut sugar is said to hover right around 35. This, coupled with the fact that it also contains good amounts of a dietary fiber called inulin, means that coconut sugar is less likely to spike blood sugar levels and can even improve glycemic control. It's also packed with vitamins and minerals, meaning it offers a lot more than taste and sugary vibes. Should you sustain yourself solely on the stuff? Probably not. However, we all need a little sweetness in our lives, and coconut sugar is a better option than most. Plus, it can typically be used as a 1:1 substitute for table sugar and sometimes even brown sugar, which is why it's my go-to sweetener for most desserts.

Grade B 100 Percent Pure Maple Syrup | Mrs. Butterworth can keep workin' those curves in the syrup aisle; however, I urge you to walk on past her and her corn syrup posse and reach for a bottle of the real stuff. Truth be told, up until a few years ago, I had no idea that there was a difference between "syrup" and pure maple syrup. I have a feeling my aunt and uncle from Vermont are shaking their heads as they read these words, but rest assured, I know better now. Pure maple syrup is just as it sounds; it's the pure syrup extracted from maple trees. It's divided into two grades: Grade A and Grade B. Although either option will get the job done, I recommend Grade B if you can get your hands on it. It has a richer flavor and a deeper amber color, and it boasts a higher mineral content than Grade A.

Medjool Dates | Medjool dates are a specific type of date known for their sticky, gooey properties. In raw dessert and snack recipes, they serve the dual purpose of sweetening and binding. I'm often asked if Medjool dates can be substituted with other types of dates, and typically they can't. On the off chance that you're able to find some exceptionally gooey standard dates, you could give it a try, but I recommend sticking with Medjool dates to ensure the best results.

Where to Find Them | *Medjool dates are often sold in bulk at specialty markets (e.g., Whole Foods) and can also be found in small tubs or containers in the produce section at many conventional grocery stores.*

Brown Rice Syrup | Brown rice syrup, also called rice malt syrup, is both a sweetener and a binder. It's incredibly thick and sticky—similar to molasses or honey—with a soft, mild flavor, and it lends the most lovely chewiness to the Peanut Butter Cookies on page 281.

Where to Find It | *Brown rice syrup can be a bit trickier to find than the above-mentioned sweeteners, so I typically purchase a jar online (www.amazon.com) rather than chasing it down in stores; however, it can often be found in specialty markets like Whole Foods.*

FLOUR IT

Oat Flour | Oat flour, how do I love thee? Let me count the ways. Theatrics aside, there's a lot to love about oat flour. First off, in a pinch, you can make homemade oat flour by giving a cup or two of old-fashioned rolled oats a 3- to 5-minute whirl around your food processor. Second, just like rolled oats, oat flour is naturally gluten-free. Just be sure to use oat flour that's certified gluten-free if you're intolerant or sensitive, because noncertified varieties run the risk of being cross-contaminated during packaging. Another reason to love it: it works magic in gluten-free baking. If you have any doubts, whip up a batch of the incredibly popular Peanut Butter Cookies on page 281 or the delectably savory Cheesy Garlic-Herb Oat Crackers on page 98. Other than the occasional use of spelt flour or blanched almond flour, oat flour is my go-to for baked goods. (*Tip*: When measuring oat flour, avoid packing or condensing it. Instead, gently scoop it into a measuring cup, shake off the excess, and use a metal spatula to level it off.)

Whole Spelt Flour | In the very rare case that a recipe in this book isn't gluten-free, it's because it contains whole spelt flour. The gluten in spelt is delicate and less elastic than the gluten found in more common gluten-containing flours (e.g., all-purpose or whole wheat). For this reason, it's often better tolerated by individuals with gluten sensitivities. (However, when in doubt, it's always best practice to check with your doctor.) Spelt's fragile gluten structure also means that it requires less kneading when used in breads and pastries, so be careful not to get knead-happy if you're making Simple Sweet Potato Cinnamon Rolls with Maple Glaze (page 55).

Where to Find It | *Spelt flour comes in both white spelt and whole spelt varieties, but the recipes in this book exclusively call for whole spelt flour. Most conventional grocery stores carry it, as do specialty*

markets like Whole Foods. I recommend Bob's Red Mill or Vita Spelt if you can find one or the other—
if you find both, lucky you! Spelt jackpot.

Blanched Almond Flour | Blanched almond flour is made by grinding blanched (i.e., skinned) almonds into flour. It's commonly used as the primary flour in Paleo baked goods; however, in this book, it's always used in conjunction with another flour to balance texture and density. Blanched almond flour is different than almond meal and the two cannot always be used interchangeably, so double-check which one you're purchasing and using for recipes. Be sure to have it on hand to whip up the Sweet Potato Pizza Crust (page 296) or Puffy Potato Pizza Crust (page 295) whenever a pizza craving strikes!

Coconut Flour | I feel like there should be a bright yellow WARNING symbol next to this one. Coconut flour has gained quite a bit of popularity in recent years, and it's a great addition to baked goods when used sparingly; however, take note: it cannot be used as a 1:1 substitute for other flours. If you've made this mistake in the past (my hand is raised), then you'll never make it again. But for those who haven't been subjected to eating a baked good formed solely from a coconut-flour base, let me explain: imagine taking a gulp of desert sand with a parched mouth. Coconut flour is highly absorbent—I'm talking spongelike absorbency—so using it as a 1:1 replacement for other flours results in the driest, crumbliest baked goods you'll ever encounter. Thus, it should always be used sparingly and in conjunction with another flour. A delicate sprinkle of the stuff goes a long way.

Arrowroot Starch/Flour/Powder | Arrowroot: Is it a starch, a flour, or a powder? Well, it turns out that's up to you and your grocery store to decide, because this thickening agent has more aliases than a secret service agent. I typically find it under the guise of a starch; however, I can vouch for its other identities, too. The most important thing to remember is that those three names identify the very same product, so purchase whichever one you find first. This root-derived thickening agent is most often used as a purer, cleaner alternative to cornstarch; however, it also works well as a binding agent in gluten-free baked goods. Although it has more up-front thickening power than cornstarch, arrowroot is delicate and prone to losing its ability to thicken if overheated. Observe its thickening magic in the Cashew // Hemp Seed Mozzarella Cheese on page 305.

Where to Find It | *Check the baking aisle of your grocery store. If you can't find it there, check the spice section, as it occasionally lingers among the spice jars. I use Bob's Red Mill's "Arrowroot Starch" because it's readily available in the stores I frequent; however, there are many wonderful brands out there, so keep your eyes peeled.*

Frozen Ripe Bananas | Let's talk about bananas for a second. I love them. Not only because they're delicious and capable of morphing into ice cream when frozen but also because they're one of the best mood-boosting foods out there thanks to their tryptophan and vitamin B_6 content. How do these two positively affect mood? Carbohydrates (e.g., sweet bananas) allow the brain to absorb tryptophan, and B_6 swoops in to help convert tryptophan into serotonin. There are few foods that I feel an instant energy and mood boost from, but bananas are one of them. I've been known to bound around the house and pop into obscure yoga poses after a late-night bowl of banana ice cream. Dan calls this "the banana high."

Another reason to be smitten with bananas: They're packed with bloat-busting potassium. Potassium and sodium take turns keeping each other balanced within our cells. However, because we have a tendency to shake the salt shaker like there's no tomorrow, the duty to regulate typically defaults to potassium. The next time you notice your body holding on to excess water weight, drink plenty of hydrating fluids and eat some bananas—the combination will flush the extra water right out of your system.

I always keep at least five ripe, peeled bananas tucked away in my freezer so that I can whip up smoothies and banana ice cream with only a moment's notice. Here are two things to keep in mind: First, make sure your bananas are very ripe and speckled before freezing. This ensures the sweetest flavor, makes them easier to digest, and allows them to blend up with the creamiest texture. Second, peel them *before* freezing or you'll need a chisel to chip away the frozen peel.

Unsweetened Almond Milk | You'll notice that recipes requiring milk call for "unsweetened almond milk." That being said, there is some flexibility here. With the exception of more intensely flavored plant-based milks (e.g., hemp milk), most other types (e.g., oat milk, cashew milk, etc.) can be used in place of almond milk. I've included recommendations for making nut-free swaps whenever applicable; just be sure to always opt for plain, unsweetened varieties.

Apple Cider Vinegar | Unlike most vinegars, apple cider vinegar (ACV) has an alkalizing effect in the body. Want proof? The next time you have heartburn or acid reflux, take a shot of organic ACV mixed with a small splash of filtered water. It'll burn going down and nearly make you toss your cookies, but within just a few minutes you'll experience a welcome reprieve from indigestion. Aside from the occasional use of balsamic vinegar or champagne vinegar, ACV is typically my go-to choice. If another vinegar (e.g., white wine vinegar) can be used in its place, you'll find it noted in the recipe, so feel free to substitute in those instances.

Tofu | I'm including tofu only so that I can mention that it's not my favorite ingredient. It's a great source of plant-based protein, so I'll typically have it a few times each month, but it's not a staple in my diet. When the craving strikes, I opt for sprouted tofu, because it's less processed and sup-posedly a bit easier to digest. I'll be honest—I can't really tell the difference, but I figure it can't hurt to lean toward a less processed option when given the choice. My favorite way to eat tofu? Spiced up and outfitted with all the fixings in my Southwest Tofu Scramble (page 60).

Nutritional Yeast | Nutritional yeast—aka "nooch" to those in the know—is an inactive form of yeast that offers an invaluable cheesy flavor to plant-based dishes. For recipes in this book, I exclusively call for nutritional yeast flakes; however, it also comes in a powdered form. Just be careful not to confuse it with brewer's yeast or you'll end up with a hot mess of something or other on your hands.

Many brands of nutritional yeast are fortified with vitamin B_{12}, which is useful for those who take the purely plant-powered path because it's vital for human health yet one of the only vitamins that runs a bit scarce in a vegan diet. Vitamin B_{12} is the by-product of bacteria, so meat and cheese eaters consume plenty of it because the animals these foods come from have B_{12}-emitting bacteria within their digestive tracts. Back in the day, the soil that fruits and veg-gies grew in was packed with B_{12}-emitting bacteria too, but modern farming practices tend to strip the soil, which means it's usually necessary for those following a vegan diet to supplement. I take a daily spritz of B_{12} and also incorporate B_{12}-fortified nutritional yeast into a few meals each week.

Where to Find It | *Nutritional yeast flakes can be purchased in bulk or prepackaged canisters at health food stores and most specialty markets (e.g., Whole Foods). If all else fails, they can also be found online (www.amazon.com).*

Tamari | Tamari is a gluten-free version of soy sauce. You'll notice that recipes call for "reduced-sodium tamari," so make sure that's the kind you purchase or you'll need to significantly reduce the amount you use so that you don't end up with an overly salty meal. For a soy-free alternative, use coconut aminos instead of tamari. Just be sure to compare the sodium content between the two and adjust accordingly to suit your tastes.

Brown Rice Pasta | Brown rice pasta is a fantastic gluten-free pasta option. Stick with brands that list just one ingredient (i.e., brown rice), as some contain unnecessary additives and preservatives.

Young Green Jackfruit + Hearts of Palm | Also known as the pulled-meat-lover-turned-vegan's dream, these two items have a lot in common: young green jackfruit (a fruit) and hearts of palm (a vegetable) can be found in cans or jars, have similar flavors, and can be simmered in sauce until tender and then shredded into a plant-based alternative to pulled meat. Give one or the other a whirl in a BBQ Pulled Jackfruit with Cashew Cheddar Cheese + Seeded Ranch Dressing (page 201) or Pulled Hearts of Palm Tamales with Chipotle Crema + Pineapple Pico de Gallo (page 239).

SPICE IT UP: MY FAVORITE SPICES + DRIED HERBS

Basil | Black salt | Cardamom | Cayenne pepper | Chili powder | Cinnamon | Coriander | Crushed red pepper flakes | Cumin | Ginger | Oregano | Pink Himalayan sea salt | Sage | Smoked paprika | Thyme | Turmeric

GET FRESH: MY MOST FREQUENTED FRESH FRUITS, VEGETABLES + HERBS

Avocados | Bananas | Berries | Cherry tomatoes | Grapes | Green apples | Lemons | Limes | Mango | Baby arugula | Baby spinach | Beets | Carrots | Cauliflower | Cucumbers | Kale | Mushrooms: shiitake, cremini, portobello | Romaine | Sweet potatoes | Yukon gold potatoes | Zucchini | Basil | Cilantro | Flat-leaf parsley | Rosemary | Thyme

GET RIPPED: MY FAVORITE PLANT-BASED PROTEIN SOURCES

Almonds | Black beans | Brown rice | Cashews | Chickpeas | Green split peas | Lentils | Old-fashioned rolled oats | Pepitas | Shelled hemp seeds | Sunflower seeds | Yellow split peas

MY OTHER ALWAYS-STOCKED PANTRY ITEMS

Canned beans | Crushed + whole peeled tomatoes | Dried tart cherries | Frozen berries (for winter smoothies) | Jarred roasted red peppers | Maca powder | Oil-packed + dry-packed sun-dried tomatoes | Raisins | Sparkling water

KITCHEN GEAR: SLICE, DICE, CHOP, BLEND + PROCESS

Food Processor | Please, don't run away! I know what you're thinking: food processors are expensive luxury items. Trust me, up until the age of twenty-seven, I thought the exact same thing and would never have thought I'd be pushing processors. However, a food processor is really, truly a necessity if you want to enjoy a satisfying range of meals in this book and when following a plant-based lifestyle in general. I use a standard 14-cup processor unless otherwise noted (e.g., "small food processor"), and although other sizes (e.g., 20-cup, 8-cup) will work in a pinch, large processors will require more stopping and scraping and smaller processors will require you to work in batches. If you don't own a food processor and are feeling the urge to kick me in the shin at this very moment, take it from someone who once felt the exact same way: once you have a food processor, you never go back. Mine never leaves the kitchen counter, and there isn't a week that goes by that I don't use it.

Multispeed Blender | Don't worry, I'm not going to push some fancy-schmancy blender on you. Although snazzy Vitamix or Blendtec blenders are great, it's not necessary to own one in order to make your way through the recipes in this book. How do I know that? Because I wrote and tested every recipe without one. I use a multispeed KitchenAid blender that Dan and I received as a wedding gift, and it works like a charm. I *do* recommend using a multispeed blender if you can make the investment. But no worries if you can't—just be sure to follow the tips and tricks for blending without a high-speed blender, and you should be just fine.

Parchment Paper | Keep your pans clean and your roasted and baked goods unscathed. That would be my slogan for parchment paper. (Perhaps I should have gone into marketing.) In all serious-ness though, parchment paper is an incredibly useful and necessary kitchen staple. In some instances, a silicone baking sheet can be used instead; however, parchment paper tends to be more reliable, especially with baked goods (e.g., cookies, bars). One word of warning: Parchment paper and waxed paper are not the same thing and cannot be used interchangeably. Unless you're one of the nonexistent few who enjoys destroying your carefully crafted creations as well as your baking pans—in that case, give waxed paper a whirl, but don't say I didn't warn you.

Spiralizer | This is not a required kitchen tool, and I've provided an alternative option (i.e., vegetable peeler) whenever applicable; however, if you've ever considered investing in a spiralizer, then I will happily vouch for the usefulness of this handy gadget. I purchased a Paderno three-blade spiralizer on Amazon for around $35 a few years back. It felt like a splurge at the time, because I was buying it specifically for one recipe and wasn't sure I'd ever feel compelled to use it again. To my surprise, it's become one of my favorite tools, and I use it several times each week to make zucchini noodles. In the winter, I simmer the noodles with marinara for a warming plant-pure spaghetti; in the summer, I leave them raw and toss them into salads for a fun, noodle-y crunch.

Juicer | Juicers are typically an investment and many models will set you back $200 or more. For this reason, there is just one juice recipe in this book; however, if you've been regularly pur-chasing those store-bought, fresh-pressed juices for $10 a pop, you'll see a quick return on your investment by juicing from the comforts of your own home. If you want one that won't break the bank, look into purchasing a centrifugal juicer. But if you can afford a bit of a splurge, consider a twin-gear or masticating juicer—they provide a higher yield of juice with less oxidation. More juice with less oxidation equals lots of goodness in your body.

HELPFUL SYMBOLS

As you flip through the pages of this book, you'll notice a variety of colorful symbols that appear just below the recipe titles. Each symbol offers practical information, such as dietary notes or the need for advance preparation, and I hope you'll find them useful as you navigate these recipes.

Prepare ahead—the recipe requires extended periods (i.e., 1 hour or more) of chilling, soaking, or freezing

GF Gluten-free	GF Gluten-free option
GRF Grain-free	GRF Grain-free option
SF Soy-free	SF Soy-free option
NF Nut-free	NF Nut-free option
OF Oil-free	OF Oil-free option
RSF Refined-sugar-free	RSF Refined-sugar-free option
R Raw	R Raw option

USEFUL NOTES

Whenever possible, I've included notes with tips and information regarding dietary modifications, substitutions, simplifications, or interesting facts. Be sure to keep an eye out for asterisks (*) within the ingredients lists, because they'll alert you to any must-read notes.

TIME RANGES

Each of us moves through the kitchen in a unique way, with some of us preferring a fast pace and some of us preferring a moderate or leisurely pace. In an effort to account for these variances and offer a bit more flexibility, the recipes include the following time ranges (as opposed to exact time estimates):

15 minutes or less

30 minutes or less

45 minutes or less

1 hour or less

1 hour +

CONVERSION CHART

1 cup = 16 tablespoons

3/4 cup = 12 tablespoons

2/3 cup = 10 tablespoons plus
   2 teaspoons

1/2 cup = 8 tablespoons

1/3 cup = 5 tablespoons plus
   1 teaspoon

1/4 cup = 4 tablespoons

BREAKFAST + BRUNCH

SIMPLE + ENERGIZING WEEKDAY BREAKFASTS

SuperSeeded Oatmeal-Raisin Granola Clusters 35

Raw Apple-Cinnamon Breakfast Parfait with Cinnamon Soft-Serve 38

Energizing Triple-Seed Morning Pudding with Berry Compote 41

Blueberry Breakfast Ice Cream with Pecan Streusel 42

Bright Morning Citrus Salad with Herbed Syrup 45

Cherry, Almond Butter + Oat Breakfast Cookies 46

Get Glowing Strawberry-Mango Chia Pudding 49

LINGER + SAVOR WEEKEND BRUNCHES

Buckwheat Breakfast Risotto with Garlicky Mushrooms 50

Savory Sage + Green Pea Breakfast Patties with Apple-Chia Compote 53

Simple Sweet Potato Cinnamon Rolls with Maple Glaze 55

Cheesy Herb + Sun-Dried Tomato Good Morning Biscuits 59

Southwest Tofu Scramble with Avocado Crisps 60

Avocado Toast with Burst Heirloom Tomatoes + Balsamic Drizzle 63

Caramelized Banana Upside-Down Oatmeal Bake
with Chai-Spiced Date Caramel 65

I adore breakfast. It's an opportunity to start the day on an energized edge, and it's also a convincing reason to hop out of bed in the morning (especially on those exceptionally dreary Mondays). And while I could be perfectly content noshing on my favorite Southwest Tofu Scramble (page 60) time and time again, I've found that a little variety infuses my morning with excitement and paves the way for a purposeful day.

Inside this two-part chapter, you'll find a curated collection of my favorite weekday grab-'n'-go breakfasts as well as savory and sweet brunch dishes that beckon a leisurely weekend pace. From Energizing Triple-Seed Morning Pudding with Berry Compote (page 41) to Simple Sweet Potato Cinnamon Rolls with Maple Glaze (page 55), this chapter has everything you need to (plant-) power your mornings and keep your taste buds singing. Let's get this day started!

Makes 7 cups (21 servings) | 1 hour +

To supersede means to take the place of something no longer useful, and this recipe for SuperSeeded Oatmeal-Raisin Granola Clusters has taken the place of all other granola recipes in my kitchen. These clusters are packed with energizing seeds and hold together in perfectly crunchy clusters thanks to two secret tricks. I'm sure you're about to fall off the edge of your kitchen stool with anticipation, so I'll cut to the chase and let you in on the double-decker secret.

Trick one: Processing some of the oats and seeds into a coarse flour. This oat-and-seed-based flour helps bind the other ingredients together.

And trick two: Aquafaba. Aqua-*whatta*? Don't fret, aquafaba is nothing more than the liquid from a can of chickpeas or white beans. And we should thank our lucky stars for this bean brine, because aquafaba behaves almost exactly like egg whites. It can be whipped into meringue and used to veganize French macarons, and is also used to bind baked goods together. Adding egg whites to granola is a little-known trick to create crunchy granola clusters, as it both binds and adds a crisp sheen. Given that aquafaba behaves similarly to egg whites, I figured it was worth a shot. And it worked like a clustery granola charm.

2 1/3 cups old-fashioned rolled oats, divided

1 cup raw shelled sunflower seeds, divided

1 1/4 cup seedless raisins*

3/4 cup raw buckwheat groats

1/3 cup raw pepitas

1/4 cup coconut sugar

2 tablespoons shelled hemp seeds

1 tablespoon ground cinnamon

1/3 cup natural creamy unsalted almond butter*

1/4 cup pure maple syrup

1/4 cup virgin coconut oil, melted

2 tablespoons aquafaba (canning liquid in chickpeas or white beans)*

2 teaspoons pure vanilla extract

1/4 teaspoon fine-grain sea salt

Preheat the oven to 275°F and line a large baking tray with parchment paper.

Add 1/3 cup of the rolled oats and 1/2 cup of the sunflower seeds to a food processor and process for 1 minute, or until the texture resembles a meal or coarse flour. Transfer the sunflower-oat meal to a large mixing bowl and add the remaining 2 cups rolled oats, remaining 1/2 cup sunflower seeds, raisins, buckwheat groats, pepitas, coconut sugar, hemp seeds, and ground cinnamon. Use a large wooden spoon to mix.

In a small mixing bowl, whisk together the almond butter, maple syrup, coconut oil, aquafaba, vanilla, and sea salt until smooth and glossy. Pour over the oat mixture and get stirring. At first it will seem like there isn't enough to coat the granola, but I promise there is plenty! It just requires a bit of muscle and a few minutes. Once every bit of the granola is evenly coated, turn it out onto the lined baking tray and use the back of a spoon or spatula to gently spread it out into a 3/4-inch-thick layer across the pan.

Bake for 15 minutes, rotate the pan, and bake for another 22–28 minutes. The granola is done when it's wafting a toasted scent, the top is a very light golden-brown, and it feels firm—but not yet crisp—to the touch. An important thing to note: granola is tricky because it doesn't become crisp and crunchy until it has had a chance to cool, so rely on look and scent more than touch or you'll end up with burnt granola clusters. Once the granola is ready, remove the pan from the oven and place it on an oven-safe cooling rack. The air circulating beneath and around the pan will efficiently cool and crisp the granola.

(continued on next page)

Allow the granola to cool completely on the pan until it's not even the slightest bit warm to the touch. If you start moving it around or try to break it into clusters while it's warm, it will crumble into regular granola. I recommend a minimum of 45 minutes of cooling time at room temperature, but try to hold out for 1 hour if you can. Once the granola is completely cool, break it into pieces of desired size and store in large airtight glass jars to maintain its crunch.

Not Keen on Raisins? | *If you're not a fan of raisins, simply swap them out for another dried fruit—dried blueberries, dried cranberries, and dried cherries all work wonders in this recipe.*

No Nuts? No Problem | *To keep this nut-free, simply swap out the almond butter for sunflower butter.*

How to Procure Aquafaba | *Open a can of chickpeas or white beans and measure out 2 tablespoons of the liquid that surrounds the beans. The leftover beans can be used to make* Lemony Hummus *(page 304).*

Serve It Up | *Sprinkle over coconut yogurt and fresh berries for a tasty parfait. You can also spoon a bit of the granola into a bowl and top with a generous splash of cold almond milk. Sweet cereal perfection.*

RAW APPLE-CINNAMON BREAKFAST PARFAIT WITH CINNAMON SOFT-SERVE

Serves 2 | 30 minutes or less

One of the most popular breakfast recipes on the Blissful Basil blog is a Raw Apple-Cinnamon Breakfast Bowl. It's oat-free and made from a simple combination of apples, dates, cinnamon, nutmeg, and chia seeds, yet it resembles a big bowl of oats both in look and in its ability to satisfy. This version relies on that same apple-laden base, but it's kicked up a notch or two by the addition of a raw cinnamon soft-serve. The soft-serve is made by blending frozen bananas and ground cinnamon until frosty, thick, and creamy. Both the apple-cinnamon mixture and the cinnamon soft-serve get layered into a jar and topped as desired. The result is a delightfully raw breakfast that boasts a high micronutrient content without sacrificing a smidgen of flavor.

RAW APPLE-CINNAMON + CHIA LAYER

3 small apples (Honeycrisp, Pink Lady, or other crisp red), peeled and cored, divided

3–5 Medjool dates, pitted*

1/2 teaspoon ground cinnamon

Pinch of nutmeg

2 tablespoons chia seeds

CINNAMON SOFT-SERVE

2 large ripe and speckled bananas, peeled, sliced, and frozen

1 teaspoon ground cinnamon

Unsweetened almond milk, as needed*

OPTIONAL TOPPINGS

Chopped raw walnuts

Raisins

Dried cranberries

Shelled hemp seeds

For the Raw Apple-Cinnamon + Chia Layer

Finely dice 1 of the apples and add it to a medium airtight container.

Cut the 2 remaining apples into large pieces and add them to a food processor along with the dates, cinnamon, and nutmeg. Pulse the mixture several times and then process for 2–3 minutes, or until the mixture resembles applesauce, stopping to scrape down the sides as needed.

Transfer to the container with the finely diced apple and stir in the chia seeds. It's best to refrigerate this for 1–2 hours to allow the chia seeds to work their thickening magic; however, in a pinch, you can skip the chill time and move straight to the next step.

For the Cinnamon Soft-Serve

Add the frozen bananas and the cinnamon to a food processor and process until smooth and creamy. If needed, add a bit of unsweetened almond milk, 1 tablespoon at a time, to encourage the bananas to blend, adding as little as possible to maintain a thick soft-serve texture. Be careful not to add too much liquid or you'll end up with a cinnamon smoothie instead of cinnamon soft-serve.

To Assemble

In 2 medium jars or glasses, layer the soft-serve and apple-cinnamon chia mixture, one after the other, garnishing the layers with toppings as you go, if desired. Serve immediately.

Firm Dates? No Problem | *If your dates are firm, as opposed to soft and gooey, soak them in warm water for 30 minutes before processing.*

No Nuts? No Problem | *To keep this nut-free, simply swap out the unsweetened almond milk for a nut-free plant-based milk, such as unsweetened soy milk or unsweetened rice milk.*

ENERGIZING TRIPLE-SEED MORNING PUDDING
WITH BERRY COMPOTE

Serves 4 | 1 hour +

This pudding is similar to the Get Glowing Strawberry-Mango Chia Pudding (page 49), only it ups the seed ante with the additions of flax and hemp seeds. All three seeds offer unique nutritional benefits, which is why they're especially wonderful when combined within the cozy confines of one dish.

Here's a quick rundown of all the nutritional goodness going on here: Chia seeds are digestion-friendly and detoxifying. Flaxseeds offer a generous amount of anti-inflammatory omega-3 fatty acids. And hemp seeds are a complete protein source, containing a digestible balance of all twenty amino acids. (Check out pages 22 and 23 for more fun facts on these plant-powerful seeds!)

I typically prepare this recipe on Sunday evening to enjoy for an energizing breakfast throughout the week. It's an excellent grab-'n'-go option, because it can be effortlessly layered into jars and topped before heading out the door in the morning. And that berry compote? Well, it makes even the earliest wake-up call a bit more palatable.

TRIPLE-SEED PUDDING

2 cups unsweetened almond milk*

1/3 cup chia seeds

2 tablespoons shelled hemp seeds

2 tablespoons flaxseeds

2 tablespoons pure maple syrup

1 1/2 teaspoons pure vanilla extract

1/2 teaspoon ground cinnamon (optional)

BERRY COMPOTE

1 1/2 cups blueberries (fresh or thawed frozen)

1 1/2 cups blackberries (fresh or thawed frozen)

1/3 cup filtered water

2 tablespoons pure maple syrup

For the Triple-Seed Pudding

In an airtight container, vigorously whisk together the almond milk, chia seeds, hemp seeds, flaxseeds, maple syrup, vanilla, and cinnamon. Refrigerate for 8 hours or overnight to thicken.

For the Berry Compote

In a medium saucepan, combine the blueberries, blackberries, water, and maple syrup over medium-high heat. Bring to a boil, decrease the heat to medium-low, and simmer, uncovered, for 12–15 minutes, or until the berries have broken down and the liquid is thick and syrupy, stirring occasionally. Remove from the heat and allow the compote to cool completely. Transfer to an airtight glass jar and refrigerate until ready to assemble.

To Assemble

In 4 small glasses or jars, layer the pudding and compote, one after the other. If desired, garnish with fresh berries. Serve chilled.

No Nuts? No Problem | *To keep this nut-free, simply swap out the unsweetened almond milk for a nut-free plant-based milk, such as unsweetened soy milk or unsweetened rice milk.*

Serves 1 | 15 minutes or less

This dreamy treat conjures up memories of my childhood favorite: ice cream soup. Ice cream soup was a delectable dish that my dad taught my brother Brad and me how to make when we were just wee ones. And it was a game-changer. Brad and I followed our dad's methodology to a T; we'd scoop heaps of ice cream into our favorite peach-hued bowls, grab our spoons, and get stirring. We'd stir and stir until the scoops of ice cream softened into a thick and frosty concoction with just the slightest glisten of melted ice cream beginning to collect around the edges of the bowl. Then, we'd slurp up spoonful after spoonful of the chilled treat, ensuring that every last drop made its way into our bellies. All these years later, I still prefer ice cream soup over ice cream scoops, and the texture of this blueberry breakfast ice cream reminds me of that perfect balance of frozen, frosty, creamy, and melted.

BLUEBERRY BREAKFAST ICE CREAM

2 large ripe and speckled bananas, peeled, sliced, and frozen

1 cup frozen blueberries

Unsweetened almond milk, as needed*

PECAN STREUSEL

2 tablespoon raw pecans, very finely chopped*

1 teaspoon coconut sugar

1/2 teaspoon ground cinnamon

OPTIONAL TOPPINGS

Fresh or frozen blueberries

Raw buckwheat groats

Pepitas

For the Blueberry Breakfast Ice Cream

Add the bananas and blueberries to a food processor. Process for 2–3 minutes, or until smooth, stopping to scrape down the sides once or twice. If needed, add a bit of unsweetened almond milk, 1 tablespoon at a time, to encourage the bananas to blend, adding as little as possible to maintain a thick soft-serve texture. Be careful not to add too much liquid or you'll end up with a blueberry smoothie instead of blueberry soft-serve.

For the Pecan Streusel

In a small bowl, whisk together the chopped pecans, coconut sugar, and cinnamon.

To Assemble

Scoop the ice cream into a bowl. Sprinkle with the streusel and add toppings as desired.

No Nuts? No Problem | *To keep this nut-free, simply swap out the unsweetened almond milk for a nut-free plant-based milk, such as unsweetened soy milk or unsweetened rice milk, and swap out the pecans for raw shelled sunflower seeds.*

BRIGHT MORNING CITRUS SALAD WITH HERBED SYRUP

Serves 4 | 30 minutes or less

It was a hot summer morning in 1989. My mom was gracefully navigating the cabinets in our kitchen, and I was meticulously crafting a cereal-box barrier to prevent my brother Brad from traversing into my personal counter space. After helping us fill our bowls with mounds of Kix cereal, my mom asked, "Would you like a glass of grapefruit juice?" Brad's sweet brown eyes widened with fear as he shook his head and let out a definitive "Yuuuuck." I, none the wiser, figured "grapefruit juice" was simply the adult name for "grape juice" and eagerly accepted the offer. One sip and my face was contorted into a bitter pucker. This was *not* grape juice. That moment single-handedly deterred me from all things grapefruit. That is, until a mysterious citrus craving struck one day while I was in college, and I've loved the pretty pink fruit ever since.

This simple yet special fruit salad is an ode to my once-foe, now-favorite citrus fruit. Segmented oranges and grapefruit are tossed in rosemary- and thyme-infused syrup. The combination of tart citrus fruit, sweet maple syrup, and savory herbs creates an addictive concoction. It's delicious all on its own but perhaps even more so when served over tangy vanilla coconut yogurt.

HERBED SYRUP

1/3 cup pure maple syrup

1/3 cup filtered water

1/4 cup roughly chopped fresh rosemary leaves

1/4 cup loosely packed sprigs of fresh thyme

CITRUS SALAD

4 oranges, peeled and ends trimmed

3 grapefruit, peeled and ends trimmed

OPTIONAL BASE

Coconut or almond yogurt

For the Herbed Syrup

In a medium saucepan, combine all the syrup ingredients over medium heat and gently whisk. Bring to a boil, decrease the heat, and simmer, uncovered, for 15–20 minutes, or until reduced to a syrupy consistency, stirring occasionally. Cool completely.

Place a sieve or fine-mesh colander over a medium bowl. Pour the syrup through the sieve or colander to separate the syrup from the herbs and stems. Use the back of a spoon to press the herbs, releasing any remaining liquid. Discard the herbs and stems.

For the Citrus Salad

While the syrup is simmering, use a paring knife to cut the oranges and grapefruit into segments by slicing alongside the membrane of the fruit. Add the citrus segments to a large nonreactive (i.e., nonmetallic) airtight container.

To Assemble

Pour the herbed syrup over the citrus fruit and toss to coat. Enjoy the salad all on its own or spooned over coconut yogurt.

Leftovers will keep for up to 4 days in the refrigerator.

Makes 12 cookies | 30 minutes or less

Breakfast cookies for one, breakfast cookies for all. The world needs more breakfast cookies, don't you think?

These soft, chewy, and satisfying cookies are a great grab-'n'-go breakfast. They call for oat flour and rolled oats as the base and coconut sugar to sweeten. Coconut sugar has a glycemic index (GI) of about 35, which puts it in the low range. Using a low-GI sweetener paired with fiber-rich oats, almond butter, and dried cherries means these cookies will keep blood sugar smooth and steady rather than spiking it. The only problem will be convincing yourself not to eat the entire batch!

1/2 cup natural creamy unsalted almond butter*

1/2 cup coconut sugar

2 teaspoons pure vanilla extract

3/4 cup oat flour

1/2 cup old-fashioned rolled oats

1 teaspoon baking soda

1/8 teaspoon fine-grain sea salt

1/4 cup filtered water

1/3 cup unsweetened dried cherries, roughly chopped

Preheat the oven to 350°F. Line a large baking sheet with parchment paper.

In a large mixing bowl, combine the almond butter, coconut sugar, and vanilla. Using a hand mixer or stand mixer fitted with the paddle attachment, beat on high for 1 minute.

In a small mixing bowl, whisk together the oat flour, oats, baking soda, and sea salt. With the mixer off, slowly pour the dry ingredients over the wet, then add the water on top of the dry ingredients. Once added, turn the mixer on low, gradually increase the speed to medium-high, and beat until just incorporated. Switch off the mixer and stir in the dried cherries.

Roll about 2 tablespoons of the dough into a ball and place on the lined baking sheet. Repeat with the remaining dough, leaving about 2 inches of space between each ball. You should have about 12 cookies.

Bake for 10–12 minutes, or until just turning golden. These cookies stay tightly packed and don't spread out much, so go by color and scent rather than overall look. Remove from the oven. Allow the cookies to cool completely on the pan before moving or enjoying.

No Nuts? No Problem | *Use sunflower butter instead of almond butter to keep these breakfast treats nut-free.*

GET GLOWING STRAWBERRY-MANGO CHIA PUDDING

Serves 4 | 1 hour +

This breakfast pudding packs a punch of vitamins C and B$_3$, zinc, potassium, and omega-3s. If you haven't tried chia pudding yet, you're in for a (seeded) treat. Chia seeds become gelatinous when they come into contact with liquid, thickening and transforming liquids into puddings, jams, and shakes. Their gelatinous quality also makes them excellent detoxifying agents because they bind to toxins in the gut and move them through the body for elimination. Chia pudding needs at least 8 hours to thicken, so I like to make this recipe on Sunday night. Then, when Monday morning rolls around, I spoon the chia pudding and strawberry-mango purée into four small mason jars, creating healthy grab-'n'-go breakfasts to enjoy throughout the week.

VANILLA CHIA PUDDING

2 cups unsweetened almond milk*

1/2 cup chia seeds

3 tablespoons pure maple syrup or to taste

1 1/2 teaspoons pure vanilla extract

STRAWBERRY-MANGO PURÉE

2 cups fresh strawberries, hulled

1 cup diced fresh mango (about 1 large mango)

1–2 Medjool dates, pitted

OPTIONAL TOPPINGS

Sliced strawberries

Diced mango

Coconut flakes

Pepitas

For the Vanilla Chia Pudding

In an airtight jar or container, whisk together the almond milk, chia seeds, maple syrup, and vanilla until the chia seeds are evenly distributed throughout the liquid. Refrigerate overnight, or for at least 8 hours, to thicken.

In the morning, vigorously whisk the pudding to redistribute the chia seeds. If it's too thin, whisk in more chia seeds, 1 tablespoon at a time, to thicken. If it's too thick, whisk in more almond milk, 1 tablespoon at a time, to thin.

For the Strawberry-Mango Purée

You can make the purée the night before or just before serving.

In a high-speed blender, combine the strawberries, mango, and dates and blend until smooth. Refrigerate until ready to assemble.

To Assemble

In 4 small bowls or jars, layer the chia pudding and the purée. Add optional toppings as you please. Serve chilled.

No Nuts? No Problem | *To keep this nut-free, simply swap out the unsweetened almond milk for a nut-free plant-based milk, such as unsweetened soy milk or unsweetened rice milk.*

BUCKWHEAT BREAKFAST RISOTTO WITH GARLICKY MUSHROOMS

Serves 4 | 45 minutes or less

This savory buckwheat breakfast dish is simmered like a porridge, yet the taste and texture are reminiscent of risotto. Creamy risotto without the need to incessantly stir? I'll take it. It's topped with mushrooms that have been dry sautéed and tossed with the tiniest bit of olive oil, a generous heap of minced garlic, a sprinkle of parsley, and a dash of sea salt. I typically find fresh parsley to be an overbearing flavor, but when it's cooked with garlic, mushrooms, and a bit of olive oil, it's absolutely magical.

BUCKWHEAT BREAKFAST RISOTTO

1 cup raw buckwheat groats

2 cups boiling water

1 tablespoon cold-pressed olive oil

1 medium yellow onion, finely diced (about 1 1/4 cups)

1 clove garlic, minced

2 1/2 cups unsweetened almond milk*

3/4 teaspoon sea salt or to taste

Freshly ground black pepper

1 tablespoon nutritional yeast flakes

GARLICKY MUSHROOMS

1 pound cremini mushrooms, brushed or wiped clean and thickly sliced

1/2 tablespoon cold-pressed olive oil

Small handful flat-leaf parsley, chopped

2 cloves garlic, minced

1/4 teaspoon sea salt or to taste

OPTIONAL TOPPINGS

2 tablespoons Nut // Seed Parmesan Cheese (page 299) or to taste*

1 lemon, halved (optional)

For the Buckwheat Breakfast Risotto

In a medium bowl, soak the buckwheat groats in the boiling water for 10 minutes to rid them of their filmy coating. Then, strain and rinse the buckwheat with cold water until the water runs clear.

Meanwhile, heat a large sauté pan over medium heat. Add the olive oil, onion, and garlic, and cook for 6 minutes, or until the onion is soft and translucent, stirring occasionally. Stir in the buckwheat and cook for another 2 minutes, or until most of the liquid has cooked off. Then, stir in the almond milk, sea salt, and black pepper to taste (some brands of almond milk will separate at this point, so don't worry if yours does).

Bring to a boil, decrease the heat to medium-low, and simmer, uncovered, for 15 minutes, or until most of the almond milk has been absorbed and the buckwheat is thick and creamy, stirring occasionally at first and with greater frequency toward the end of cooking.

Remove from the heat and stir in the nutritional yeast. Season with more sea salt and black pepper, if desired.

For the Garlicky Mushrooms

While the buckwheat is simmering, heat another large sauté pan over high heat. Once the pan is hot, add the mushrooms, decrease the heat to medium-high, and cook for 6 minutes, or until there is just the tiniest amount of liquid remaining and the mushrooms have a deep, golden-brown glisten to them, nudging them around as needed to prevent burning. It will initially seem like the mushrooms might burn, but this is about the point when they will release their liquid.

Then, decrease the heat to medium-low and add the olive oil, parsley, garlic, and sea salt. Cook for another 2 minutes, or until the garlic scent mellows and the parsley wilts, stirring frequently. Remove from the heat and set aside.

To Assemble

Spoon the buckwheat risotto into bowls, top with the mushrooms, and sprinkle with the Parmesan. If desired, spritz with fresh lemon juice for a pop of brightness. Serve immediately.

No Nuts? No Problem | *To keep this nut-free, simply swap out the unsweetened almond milk for a nut-free plant-based milk, such as unsweetened soy milk or unsweetened rice milk, and opt for seed-based Parmesan.*

SAVORY SAGE + GREEN PEA BREAKFAST PATTIES WITH APPLE-CHIA COMPOTE

Serves 4 | 1 hour +

I used to have a thing for frozen meatless breakfast patties, but as my plant-powered years have unfolded, I've become more attuned to how different foods make me feel, and those frozen breakfast patties make me feel suboptimal at best. I have an inkling the culprit is the long list of unpronounceable, laboratory-born ingredients, so I came up with a suitable alternative.

These plant-pure patties have a rich punch of sage reminiscent of a classic breakfast patty, a subtle sweetness from grated green apple, a protein- and fiber-packed heartiness from green split peas, and just the right amount of chewiness from brown rice. An apple-chia compote brightens the dish and complements the earthiness of the patties.

SAVORY SAGE + GREEN PEA BREAKFAST PATTIES

1 cup uncooked green split peas, thoroughly rinsed

1/2 cup uncooked brown rice, thoroughly rinsed

5 cups water

1 large Granny Smith apple, peeled

1/4 cup oat flour

3 scallions, trimmed and thinly sliced

1 clove garlic, minced

2 tablespoons finely chopped fresh sage leaves

1 tablespoon apple cider vinegar

1 teaspoon fine-grain sea salt

1/4 teaspoon ground sage (optional)

1/4 teaspoon dried thyme

Freshly ground black pepper

For the Savory Sage + Green Pea Breakfast Patties

Combine the green split peas, brown rice, and water in a large saucepan over medium-high heat. Bring to a boil, cover, and decrease the heat to medium-low. Simmer for 40–45 minutes, or until the split peas are very tender. If needed, add more water to keep the peas submerged. Remove from the heat and strain off as much of the excess water as possible.

Preheat the oven to 400°F. Line a large baking tray with parchment paper.

Grate the peeled apple down to the core. Gather the grated apple in your hands and squeeze to release any excess juice. You should have about 1/2 cup grated apple pulp after releasing the juice.

In a large mixing bowl, stir together the cooked split peas and brown rice, grated apple, oat flour, scallions, garlic, fresh sage, apple cider vinegar, sea salt, ground sage (if using), dried thyme, and black pepper to taste. The mixture should be moist but not runny. If it's runny, add in more oat flour, 1 tablespoon at a time, to thicken. The dough will be sticky—and consequently, a bit difficult to work with—but a moist, sticky dough will yield tender patties.

Lightly grease a 1/3-cup measuring cup and use it to scoop out the dough. Gently pack the dough into the cup and turn it out onto the lined baking tray, carefully shaping into a patty that's 1 inch thick and about 2 1/2 inches in diameter. Repeat with the remaining dough. You should have about 8 patties.

Bake for 14 minutes, use a metal spatula to gently flip each patty, and bake for another 12–16 minutes, or until both sides are crisp and flecked with a golden-brown hue.

(continued on next page)

APPLE-CHIA COMPOTE

3 large Granny Smith apples (about 1 1/2 pounds), peeled, cored, and finely diced

1 1/2–2 cups pure apple juice, plus more if needed

1 tablespoon pure maple syrup

1 tablespoon fresh lemon juice

1 tablespoon chia seeds, plus more if needed

OPTIONAL TOPPINGS

Microgreens

Sliced radishes

For the Apple-Chia Compote

Make the compote while the split peas are simmering.

In a medium saucepan, stir together the diced apples, 1 1/2 cups of the apple juice, the maple syrup, and the lemon juice over medium-high heat. Bring to a boil, decrease the heat to medium-low, and simmer, uncovered, for 15 minutes, stirring occasionally. Then, cover and continue to simmer, stirring occasionally, for another 10–15 minutes, or until the apples just begin to break down and the compote thickens. If needed, add more apple juice, 1/4 cup at a time, to prevent the apples from sticking to the pan and scorching.

Remove from the heat and stir in the chia seeds. Let cool. If desired, add more apple juice, 1 tablespoon at a time, to thin or more chia seeds, 1 tablespoon at a time, to thicken.

To Serve

Spread a generous amount of the compote out over 4 plates. Top each with 2 warm patties. Garnish with the microgreens and radishes (if using).

Refrigerate leftovers in separate containers for up to 4 days. The patties can be frozen for up to 1 month.

Plant-Powered Protein | *Just one patty contains 7 grams of protein and 8 grams of fiber!*

SIMPLE SWEET POTATO CINNAMON ROLLS WITH MAPLE GLAZE

If you've heard me talk about Dan's recipe rating system, then you know it's nearly impossible to receive a 10 out of 10 from him. And 8s and 9s aren't handed out like candy either. In his words, "I can't give everything a 10, because it would become meaningless. A 10 rating is reserved for just a few recipes a year." All right, Zagat, slow your ~~cinnamon~~ roll. I've actually come to appreciate his rigorous system because when I receive a 10, I feel like I've struck recipe gold. I'm sure you know where I'm going with this, but these cinnamon rolls received a 10 rating along with a request to make them every weekend.

The sweet potato dough comes together with a small handful of ingredients and only requires about 2 minutes of kneading, but there's no replacement for a warm place and a couple of hours of rise time, so be sure to plan ahead. The dough is slathered with a cinnamon and coconut sugar filling before being rolled, sliced, and baked. The finishing touch is a generous drizzle of sweet maple glaze. With light, puffy exteriors and warm, gooey interiors, I have a feeling these cinnamon rolls will earn a perfect 10 in your home, too.

SWEET POTATO CINNAMON ROLLS

1 1/4 cups peeled and small-diced (1/3-inch cubes) sweet potato (about 1 medium sweet potato)

3/4 cup warm water (105°F–115°F)

2 1/4 teaspoons active dry yeast (1 packet)

1 tablespoon pure maple syrup

2 3/4 cups whole spelt flour, plus more as needed and for dusting

2 tablespoons melted virgin coconut oil, divided, plus more for greasing

1 tablespoon plus 1 teaspoon ground cinnamon, divided

1/4 teaspoon sea salt

1/2 cup coconut sugar

MAPLE GLAZE

1/4 cup pure maple syrup

1/4 cup room-temperature virgin coconut oil, melted

1 tablespoon natural creamy almond butter*

1/2 teaspoon pure vanilla extract (optional)

For the Sweet Potato Cinnamon Rolls

The sweet potato needs to be measured precisely, so make sure you have exactly 1 1/4 cups of small-cubed potato. Steam the diced sweet potato for 30 minutes, or until fall-apart tender. (Avoid steaming in the microwave, because it will dry out the sweet potato rather than infusing it with moisture.)

In a small bowl, gently whisk together the warm water, yeast, and maple syrup. Let stand for 5 minutes, or until a foam develops on the surface.

Meanwhile, lightly grease a large glass mixing bowl with coconut oil.

Add the steamed sweet potato to a food processor and process for 1 minute, or until puréed, stopping to scrape down the sides as needed. Add the yeast mixture, spelt flour, 1 tablespoon of the coconut oil, 1 teaspoon of the cinnamon, and the sea salt. Pulse 5 times and then process for 15 seconds, or until the dough begins to roll into a loosely formed ball.

The dough should be soft and sticky yet pulled together. If it's too loose or wet, add more spelt flour, 1/4 cup at a time, and pulse to incorporate. Alternatively, if it's too dry or dense, add more warm water, 2 tablespoons at a time, and pulse to incorporate.

(continued on next page)

Pull the dough from the food processor and turn out onto a clean work surface that has been dusted with spelt flour. Knead for 1 1/2–2 1/2 minutes, until the dough is smooth and springy, adding more spelt flour as needed. You'll know it's ready when it begins to hold its shape and springs back, slightly but not completely, when pressed. The gluten in spelt is delicate, so be careful not to overknead or you'll end up with dry, crumbly cinnamon rolls.

Shape the dough into a ball and place it in the prepared bowl. Cover the bowl with a clean kitchen towel and let the dough rise in a warm place for 1 1/2 hours, or until doubled in size.

When the dough has just a few minutes left to rise, lightly grease an 8 × 8-inch baking pan with coconut oil. Whisk together the coconut sugar and remaining 1 tablespoon cinnamon in a small bowl.

Punch down the dough and turn it out onto a clean, lightly floured work surface. Use a rolling pin to roll the dough into a 1/2-inch-thick rectangle (approximately 8 × 18 inches).

Lightly brush the top of the dough with the remaining 1 tablespoon melted coconut oil and sprinkle with the coconut sugar mixture.

Starting at the front of the long edge of the rectangle, carefully roll the dough away from you until you have a tightly wound roll. Use your fingers to pinch the seam closed. Use a sharp serrated knife to slice into nine 2-inch-thick rolls.

Gently place the rolls in the greased baking pan, swirled-side up, leaving 1/4–1/2 inch of space between each. Loosely cover the pan with parchment paper and let the rolls rise in a warm place for 30 minutes, or until doubled in size. Meanwhile, preheat the oven to 350°F.

Bake for 18–24 minutes, or until the rolls are just barely turning golden and the tops feel firm to the touch.

For the Maple Glaze

In a small bowl, vigorously whisk together the maple syrup, coconut oil, almond butter, and vanilla (if using) until smooth and emulsified.

To Serve

Serve the cinnamon rolls warm with a generous drizzle of maple glaze.

No Nuts? No Problem | *To keep these sweet rolls nut-free, swap out the almond butter for sunflower butter.*

Sunday Brunch for Body + Soul | *Allow this recipe to lure you out of bed a bit early on a Sunday morning, and cozy up with a good book or leisurely move through yoga poses as the dough rises. By the time the world opens its eyes, you'll have warm cinnamon rolls and a nourished heart.*

CHEESY HERB + SUN-DRIED TOMATO GOOD MORNING BISCUITS

Makes 6 biscuits | 1 hour or less

There are few foods that comfort like warm, freshly baked biscuits, and these puffy little rounds are no exception. Cheesy nutritional yeast, salty sun-dried tomatoes, and herbs are woven throughout an oat-flour biscuit base. Instead of shortening, olive oil lends moisture and allows the biscuits to bake up with crisp, golden exteriors and soft, tender interiors. They waft the most drool-worthy, herbaceous, and savory scent, which makes those 20-plus minutes of baking time a bit hard to endure yet entirely worthwhile.

1 tablespoon flaxseed meal (ground flaxseed)

1 tablespoon filtered water

1/2 cup unsweetened almond milk

3 tablespoons olive oil

1 tablespoon apple cider vinegar

1 1/2 cups homemade oat flour*

1/4 cup blanched almond flour

1/4 cup nutritional yeast flakes

1 1/2 teaspoons aluminum-free baking powder

1 teaspoon chopped fresh rosemary

1 teaspoon dried basil

1/4 teaspoon dried oregano

1/2 teaspoon fine-grain sea salt

1/8 teaspoon freshly ground black pepper

2 tablespoons finely chopped oil-packed sun-dried tomatoes, thoroughly drained

Preheat the oven to 450°F. Line a small baking tray with parchment paper. In a medium mixing bowl, whisk together the flaxseed meal and water, and set aside for 10 minutes to thicken. Then, whisk in the almond milk, olive oil, and apple cider vinegar.

In a large mixing bowl, whisk together the oat flour, almond flour, nutritional yeast, baking powder, rosemary, basil, oregano, sea salt, and black pepper. Stir in the sun-dried tomatoes.

Form a well in the oat flour mixture and pour the almond milk liquid into it. Gently fold and stir until combined into a soft, loose dough. Let the dough rest for 10–15 minutes. This gives the oat flour time to absorb the liquid, thereby thickening the dough.

Line a clean work surface with parchment paper and dust it with oat flour. Lightly grease a 3-inch circular cookie cutter or the opening of a small juice glass.

Turn out the dough onto the parchment paper and gently form it into a 3/4-inch-thick disk. Use the cookie cutter or glass to punch biscuits out of the dough. Gently reform the dough and repeat until you have 6 biscuits. If you don't have enough dough to properly punch out the sixth biscuit, use your hands to roll it into a ball and gently flatten into a biscuit. Place the biscuits next to one another in the center of the parchment-lined baking tray, allowing them to lightly touch to encourage even rising.

Bake for 20–24 minutes, or until the tops of the biscuits are light golden and the bottoms are just barely light golden brown. Serve the biscuits warm from the oven with a pat of vegan butter.

Opt for Homemade Oat Flour | *I recommend using homemade oat flour for this recipe because it's slightly coarser than store-bought oat flour and prevents the biscuits from drying out. To make it, add a few cups of old-fashioned rolled oats to a food processor and process for 4 minutes, or until it resembles flour. Measure off the 1 1/2 cups needed for this recipe, and store any leftover oat flour in an airtight container.*

Serves 2–4 | 45 minutes or less

Tofu has long been the catalyst for a slew of vegan jokes, and I used to stand proudly in the tofu-hating camp. But after giving up eggs, I finally caved and gave the whole scrambled tofu thing a try. Believe it or not, tofu can take on a flavor and texture that is just as enticing as scrambled eggs. The added perk? It's just as protein-packed without any of the cholesterol. For this scramble, you'll toast a variety of dried spices in olive oil before crumbling the tofu into the pan. Toasting the spices in oil draws out the depth of their flavor, and the aroma that wafts from the pan is mouthwatering. After cooking the tofu until golden, you'll top it with a dollop of garlicky avocado mash, salsa, tomatoes, scallions, and cilantro. A lime wedge garnish pulls it all together.

SOUTHWEST TOFU SCRAMBLE

14- or 16-ounce block extra-firm tofu, drained and rinsed

1 tablespoon smoked paprika

1 1/2 teaspoons garlic powder

1 teaspoon ground coriander

3/4 teaspoon sea salt or to taste

1/2 teaspoon dried oregano

1/2 teaspoon ground cumin

1/2 teaspoon ground turmeric (optional)

1/4 teaspoon dried thyme

1/8 teaspoon cayenne pepper (optional)

2 tablespoons olive oil

1 tablespoon fresh lime juice

AVOCADO MASH

2 small ripe avocados, halved, pitted, and peeled

Juice of 1/2 lime, or to taste

1 clove garlic, minced

Sea salt

For the Southwest Tofu Scramble

Wrap the tofu in a few layers of paper towels, place it on a rimmed plate or baking tray, and set a very heavy pan, skillet, or cookbook on top of it for 15 minutes to release excess water. (You can also use a tofu press if you have one.)

Meanwhile, combine the smoked paprika, garlic powder, coriander, sea salt, oregano, cumin, turmeric (if using), thyme, and cayenne pepper (if using) in a small bowl. Set the bowl and the pressed tofu within reach of the stove.

Add the spice mixture and olive oil to a skillet over medium heat, and cook for 30–60 seconds to bloom the spices, stirring frequently.

Crumble the pressed tofu into the skillet, and stir to coat in the spices. Cook for 10–12 minutes, or until the tofu is deep golden and any liquid has cooked off, stirring occasionally at first but with greater frequency in the last few minutes.

Remove from the heat and stir in the fresh lime juice. Season with more sea salt, if desired.

For the Avocado Mash

Meanwhile, add the avocado, lime juice, garlic, and sea salt to a small bowl. Mash together with the back of a fork. Reserve half of the mash for topping the scramble and the other half for spreading over the tortilla crisps.

AVOCADO CRISPS

4 small corn tortillas

1/2 batch Avocado Mash (recipe above)

Sea salt

TOPPINGS

1/2 cup salsa

1/2 cup diced cherry tomatoes

1/4 cup thinly sliced scallions

1/4 cup fresh cilantro, stemmed

1 lime, cut into wedges

For the Avocado Crisps

Heat a small skillet over high heat, and toast each tortilla for 2–3 minutes on each side, or until they're crisp with flecks of deep golden brown. Slather each with some of the reserved avocado mash and season with sea salt to taste.

To Assemble

Divide the tofu scramble among bowls. Top with the reserved avocado mash and the salsa, tomatoes, scallions, and cilantro. Serve with the crisps and lime wedges for spritzing.

AVOCADO TOAST WITH BURST HEIRLOOM TOMATOES + BALSAMIC DRIZZLE

Makes 4 pieces | 30 minutes or less

Avocado toast is quite possibly the most glorious meal to have ever hit the vegan brunch table. Creamy avocado is fanned or mashed over toast, serving as nature's dreamiest butter. Traditional avocado toast typically just involves a piece of toast topped with thinly sliced or mashed avocado, a spritz of fresh lemon or lime juice, an optional drizzle of cold-pressed olive oil, and a sprinkle of salt and pepper. But in this brunchy, jazzed-up take on avocado toast, sliced avocado is fanned across hearty toasted bread and topped with juicy heirloom cherry tomatoes that have been pan-cooked with garlic and herbs until they burst open. The finishing touch is a sprinkle of fresh basil and a generous drizzle of tangy balsamic reduction.

BALSAMIC DRIZZLE

1 recipe Balsamic Reduction (page 297)

BURST HEIRLOOM TOMATOES

1 tablespoon olive oil

2 cloves garlic, smashed, peeled, and roughly chopped

1/2 teaspoon dried oregano

1/2 teaspoon dried basil

1/4 teaspoon dried parsley

1/8 teaspoon crushed red pepper flakes (optional)

2 heaping cups heirloom or standard cherry tomatoes

Sea salt

TOAST AND TOPPINGS

4 pieces gluten-free or sprouted bread, toasted*

1 medium avocado, halved, pitted, peeled, and thinly sliced

1/4 cup fresh basil leaves, chopped

Sea salt and freshly ground black pepper

For the Balsamic Drizzle

If you don't have it handy in your pantry, start by preparing the Balsamic Reduction.

For the Burst Heirloom Tomatoes

Heat the olive oil in a medium skillet over medium-low heat until it just begins to thin out and coat the pan.

Add the garlic, oregano, basil, parsley, and red pepper flakes (if using), and briefly sauté until fragrant, about 1 minute.

Add the cherry tomatoes and a sprinkling of sea salt, increase the heat to medium-high, and cook for 6–8 minutes, or until the tomatoes burst open and just begin to wrinkle. Use a large wooden spoon to occasionally nudge the tomatoes and garlic around the pan to prevent burning, watching out for the hot oil and juices as the tomatoes burst.

To Assemble

Fan the sliced avocado out over each piece of toasted bread. Top with the burst tomatoes, chopped basil, and a drizzle of the balsamic reduction. Season with sea salt and black pepper to taste. Serve immediately.

No Gluten? No Problem | *Use gluten-free bread to keep this dish gluten-free.*

CARAMELIZED BANANA UPSIDE-DOWN OATMEAL BAKE WITH CHAI-SPICED DATE CARAMEL

Serves 8–10 | 1 hour +

If bananas Foster sobered up and had a baby with an oat-crusted pineapple upside-down cake, this is what it would taste like. This brunch-appropriate twist on a banana upside-down cake with a chai-spiced caramel is, without even the tiniest inkling of doubt, my favorite sweet breakfast. The chai-spiced caramel is completely optional, but I recommend it for special occasions, as it dresses up the oat bake and adds a lovely layer of warmth and decadence. When you need to wow a crowd—say, a holiday breakfast or reunion brunch with friends—this dish delivers. But it's just as lovely on an average weekday. So when I need to spice up my breakfast routine and treat myself, I'll make this oat bake on Sunday and enjoy it by the slice throughout the week.

CARAMELIZED UPSIDE-DOWN BANANAS

1/2 cup coconut sugar

1/4 cup virgin coconut oil, melted, plus more for greasing the pan

2 ripe bananas, peeled and sliced into 1/4-inch-thick coins

OATMEAL BAKE

1 1/2 cups unsweetened almond milk*

1/2 cup plus 2 tablespoons mashed ripe banana (about 2 small bananas)

1/4 cup pure maple syrup

2 teaspoons pure vanilla extract

2 cups old-fashioned rolled oats

1/4 cup raw walnut halves, chopped (optional but recommended)

1 teaspoon aluminum-free baking powder

1 teaspoon ground cinnamon

1/8 teaspoon fine-grain sea salt

Preheat the oven to 350°F. Line a large baking tray with foil. Lightly grease a round 9-inch springform pan with coconut oil, and place it on top of the baking sheet. (The lined tray is simply there to catch any sugary liquid that bubbles out of the springform pan during baking.)

For the Caramelized Upside-Down Bananas

In a small mixing bowl, whisk together the coconut sugar and melted coconut oil, and spread it evenly into the greased springform pan.

Arrange the sliced bananas on top of the coconut sugar mixture, forming a circular pattern. This layer will eventually be the top of the oat bake, so take your time with this step.

For the Oatmeal Bake

In a medium mixing bowl, whisk together the almond milk, mashed banana, maple syrup, and vanilla until combined.

In a large mixing bowl, whisk together the rolled oats, walnuts (if using), baking powder, cinnamon, and sea salt.

Add the wet mixture to the dry and use a spatula to stir until just combined. Set the oat batter aside for 5–10 minutes to thicken, stirring occasionally.

Slowly spoon the oat batter into the springform pan, ensuring that the sliced bananas stay put. Use the back of the spoon to gently smooth out the batter.

(continued on next page)

CHAI-SPICED DATE CARAMEL (OPTIONAL)

1/2 cup boiling water

1 chai tea bag

2/3 cup pitted and packed Medjool dates (about 8 dates)

2 teaspoons virgin coconut oil

1 teaspoon pure vanilla extract

1/2 teaspoon ground ginger

1/2 teaspoon ground cinnamon

1/4 teaspoon ground cardamom

1/8–1/4 teaspoon ground cloves

1/4 teaspoon fine-grain sea salt or to taste

Bake for 35–45 minutes, rotating the baking tray 180 degrees at the half-way point, or until the surface is a light golden brown, the edges are slightly pulled away from the sides of the pan, and the top springs back when gently pressed. It won't look 100 percent set, but the oats will continue to set as they cool.

Let cool for 20 minutes

Once the pan is cool enough to handle, release and remove the sides of the springform pan. Place a serving platter face-side down on top of the oat bake. Get a firm grip on the bottom of the pan, and carefully flip the oat bake onto the platter in one motion. Run a knife or metal spatula between the base of the pan and the bananas to release.

For the Chai-Spiced Date Caramel (Optional)

Combine the boiling water and tea bag in a heat-safe pitcher-style measuring cup. Steep for 5 minutes, discard the tea bag, and cool the tea in the freezer for 5 minutes.

Add the cooled tea to a food processor along with the remaining ingredients. Process for 4–6 minutes, or until you have a smooth sauce, stopping to scrape down the sides as needed. If your sauce is too thick, add more water, 1 tablespoon at a time, to thin. Alternatively, if your sauce is too thin, add more pitted dates, one at a time, to thicken. This is a spoonable caramel sauce rather than one that drizzles, so keep that in mind as you make adjustments.

To Serve

Slice the oat bake into as many pieces as desired. Spoon a bit of the chai-spiced caramel (if using) onto a plate and nestle a slice of the oat bake on top.

Refrigerate leftovers for up to 5 days.

No Nuts? No Problem | *To keep this nut-free, simply swap out the unsweetened almond milk for a nut-free plant-based milk, such as unsweetened soy milk or unsweetened rice milk.*

SMOOTHIES + JUICES

Inhale 1 . . . 2 . . . 3 . . . 4 . . . 5. Exhale 5 . . . 4 . . . 3 . . . 2 . . . 1. And as that last bit of air exits your lungs, allow your preconceived smoothie and juice notions to make their grand departure, too. Out with the predict-able (strawberry-banana snoozefest) and in with the attention-grabbing and mouthwatering (Electric Turmeric-Lemonade Smoothie, page 72).

Looking for something green and glorious? Check out the Hellooo, World! Green Smoothie on page 87. Or perhaps you need an after-noon pick-me-up? A Double-Chocolate Hazelnut Espresso Smoothie (page 80) should do the trick. Feeling under the weather, worn out, or run-down? Make the Sunshiny Citrus Smoothie on page 84, and slurp down a glass of vitamin C liquid gold. Craving a green juice that'll put a spring back in your step on an extra-mopey Monday? Check out the Zip-py Pineapple + Fennel Juice on page 79. Or perhaps you're in the mood for an ultra-bubbly smoothie that marches to the effervescent ~~beat~~ fizz of its own drum? In that case, go with the Beguiling Berry-Fizz Bubble Tea on page 69.

Makes 2 (14-ounce) smoothies | 1 hour +

Bubble tea first sprang to life in Taiwan in the early 1980s. There's debate over who invented the beloved beverage, but a man named Liu Han-Chieh seems to be the most widely credited creator. His variation was made with a base of tea, milk, ice, and tapioca pearls; however, over the years, fruit-based variations were also introduced. I first enjoyed the refreshing, fun, and chewy beverage after a sand- and fun-filled day at the beach with Dan. As we walked home from the breezy lakeshore, we passed a bubble tea shop and decided to stop in to see what all the excitement was about. Dan ordered strawberry and I ordered watermelon. And you would have thought the two of us had been deprived of liquid for days given the urgency of our gulps. Sweet, refreshing, icy, and satisfying all at once. If there were such a thing as love at first sip, bubble tea would hold that title for me. And this berry-filled, fizzy twist is every bit as enticing. Tapioca pearls are nestled at the bottom of this smoothie, yielding a fun and refreshing treat that will keep you coming back for more. Cheers to love at first sip!

TAPIOCA PEARLS

7 cups water, divided

1/4 cup large tapioca pearls*

2 tablespoons pure maple syrup

BERRY-FIZZ SMOOTHIE

1 cup frozen raspberries

1 cup frozen blueberries

1 cup filtered water

4 pitted Medjool dates or to taste*

1/2–1 cup lime sparkling natural mineral water

For the Tapioca Pearls

In a large saucepan, bring 4 cups of the water to a rolling boil over high heat. Add the tapioca pearls and stir to disperse. Allow the water to return to a boil. Once the tapioca pearls begin to float to the top, lower the heat to medium and cover the pan, leaving the lid slightly ajar. Cook for 30 minutes, stirring every 10 minutes.

Turn off the heat, cover the pan completely, and allow the tapioca pearls to steep for 25 minutes, or until translucent. It's okay if their centers are still flecked with a tiny bit of white.

Meanwhile, pour the remaining 3 cups water into a large jar and stir in the maple syrup.

Drain and thoroughly rinse the steeped tapioca pearls with cool water. Transfer them to the jar of sweetened water and refrigerate until ready to use. They'll keep for about 4 days in the refrigerator.

For the Berry-Fizz Smoothie

Combine the raspberries, blueberries, filtered water, and dates in a high-speed blender and blend on high until completely smooth. Stir in the sparkling mineral water, adding 1/2 cup for a sweeter smoothie or 1 cup for a lighter, more effervescent smoothie.

To Assemble

Spoon a generous amount of the tapioca pearls into 2 glasses and pour the berry smoothie on top. Serve immediately with a wide bubble-tea straw large enough to slurp up the pearls.

(continued on next page)

Mind Your Tapioca Pearls | *Be sure to check the ingredient list when you're buying tapioca pearls—it should have one ingredient: tapioca starch. If there is a long list of nonsense, take a pass, because they won't cook up as well and are probably full of chemicals.*

Be Kind to Your Blender | *If you're not using a high-speed blender (e.g., Vitamix or Blendtec), soak the dates in hot water for 30 minutes to soften before blending.*

Simplify It! | *If you're short on time, feel free to make just the Berry-Fizz Smoothie (sans tapioca pearls). Truth be told, it's my favorite smoothie in this book and it requires all of about 5 minutes to make.*

Makes 1 (24-ounce) or 2 (12-ounce) smoothies
15 minutes or less

Well, hello there. Allow me to introduce you to one of my all-time favorite smoothies. She's got an electric glow and a sweet tartness that'll keep you on your toes. Plus, she'll detox the weekend right out of you. She goes by Electric Turmeric-Lemonade Smoothie, but you can call her Lemonade for short.

In all seriousness though, this smoothie offers an anti-inflammatory and detoxifying boost thanks to its turmeric and fresh lemon juice. Curcumin, the yellow-orange pigment in turmeric, is considered an anti-inflammatory powerhouse. Although it does add a subtle kick to the smoothie, it's mellowed by a gentle nuzzle of sweetness from mango and green grapes. And despite its acidic bite, fresh lemon juice acts as a powerful alkalizer inside the body, cleaning house and nudging the liver to dump accumulated toxins.

1 1/2 cups peeled and diced ripe fresh mango (about 1 large mango)

1/2 cup seedless green grapes

1/2–1 cup ice

1/2 cup coconut water or filtered water

2 tablespoons fresh lemon juice

1/4 teaspoon ground turmeric

1–2 Medjool dates, pitted (optional, to sweeten)*

Add all the ingredients to a high-speed blender, and blend until smooth.

Sweeten to Taste | *The sweetness of your mango and green grapes will determine whether or not you need to add the dates.*

Be Kind to Your Blender | *If you're not using a high-speed blender (e.g., Vitamix or Blendtec), soak the dates in hot water for 30 minutes before blending.*

Makes 1 (16-ounce) smoothie | 15 minutes or less

Get your happy, dewy glow on with this breakfast-appropriate shake. Tahini, also known as sesame butter, is rich in calcium and vitamin E. Pair it with tryptophan- and potassium-laden bananas and a spoonful of protein-rich hemp seeds, and you've got yourself a shake full of goodness. Hello, glowing hair, dewy skin, and feel-good vibes. Let's get this day started, shall we?

1 ripe and speckled banana, peeled, sliced, and frozen

1 cup unsweetened almond milk*

1/2 cup ice (optional)

2 Medjool dates, pitted*

1 tablespoon tahini

1 tablespoon shelled hemp seeds

1 teaspoon pure vanilla extract

Add all the ingredients to a high-speed blender, and blend until smooth and creamy.

No Nuts? No Problem | *To keep this nut-free, simply swap out the unsweetened almond milk for a nut-free plant-based milk, such as unsweetened soy milk or unsweetened rice milk.*

Be Kind to Your Blender | *If you're not using a high-speed blender (e.g., Vitamix or Blendtec), soak the dates in hot water for 30 minutes to soften before blending.*

ENERGIZING CARROT-CAKE SMOOTHIE

Makes 1 (20-ounce) or 2 (10-ounce) smoothies | 15 minutes or less

The thought of carrot cake conjures up a hazy memory from childhood. We were in a restaurant when I was offered a piece of carrot cake. I promptly turned it down. Carrots? Cake? My young brain couldn't fathom a delicious outcome with the word *carrot* juxtaposed with *cake*.

But my curiosity was piqued as I caught a glimpse of the mysterious cake slathered with thick white icing. I eagerly took a bite of my mom's and felt a sense of joy wash over me, and I've never again doubted the scrumptiousness of this aptly named dessert.

Although a far departure from its icing-slathered form, this smoothie is home to all the classic carrot cake elements: warming spices, creaminess, a soft orange glow, and just the right amount of nuttiness.

2 ripe and speckled bananas, peeled, sliced, and frozen	Add all the ingredients to a high-speed blender, and blend until smooth and creamy.
1 medium carrot, peeled and roughly sliced	
1 cup unsweetened almond milk	
2 tablespoons raw walnut pieces*	
1 Medjool date, pitted*	
1 teaspoon peeled and minced ginger root or 1/2 teaspoon ground ginger	
1 teaspoon ground cinnamon	
1 teaspoon pure vanilla extract (optional)	
Pinch of ground nutmeg	

Be Kind to Your Blender | *If you're not using a high-speed blender (e.g., Vitamix or Blendtec), soak the walnuts and date in hot water for 30 minutes to soften before blending.*

Food for Thought | *Walnuts are excellent brain food thanks to their omega-3 content. Plus, they look like little brains, which seems like Mother Nature's hint that these nuts will keep your noggin healthy.*

Makes 2 (14-ounce) juices | 15 minutes or less

Between the hours of 5:00 A.M. and 7:00 A.M., you'll find me singing, dancing, and offering tidbits of optimism to anyone who will listen (usually our orange tabby cat, Jack). Sometimes my morning-person excitement might even be inappropriately joyful. Such as the time I kissed Dan good-bye and encouraged him to "Have a stupendous day!" only to be reminded that he actually needed to fire someone at work that morning. Oops.

While my early-morning hours are outfitted in energy and excitement, my early-afternoon hours are the exact opposite. I typically hit a two-hour energy slump around 12:00 P.M. every day, and it takes all the willpower I have not to curl up under my desk for an afternoon snooze. Fortunately, I've found two things that combat the afternoon sleepies: hydration and a kick of spice. Luckily, this juice offers a bit of both. Whether you're a morning person or an afternoon person, take a swig of this sweet and spicy blend the next time your energy slumps to alert your senses and put a spring back in your step.

1 large cucumber (about 10 ounces), peeled

3 heaping cups fresh pineapple chunks (about 1 medium pineapple, peeled)

1 bulb fennel (about 10 ounces), ends trimmed

1 cup loosely packed fresh cilantro, stemmed

1/2–1 small jalapeño, ends trimmed, halved, and seeded

Cut all the ingredients to a length and width that will fit through your juicer.

One at a time, run each piece through the juicer. If you have a centrifugal juicer—as opposed to a masticating or twin gear juicer—I recommend collecting the pulp and running it through another one or two times to yield as much juice as possible.

Repurpose That Pulp! | *Freeze the pulp and add it to smoothies, oatmeal, or salads throughout the week. Talk about a fiber and flavor boost!*

Makes 1 (18-ounce) or 2 (9-ounce) smoothies | 15 minutes or less

What a mouthful. This one is easier to make than it is to say. Chocolate × 2 + toasted hazelnuts + espresso = goodness in a glass with a kick of caffeine. This afternoon pick-me-up smoothie tastes like frosty scoops of double-chocolate chunk ice cream blended with ribbons of Nutella and a splash of aromatic espresso. The ~~cherry~~ cacao nibs on top? This plant-powerful treat is made from pure, nourishing foods, meaning every ounce keeps it real. No, you're not dreaming. But now that you mention it, you might actually be drooling. Yes, really—there on the right side of your mouth. Little to the left. Yep, you got it.

1 ripe and speckled banana, peeled, sliced, and frozen

1 cup unsweetened almond milk

1/2 cup ice

1/4 cup toasted hazelnuts*

2–4 ounces brewed espresso or strong coffee, chilled

3–4 Medjool dates, pitted and soaked

1 1/2 tablespoons raw cacao powder

1 teaspoon pure vanilla extract

1/8 teaspoon sea salt

2 tablespoons cacao nibs

Add the frozen banana, almond milk, ice, hazelnuts, espresso, dates, cacao powder, vanilla, and sea salt to a high-speed blender, and blend until smooth and creamy.

Add in the cacao nibs and blend for a few seconds to roughly chop and incorporate them into the smoothie.

Toast Your Hazelnuts | *Preheat the oven to 400°F. Spread 1/4 cup raw hazelnuts in a small, ungreased baking pan, and bake for 6–10 minutes, or until they're wafting a warm, toasted scent.*

ALMOND BUTTER MACA MADNESS SMOOTHIE (TRIPLE REMIX)

Makes 1 (24-ounce) or 2 (12-ounce) smoothies | 15 minutes or less

The original version of this smoothie is my absolute favorite smoothie ever, and it's become one of the most popular smoothies on the Blissful Basil blog. So it only made sense to include it in the book. However, I couldn't help but expand upon the original version, so you're getting a triple remix: Original, Cacao Crunch, and Vanilla Chai Spice.

  This smoothie is so creamy and rich that it boldly walks the line between smoothie and shake. If you haven't been introduced to raw maca root powder yet, this is a great way to get acquainted. It's rich in vitamins B, C, and E; it helps balance hormones and mood; it increases energy and stamina; and it has skin-clarifying properties.

ORIGINAL

2 ripe and speckled bananas, peeled, sliced, and frozen

1 cup unsweetened almond milk*

1 tablespoon almond butter*

1 tablespoon maca powder

1/2 teaspoon pure vanilla extract

CACAO CRUNCH

2 ripe and speckled bananas, peeled, sliced, and frozen

1 cup unsweetened almond milk*

1–2 tablespoons raw cacao powder

1 tablespoon almond butter*

1 tablespoon maca powder

1 tablespoon raw cacao nibs (optional)

VANILLA CHAI SPICE

2 ripe and speckled bananas, peeled, sliced, and frozen

1 cup unsweetened almond milk*

1 tablespoon almond butter*

1 tablespoon maca powder

1 teaspoon pure vanilla extract

1/4 teaspoon ground cinnamon

1/4 teaspoon ground ginger

1/8 teaspoon ground cardamom

1/8 teaspoon ground cloves

Original

Add all the ingredients to a high-speed blender, and blend until smooth and creamy.

Cacao Crunch

Add the frozen bananas, almond milk, cacao powder, almond butter, and maca powder to a high-speed blender, and blend on high until smooth. Add the raw cacao nibs (if using) and pulse to roughly chop and incorporate.

Vanilla Chai Spice

Add all the ingredients to a high-speed blender, and blend until smooth and creamy.

No Nuts? No Problem | *To keep these smoothies nut-free, swap out the almond butter and almond milk for sunflower butter and nut-free plant-based milk, such as unsweetened soy milk or unsweetened rice milk.*

Makes 2 (16-ounce) smoothies | 15 minutes or less

Fresh mango, frozen banana, orange, and grapefruit are blended with lime juice and baobab powder to create a smoothie with a sunshiny hue, an ultra-bright taste, and a pop of vitamin C. Something about the color of this smoothie really does make me happy—it's difficult not to feel a touch of optimism when you're staring into a golden abyss of blended fruit.

2 cups fresh mango chunks (about 2 medium mangoes)

1 ripe and speckled banana, peeled, sliced, and frozen

1 navel orange, peeled and quartered

1/4–1/2 large grapefruit, peeled and seeded

1 tablespoon fresh lime juice

1 teaspoon baobab powder (optional)*

Add all the ingredients to a high-speed blender, and blend until smooth. If needed, add in a bit of filtered water, 1/4 cup at a time, to encourage blending.

What in the World Is Baobab? | *Baobab is a naturally occurring raw fruit powder derived from the baobab tree. It has a lovely citrusy flavor that's reminiscent of orange sherbet, and it contains 6 times more vitamin C than oranges and 5 times more potassium than bananas!*

HELLOOO, WORLD! GREEN SMOOTHIE

Makes 1 (18-ounce) or 2 (9-ounce) smoothies | 5 minutes

It was a tough job to figure out which green smoothie to include in this book. After blending and sipping my way through more glasses of green than I could count—consider me a green-smoothie Goldilocks—I finally settled on this one. It's neither too wildly green and grassy nor too light and fruity. It's juuuust right. This green smoothie struts right down the middle in terms of flavor and hue. It garners its sweetness from frozen banana and pineapple, and it's balanced by the addition of curly kale and fennel. A small spoonful of fresh minced ginger is tossed in to encourage digestion and get things flowing. Start your blenders, gather your greens, and welcome a new day. Helloo, world!

1 ripe and speckled banana, peeled, sliced, and frozen*

1 cup tightly packed stemmed curly kale or baby spinach

3/4 cup unsweetened almond milk*

3/4 cup fresh or frozen pineapple chunks

1/4 medium fennel bulb, ends trimmed and roughly chopped

1 teaspoon fresh minced ginger

Add all the ingredients to a high-speed blender, and blend until smooth and creamy.

Not Up for Banana? | *Swap out the frozen banana for 1 cup frozen mango to keep things light, sweet, and refreshing.*

No Nuts? No Problem | *To keep this nut-free, simply swap out the unsweetened almond milk for a nut-free plant-based milk, such as unsweetened soy milk or unsweetened rice milk.*

SNACKS + APPETIZERS

SNACKS

Power Biscotti 91

Cinnamon-Almond Granola Bar(k) 94

Blueberry Muffin Energy Bites 97

Cheesy Garlic-Herb Oat Crackers 98

Soft + Chewy Trail Mix Cookies 101

Avocado Rice Cakes with Spicy Tomato Jam 102

Crispy Parmesan Brussels Sprout Chips with Lemon Aioli 105

APPETIZERS

Roasted Balsamic Cauliflower Steaks with Tomato-Basil Relish 106

Herbed Cashew Cheese Plate with Spicy Tomato Jam + Roasted Garlic 109

Crispy CauliPower Tots with Speedy Two-Minute Ketchup 111

Garlic, Rosemary + Parmesan Focaccia Bread 115

Roasted Yellow Pepper, Sun-Dried Tomato + Basil Portobello Pizzettes 116

Pile 'Em High Epic Plant-Powered Nachos 119

Yellow Split-Pea Nacho Cheese 120

Beet Balls with Spicy Tahini-Ginger Sauce 123

My memories of early childhood are filled with images of my mom and dad hosting large gatherings at our house. Their parties always struck that welcoming sweet spot: they were meticulously planned down to the last detail, yet guests were encouraged to come as they were, kick back, and relax. I remember one party in particular, a summer barbecue, in which there were nearly 100 guests. My mom prepared a feast of appetizers, snacks, and sides, and my dad served as grill master. The happiness I felt then, seeing so many family members and friends laughing and feasting together, remains embedded within the memories I carry with me today. In hindsight, that big summer barbecue was the first time I realized that there's far more joy to be collected from moments than from materials.

My mom and dad parted ways just a few years after that spectacular party. And shortly after that, they both remarried. From a distance, it appears that they fell in love with each other's opposite. But upon closer inspection, there's a very strong common thread running between all four of my parents: They value moments of connection, especially those with family, above all else. They'll do whatever they can to set the stage for these moments to take place, and nothing brings them more joy than stepping back to witness the happiness that ensues. And whether it's an afternoon snack at home with friends, a family barbecue, or a special event, those four know how to make their guests feel special and at ease. Their trick? Good food that's made with love (and lots of it), including plenty of snacks and appetizers to break the ice and get the friendly chitchat flowing.

In the spirit of the above, let's get this party started, shall we? Whether you're in need of a tasty snack to nosh on for girls' night, an energizing mid-morning nibble to fuel your little loved ones (or yourself), or a crowd-pleasing array of small bites to toast a special occasion, I've got you covered. Let the good vibes roll.

POWER BISCOTTI

Makes 16 biscotti | 1 hour +

These crunchy snacks were specially designed to be nutrient-rich down to their last grain-free bite. Rather than grain-based flour, these biscotti are made with homemade sunflower seed flour. Dried fruit, pepitas, and cacao nibs are folded in to offer pops of texture, while pure maple syrup provides just the right amount of subtle sweetness. The dough is formed into two flat, rectangular loafs and baked before being sliced and baked a second time until crisp and golden. These biscotti make a fantastic energizing snack or breakfast that you can grab on your way out the door. Or you can dunk them into coffee or tea as you settle in with a good book.

1 tablespoon flaxseed meal (ground flaxseed)

2 tablespoons filtered water

2 cups raw shelled sunflower seeds

1 tablespoon arrowroot starch

1/4 teaspoon fine-grain sea salt

1/2 cup unsweetened dried cherries, cranberries, or blueberries, roughly chopped

1/3 cup raw pepitas

2 tablespoons cacao nibs (optional)

1/4 cup pure maple syrup

1 teaspoon pure vanilla extract

Preheat the oven to 350°F. Line a large baking sheet with parchment paper.

In a small mixing bowl, whisk together the flaxseed meal and water. Set aside for 10 minutes to thicken.

Meanwhile, add the raw sunflower seeds to a food processor and process for 1 minute, or until you have a coarse flour or fine meal and all of the seeds are thoroughly ground, stopping to pulse several times to ensure even processing. The texture should be flourlike; be careful not to over-process or you'll end up with sunflower butter.

Transfer the sunflower flour to a large mixing bowl and whisk in the arrow-root and sea salt. Stir in the dried fruit, pepitas, and cacao nibs (if using).

Add the maple syrup and vanilla extract to the small mixing bowl with the flaxseed mixture and vigorously whisk to combine. Pour over the dry sunflower mixture, and use a large wooden spoon to mix well. At first it will seem like there isn't enough liquid, but keep stirring until the liquid is evenly dispersed and you have a damp dough.

Turn the dough out onto the lined baking sheet, and divide it into 2 equal pieces. Use your hands to shape and compact the dough into 2 tightly packed rectangles. Each rectangle should be approximately 4 × 6 inches, and just shy of 1 inch thick. If the dough is sticking to your hands, lightly dampen them with water to repel the mixture.

Bake for 20–24 minutes, or until the edges are light golden brown and each rectangle feels well set, yet retains a soft indentation when gently pressed. Remove from the oven and cool for 20 minutes.

Meanwhile, decrease the oven temperature to 275°F.

(continued on next page)

Once the biscotti rectangles are mostly cool, use a sharp knife to cut them widthwise into 3/4-inch-thick slices, pressing straight down and rocking the knife back and forth to slice rather than using a sawing motion. You should have a total of 16 biscotti, 8 from each rectangle, and each should be approximately 4 inches long.

Carefully return the biscotti to the lined baking pan, sliced-side down. Bake for 16–18 minutes. Then, use a metal spatula to carefully flip each biscotti, and bake for another 16–18 minutes, or until rich golden brown and crisp to the touch. They'll continue to crisp as they cool, so keep that in mind when testing for doneness.

Carefully transfer the biscotti to a wire cooling rack. Cool completely. Store in an airtight glass container to maintain crispness. They'll keep for up to 1 week at room temperature.

CINNAMON-ALMOND GRANOLA BAR(K)

Otherwise known in our house as "granola crack," this simple, power-packed snack is crunchy, nutty, and just sweet enough. It's basically a giant, homemade granola bar that gets broken into bite-size pieces. It reminds me of delectable little speculoos cookies, those crisp, rectangular shortbread cookies, only it's packed with healthy fats, vitamin E, zinc, and potassium. I like to make this on Sunday night so that I can snack on it throughout the week, but I've also been known to eat the entire batch in under 24 hours.

1 1/2 cups old-fashioned rolled oats

1/2 cup raw almonds

1/2 cup pure maple syrup

1/4 cup natural almond butter

2 tablespoons virgin coconut oil

2 teaspoons pure vanilla extract

1 1/2 teaspoons ground cinnamon

1/4 teaspoon fine-grain sea salt

Preheat the oven to 275°F. Line a 9 × 13-inch baking tray with parchment paper.

Add all the ingredients to a food processor. Pulse 10–15 times and then process for 30 seconds, or until a coarse meal forms and the oats are roughly chopped.

Scoop the granola mixture onto the lined pan and use a spatula to press and compact it, beginning at the outer edges of the pan and working your way inward. Leave a 4 × 3-inch rectangular hole in the center of the pan, forming the mixture into a doughnutlike shape (to ensure even baking). Keep compacting and smoothing the mixture until you have an evenly distributed 1/3- to 1/2-inch-thick layer.

Bake for 30 minutes, rotate the pan, and bake for another 25–30 minutes, or until the edges are light golden brown, the bottom is deep golden brown, and the surface feels dry to the touch. It will continue to crisp as it cools, so go by time and color rather than crispness to assess doneness.

Transfer the entire pan to an oven-safe wire cooling rack and cool completely.

Break into one- or two-bite pieces. Store the bark in an airtight glass container to maintain crispness. It will keep for up to 2 weeks at room temperature.

BLUEBERRY MUFFIN ENERGY BITES

Makes 12 energy bites | 15 minutes or less

When I was a teenager, I had a thing for those oversized packaged blueberry muffins sold in school cafeterias. I convinced myself I was making a healthy choice because I opted for the muffins flecked with blueberries (if that's what they were) over the ones dotted with chocolate chips. I'd diligently pick off bits of the muffin stump and protectively preserve the muffin top until the very end, saving the best for last. In retrospect, those muffins probably weren't doing much for me other than fueling my hormone-charged adolescent cravings. So I did what any oversized-muffin-lover-turned-wellness-enthusiast would: I made blueberry muffin energy bites! These energy bites pack a rich blueberry flavor, lively sweetness, and playful caramel notes. Their flavor takes me back to my giant blueberry muffin moments, minus the junk and plus a boost of plant-pure goodness with real blueberries, to boot.

1 cup pitted and packed Medjool dates

1/2 cup dried mulberries

1/2 cup raw almonds*

2 tablespoons shelled hemp seeds*

1/8 teaspoon fine-grain sea salt

1/2–3/4 cup dried wild blueberries

In a food processor, combine the Medjool dates, mulberries, almonds, hemp seeds, and sea salt. Pulse a few times and then process until the mixture begins to clump together as it moves around the blade. You want a crumbly but sticky mixture that holds together when pressed between your fingers. If needed, add a few more pitted dates to stick all that goodness together. Then, add the dried blueberries and pulse 10–15 times to chop and incorporate.

Using a 1 1/2-tablespoon cookie scoop or spoon, scoop out a tightly packed mound, roll into a ball, and drop into an airtight container. Repeat with the remaining mixture. You should have 12 energy bites. Store in the refrigerator for up to 1 week or in the freezer for up to 1 month.

No Nuts? No Problem | *To make this nut-free, swap out the raw almonds for raw shelled sunflower seeds.*

Ch-Ch-Ch-Chia! | *Feel free to swap out the hemp seeds for chia seeds. They offer a lovely little crunch as well as a detoxifying boost.*

Makes about 80 crackers | 1 hour +

Also known as an herbed-up, vegan version of my favorite college snack—hint: it starts with *Cheez* and ends with *Its*—this plant-based rendition took me ten trials to perfect, and I'm happy to say that it was 100 percent worth the fuss and a few choice words. These crackers have an irresistible flaky crispness and garlic-herb cheesiness that's even more snack-worthy and addictive than the original.

1 tablespoon flaxseed meal (ground flaxseed)

2 tablespoons filtered water

1 cup oat flour

1/2 cup nutritional yeast flakes

1 teaspoon garlic powder

1 teaspoon dried basil

1 teaspoon dried oregano

1 teaspoon fine-grain sea salt or to taste

1/4 cup cold water

1/4 cup cold-pressed olive oil

In a small bowl, whisk together the flaxseed meal and filtered water. Set aside for 10 minutes to thicken.

Add the oat flour, nutritional yeast, garlic powder, basil, oregano, and sea salt to a food processor. Pulse 15 times to incorporate. Then, add the flaxseed mixture, cold water, and olive oil. Pulse a few times and then process for 20 seconds, or until the mixture begins to clump together or rolls into a ball. Let the dough rest in the food processor for 20 minutes. (This gives the oat flour time to fully absorb the moisture from the water and oil, which makes for easier rolling.)

Preheat the oven to 350°F. Line two large baking trays with parchment paper.

Lay a large piece of parchment paper out on a clean work surface. Transfer the cracker dough to the parchment paper, form into a disk, and cover with another equal-sized piece of parchment paper.

Use a rolling pin to roll out the cracker dough to just under 1/8 inch thickness between the sheets of parchment paper.

Remove the top sheet of parchment paper and use a pizza cutter to cut the dough into 1-inch squares. If desired, use a toothpick to dot the center of each cracker with a decorative hole. Carefully transfer the crackers to the lined baking trays, forming a single layer and leaving a bit of space in between each cracker.

Bake for 8 minutes, rotate the pans, and bake for another 8–14 minutes, or until the crackers are light golden brown and feel mostly crisp to the touch. They'll continue to crisp up as they cool. If some crackers are baking quicker than others due to varying thickness, remove them in batches, transferring those that are done early to another pan to cool.

Let the crackers cool completely. Then, transfer to an airtight glass jar or glass container (to maintain crispness) and store at room temperature for up to 2 weeks.

SOFT + CHEWY TRAIL MIX COOKIES

Makes 10 cookies | 30 minutes or less

These cookies inspire a lot of love, and it's easy to see why. They represent all the best parts of trail mix in a soft and chewy package. Dan and I are equally smitten. In fact, these cookies are such a hot commodity in our house that I'm able to use them as bargaining chips in exchange for household chores. I've even used them to avoid my most dreaded chore: emptying the dishwasher. Its poorly designed silverware basket always leaves a tangle of utensils in its wake. *"Dan, I'll make trail mix cookies if you empty the silverware basket."* Before I've even reached for the rolled oats, he'll leap for the dishwasher. What he doesn't know? I'd happily make these cookies any day of the week and without any compensation just to enjoy their deliciousness, but that'll be our little secret.

1 cup old-fashioned rolled oats

1/3 cup seedless raisins or dried cranberries

1/4 cup raw pepitas

1/4 cup raw sunflower seeds

1 tablespoon chia seeds

1 tablespoon flaxseed meal (ground flaxseed)

1/2 teaspoon ground cinnamon

1/8 teaspoon fine-grain sea salt

1/3 cup brown rice syrup

2 tablespoons sunflower butter or almond butter*

1 teaspoon pure vanilla extract

Preheat the oven to 300°F. Line a large baking sheet with parchment paper.

In a large mixing bowl, stir together the rolled oats, raisins, pepitas, sunflower seeds, chia seeds, flaxseed meal, cinnamon, and sea salt.

In a small mixing bowl, use a fork to whisk together the brown rice syrup, sunflower butter, and vanilla until smooth and glossy.

Pour the wet syrup mixture over the dry oat mixture and stir to evenly coat. This takes a bit of strength and a few minutes of time, so be patient. You almost need to mash the mixture to disperse the wet ingredients.

Use a small ice cream scoop or measuring spoon to scoop out 2 heaping tablespoons of dough. Drop on the lined baking sheet and repeat until you have 10 mounds of dough. Then, lightly wet your hands with water and flatten and compact each mound into a 3/4-inch-thick cookie. If your fingers become too sticky to properly form and compact the cookies, just lightly wet your hands again.

Bake for 12–14 minutes, or until the cookies lose their tackiness. Be careful not to overbake, or you'll have crunchy cookies instead of soft, chewy ones.

Transfer the entire pan to a cooling rack. Allow the cookies to cool completely before moving. (They'll set and firm up as they cool.)

Store the cookies in an airtight container at room temperature for up to 3–4 days.

No Nuts? No Problem | *To keep this nut-free, simply swap out the almond butter for sunflower butter.*

Makes 2 rice cakes | 15 minutes or less

There will be no plain rice cakes or boring snacks on my watch. Crunchy rice cakes are topped with sliced avocado and a few generous spoonfuls of Spicy Tomato Jam (page 291). A light sprinkle of salt and pepper finishes off this simple yet immensely satisfying snack.

1/2 small avocado, halved, pitted, peeled, and thinly sliced

2 rice cakes

1/4 cup Spicy Tomato Jam (page 291)

Sea salt and freshly ground black pepper

Fan the avocado out over each rice cake, top with the Spicy Tomato Jam, and season with sea salt and black pepper to taste. Serve immediately.

Plan, Prepare, Conquer | *Make a batch of* Spicy Tomato Jam *over the weekend and enjoy this quick snack throughout the week.*

CRISPY PARMESAN BRUSSELS SPROUT CHIPS
WITH LEMON AIOLI

Serves 4–6 | 1 hour +

Kale chips everywhere are buckling under the pressure, because Brussels sprouts may very well be the veggie to steal the healthy-snack-food trophy. Broccoli chips gave it their all but came up a bit too crunchy; root veggies have been crunchin' for years, yet they're a bit tricky to master at home; and eggplant chips might as well call an audible and pass the ball to B. Sprouts. Because these crisp, golden-brown chips are a touchdown, especially when they're coated in salty Nut // Seed Parmesan Cheese (page 299). The lemon aioli is completely optional, but it dresses up the chips and adds a snazzy, lemony tang to balance out that savory Parmesan flavor.

CRISPY PARMESAN BRUSSELS SPROUT CHIPS

2 pounds large Brussels sprouts

2 tablespoons cold-pressed olive oil

1 recipe Nut // Seed Parmesan Cheese (page 299)*

LEMON AIOLI (OPTIONAL)

3/4 cup raw cashews*

1/2 cup filtered water

2 cloves garlic, peeled

2 tablespoons fresh lemon juice

1 teaspoon Dijon mustard

1/2 teaspoon sea salt

Freshly ground black pepper

For the Crispy Parmesan Brussels Sprout Chips

Preheat the oven to 250°F. Line two large baking sheets with parchment paper.

One at a time, trim the Brussels sprouts and separate the leaves. You'll need to trim the base of the sprout a few times to get as many leaves as possible from each. If the leaves appear gritty or dirty, thoroughly rinse and pat them completely dry. Transfer to an extra-large mixing bowl, drizzle with the olive oil, and massage the oil into the leaves. Prepare the Nut // Seed Parmesan Cheese, sprinkle it over the leaves, and toss to evenly coat.

Divide the leaves evenly between the baking sheets and spread them out into a single layer, separating any clumps of leaves to ensure even crisping. If necessary, reserve some of the leaves to bake in a second batch.

Bake for 45–55 minutes, or until the leaves are crisp and their edges are golden brown, tossing every 15 minutes to prevent burning. If the pans have been overcrowded and they are baking unevenly, simply remove the leaves that are done and continue baking any tender or soggy leaves until crisp.

These are best served warm immediately after baking.

For the Lemon Aioli (Optional)

Prepare the aioli while the chips are baking. Add all the aioli ingredients to a high-speed blender and blend on high for 2 minutes, or until completely smooth, stopping to scrape down the sides as needed. Keep refrigerated until serving.

No Nuts? No Problem | *To keep this recipe nut-free, opt for a seed-based Parmesan and omit the lemon aioli.*

Be Kind to Your Blender | *If you're not using a high-speed blender (e.g., Vitamix or Blendtec), soak the cashews in water for 2 hours or boil them for 10 minutes to soften before blending.*

ROASTED BALSAMIC CAULIFLOWER STEAKS WITH TOMATO-BASIL RELISH

Serves 2–4 | 1 hour +

It was a school night in the spring of 1995; I was eleven and in the throes of my preteen years, and my mom served up a recipe for Sautéed Worcestershire Chicken that she had found in *Bon Appétit*. Although the title highlights Worcestershire, it was the subtle addition of balsamic vinegar that always stood out for me. It was this dish that ignited my love for the rich and tangy vinegar.

These Roasted Balsamic Cauliflower Steaks tip their balsamic hat to that childhood favorite of mine. They're soaked in a rich balsamic marinade before being roasted and topped with a lively tomato-basil relish. I recommend finding the biggest head of cauliflower that you can or investing in two medium heads for this dish, because you'll need to cut at least four sizable "steaks" from the center.

ROASTED BALSAMIC CAULIFLOWER STEAKS

1 extra-large or 2 medium heads cauliflower, outer leaves removed

2/3 cup balsamic vinegar

1/4 cup cold-pressed olive oil

2 tablespoons tahini

2 cloves garlic, minced

1/2–3/4 teaspoon sea salt

Freshly ground black pepper

TOMATO-BASIL RELISH

1 cup cherry tomatoes, diced

1/4 cup loosely packed basil leaves, thinly sliced

1 teaspoon balsamic vinegar

1 small clove garlic, minced

Sea salt and freshly ground black pepper

For the Roasted Balsamic Cauliflower Steaks

Carefully stand the head of cauliflower on its stem and use a sharp knife to cut it in half down the center. Then, stand each half on its stem and cut as many 1/2- to 3/4-inch-thick cauliflower "steaks" as possible, moving from the center outward. You'll want at least 4 total but preferably more if possible. Reserve the remaining cauliflower for other uses.

Prepare the marinade. In a medium mixing bowl, whisk together the balsamic vinegar, olive oil, tahini, garlic, sea salt, and black pepper to taste.

In a large resealable bag, combine the cauliflower steaks and marinade and toss to evenly coat. Marinate for 30 minutes, gently turning the bag every 5–10 minutes to redistribute the marinade.

After about 15 minutes of marinating, preheat the oven to 400°F and line a large baking tray with parchment paper.

Remove the cauliflower steaks from the marinade and spread them out in a single layer on the lined baking tray. Bake for 30–35 minutes, or until golden brown and tender, gently flipping at the 15-minute mark.

For the Tomato-Basil Relish

While the cauliflower is baking, prepare the tomato-basil relish. In a small mixing bowl, gently stir together all the relish ingredients, then refrigerate until serving.

To Assemble

Divide the cauliflower steaks among plates, and season with more sea salt and black pepper, if desired. Spoon the tomato-basil relish on top of each steak and serve immediately.

HERBED CASHEW CHEESE PLATE WITH SPICY TOMATO JAM + ROASTED GARLIC

If you're suspiciously eyeing this recipe because homemade nut cheese sounds all too fussy, I get it. Up until July of 2014, just the thought of it was enough to simultaneously bore me and stress me out. But one steamy summer afternoon, a vegan cheese craving aligned with an unexpected sense of kitchen adventure and before I knew what was happening, nuts were soaking and cheesecloth was being trimmed. The result was a creamy, spreadable, nearly sliceable herbed cashew cheese that was actually crazy-easy to make. I paired it with Spicy Tomato Jam (page 291) and shared the recipe on Blissful Basil and to my sweet surprise, it's held the number one spot for appetizers ever since. This is the same recipe, but because I can't seem to leave well enough alone, it's made just a touch more magical with the addition of roasted garlic.

HERBED CASHEW CHEESE

1 cup raw cashews, soaked in water for 8 hours or more, drained

2 tablespoons nutritional yeast flakes

2 tablespoons fresh lemon juice

2 tablespoons filtered water

1 teaspoon apple cider vinegar or white wine vinegar

1 clove garlic, minced

1/2 teaspoon sea salt or to taste

Freshly ground black pepper

1/2 tablespoon chopped fresh basil, plus more for garnishing

1/2 teaspoon chopped fresh oregano, plus more for garnishing

1/4 teaspoon chopped fresh thyme, plus more for garnishing

ROASTED GARLIC

2 heads garlic

2 teaspoons olive oil (optional)*

SPICY TOMATO JAM

1 recipe Spicy Tomato Jam (page 291)

For the Herbed Cashew Cheese

Add the soaked cashews to a food processor along with the nutritional yeast, lemon juice, filtered water, vinegar, garlic, sea salt, and black pepper to taste. Process for 4 minutes, or until very smooth and creamy, stopping to scrape down the sides as needed. The texture should resemble a runny cream cheese. Add the chopped basil, oregano, and thyme and pulse a few times to incorporate.

For a thinner, softer spreadable cheese, enjoy as is.

For a thicker, denser spreadable cheese, line a small colander with tightly woven cheesecloth, scoop the cashew cheese into the cheesecloth, fold the ends over the top to cover, and place the colander over a medium bowl so that it is suspended. Refrigerate for at least 8 hours or overnight.

For the Roasted Garlic

Preheat the oven to 400°F about 1 hour before you're ready to serve the cheese plate.

On a cutting board, lay each head of garlic on its side and slice off just enough of the tip to expose the inside of the cloves. Place each head sliced-side up on a piece of foil and lightly drizzle with olive oil (if using). Wrap tightly by folding the foil inward and transfer to a small baking tray.

Roast for 35–45 minutes, or until the garlic is tender and buttery.

For the Spicy Tomato Jam

While the garlic is roasting, make the Spicy Tomato Jam.

(continued on next page)

FOR SERVING

Sliced seeded, sprouted, or
gluten-free baguette or crackers*

To Serve

If you're serving the cashew cheese without refrigerating, scoop it into a small serving jar or bowl. If you opted to refrigerate the cheese to thicken it, carefully unwrap it and discard the cheesecloth.

Place the cheese on a serving platter and garnish the top with chopped fresh herbs. Serve with the tomato jam, roasted garlic, and sliced bread or crackers.

Refrigerate the leftover cheese and tomato jam in separate airtight containers for up to 3 days.

No Oil? No Problem | *To keep this dish oil-free, simply omit the olive oil.*

No Grains? No Problem | *To keep this dish grain-free, swap out the crackers or bread for sliced vegetables, such as carrots or cucumbers.*

CRISPY CAULIPOWER TOTS WITH SPEEDY TWO-MINUTE KETCHUP

Makes about 35 tots | 1 hour +

These tots are sans taters and plus cauliflower, tahini, and flax. Cauliflower transforms your average tot into a snack that's equally delicious and slightly more nutritious than its spud-laden predecessor. This is all thanks to the detoxifying boost garnered from this beloved cruciferous veggie. I recommend serving these tots warm alongside a bowl of Speedy Two-Minute Ketchup (page 298) for the ultimate dipping experience.

OAT CRUMBS

1 cup old-fashioned rolled oats

1/4 cup nutritional yeast flakes

1 teaspoon smoked paprika

1 teaspoon fine-grain sea salt

1/2 teaspoon garlic powder

1/8 teaspoon freshly ground black pepper

CRISPY CAULIPOWER TOTS

1 large head cauliflower (7 inches in diameter), outer leaves removed

1/2 small yellow onion, finely diced (about 1/2 cup)

1/2–3/4 teaspoon fine-grain sea salt

1 tablespoon runny tahini

2 tablespoons flaxseed meal (ground flaxseed)

1 tablespoon filtered water

2/3 cup aquafaba (liquid from one 15-ounce can of chickpeas or white beans)*

FOR SERVING

1 recipe Speedy Two-Minute Ketchup (page 298)

For the Oat Crumbs

Add the rolled oats and nutritional yeast to a food processor. Process for 15–30 seconds, or until a coarse meal forms. You want a texture similar to panko bread crumbs. Transfer the oat crumbs to a large, shallow bowl or baking dish. Whisk in the smoked paprika, sea salt, garlic powder, and black pepper.

For the Crispy CauliPower Tots

Preheat the oven to 425°F. Line a large baking tray with parchment paper.

Cut the cauliflower into medium florets, trimming away most of the stem on each. You'll need 7–8 cups of florets. Add the cauliflower florets to the bowl of a food processor fitted with the S-blade (you might need to do this in batches depending on the size of your food processor), and pulse until finely riced, stopping as needed to fold in the cauliflower if it collects on the sides. The texture should be closer to couscous or quinoa than to rice.

Heat a large skillet over medium-low heat. Add the finely riced cauliflower, onion, and sea salt. Cook for 10–14 minutes, or until the cauliflower is tender and the pungency of its scent has mellowed, stirring occasionally and being careful not to burn or brown. Remove from the heat and stir in the tahini.

In a small bowl, whisk together the flaxseed meal and filtered water. Set aside for 10 minutes to thicken.

Use a fork to stir and mash the flaxseed mixture into the cooked cauliflower. It should resemble dry, slightly lumpy mashed potatoes. Allow the mixture to cool for 10 minutes, or until it can be comfortably handled.

(continued on next page)

While the cauliflower cools, pour the aquafaba into a shallow bowl or dish and create a tot-assembly station, lining up the aquafaba, oat crumbs, and lined baking tray from left to right.

Scoop out even tablespoons of the cauliflower mixture, form and gently compact each into a 1-inch tot, and place on the lined baking tray. This is a tender mixture, so take your time forming. You should have about 35 tots.

Briefly and carefully dip each tot in the aquafaba, shake off the excess, transfer to the oat mixture, and gently roll to coat. Return to the baking pan, leaving about 1 inch of space between each tot.

Bake for 30–35 minutes, or until the bottoms are deep golden brown, the tops are light golden brown, and the oat coating is crisp to the touch.

To Serve

While the tots bake, make the Speedy Two-Minute Ketchup.

Serve the tots warm from the oven alongside the ketchup. These are best enjoyed fresh from the oven.

What in the World Is Aquafaba? | *Aquafaba is the liquid from canned chickpeas or white beans, and it's typically used as a versatile replacement for egg whites. To obtain it, open a can of chickpeas or white beans, place a colander over a medium bowl, and strain to separate the canning liquid from the beans. The leftover beans can be used to make* Lemony Hummus *(page 304).*

GARLIC, ROSEMARY + PARMESAN FOCACCIA BREAD

Serves 6–8 | 1 hour +

Make way and roll out the red ~~carpet~~ kitchen towel. At the risk of sounding like a doting recipe writer, I will say that this focaccia bread is completely worthy of superstar status. It's a total crowd-pleaser, winning high praises from vegans and non-vegans alike. A base of Puffy Potato Pizza Crust (page 295) is topped with thin rounds of red onion and baked in a cast-iron skillet until it gently puffs. Then, it's brushed with a flavorful garlic-herb oil and sprinkled with Nut // Seed Parmesan Cheese (page 299) before being baked until it takes on a deep golden hue. This is a soft, tender focaccia, but you can absolutely bake it longer to create a crispier focaccia if that's what you prefer.

1 recipe Puffy Potato Pizza Crust (page 295), unbaked*

3 tablespoons cold-pressed olive oil, divided

1 small red onion, thinly sliced into rounds

2 cloves garlic, minced

2 teaspoons chopped fresh rosemary leaves

1/4 teaspoon sea salt

1/8–1/4 teaspoon crushed red pepper flakes

2 tablespoons Nut // Seed Parmesan Cheese (page 299)*

Prepare the Puffy Potato Pizza Crust dough (do not bake).

Preheat the oven to 400°F. Line the bottom of a 12-inch, well-seasoned, oven-safe skillet with a round piece of parchment paper. Lightly brush the sides of the pan and the parchment paper with 1 tablespoon of the olive oil.

Use a spatula to spread the potato pizza dough out into an even, 1/3-inch-thick circle in the skillet. Top with the red onion rounds.

Bake for 25–30 minutes, or until the dough puffs up and the edges are just turning golden brown.

Meanwhile, add the remaining 2 tablespoons olive oil, garlic, rosemary, sea salt, and red pepper flakes to a small sauté pan. Heat over medium heat for 2 minutes, or until it begins to simmer. Then, decrease the heat to low and continue to simmer for 2–4 minutes, or until the rosemary just begins to turn golden, stirring frequently and being careful not to burn the garlic. Remove the herb oil from the heat and let cool.

Prepare the Nut // Seed Parmesan Cheese.

Once the dough has finishing baking, carefully remove the skillet from the oven. Brush the top of the focaccia with the herb oil and sprinkle with the Parmesan. Bake for another 5–8 minutes, or until most of the oil has been absorbed and the top of the focaccia is a rich golden color. Use a pizza cutter to slice into 12–16 pieces.

Leftovers can be refrigerated for up to 3 days and reheated.

No Nuts? No Problem | *To keep this recipe nut-free, use sunflower flour in the dough instead of almond flour and opt for a seed-based Parmesan.*

Leftovers? | *This focaccia reheats like a dream, so don't fret on the off chance that you have leftovers. To reheat it, preheat the oven to 400°F. Then, spread the focaccia pieces on a small baking tray and bake for 8–10 minutes, or until warmed through with crisp edges.*

ROASTED YELLOW PEPPER, SUN-DRIED TOMATO + BASIL PORTOBELLO PIZZETTES

Makes 12 pizzettes | 30 minutes or less

These pizzettes are a tiny twist on my mom's favorite homemade pizza recipe, and I have a handful of memories of us making it, side by side, in the kitchen. Her original recipe calls for traditional pizza dough, which gets topped with pizza sauce, cheese, roasted yellow peppers, and sliced Roma tomatoes before being baked to crispy perfection. The final touch is a drizzle of balsamic reduction and a sprinkle of fresh basil. Believe it or not, I once thought I hated basil because of this pizza. I accused that poor herb of overpowering the other flavors and begged my mom to spare my slices from its chiffonaded wrath. And in the instances when it made its way onto my portion, I would pluck and discard each delicate piece. My mom and I have nearly identical tastes in food—we rarely come across a flavor we don't like—so she knew it was only a matter of time before I loved basil, too. She was right.

For this bite-size variation, baby portobello mushroom caps are roasted before being topped with pizza sauce, a generous dollop of Cashew // Hemp Seed Mozzarella Cheese (page 305), roasted yellow peppers, and sun-dried tomatoes. They're baked just long enough for the cheese and toppings to melt together before being finished with a drizzle of balsamic reduction and a scattering of fresh basil.

12 large cremini mushrooms or small portobello mushrooms (with a 2- to 3-inch diameter), brushed clean and stemmed

Sea salt and freshly ground black pepper

2 tablespoons Balsamic Reduction (page 297)

1 recipe Cashew // Hemp Seed Mozzarella Cheese (page 305)*

1/3 cup store-bought jarred pizza sauce*

1/3 cup drained and thinly sliced jarred roasted yellow peppers

1/4 cup drained oil-packed sun-dried tomatoes, roughly chopped

Handful fresh basil leaves, thinly sliced

Preheat the oven to 375°F. Line a large baking sheet with parchment paper.

Use a small spoon to gently scrape away the gills from each mushroom. Place the mushrooms gill-side up on the lined baking sheet and season with sea salt and black pepper to taste. Roast for 10 minutes, or until just starting to become tender and juicy. Remove from the oven and let cool slightly. Pour off any water that collected in the caps while baking.

While the mushrooms are roasting, prepare the Balsamic Reduction and Cashew // Hemp Seed Mozzarella Cheese.

Spread about 1 heaping teaspoon of pizza sauce into each mushroom cap and top with a generous dollop of the mozzarella. Garnish with the roasted peppers and sun-dried tomatoes.

Bake for another 5 minutes, or until the toppings gently melt into the mozzarella. Remove from the oven. Drizzle with the balsamic reduction and sprinkle with the fresh basil. Serve immediately.

No Nuts? No Problem | *To keep this nut-free, opt for the* Hemp Seed Mozzarella Cheese.

Give That Sauce a Once-Over | *If you're avoiding refined sugars, scan the ingredients as you're purchasing your pizza sauce and adjust accordingly—many brands contain unnecessary added sugar. My go-to is Rao's Pizza Sauce.*

PILE 'EM HIGH EPIC PLANT-POWERED NACHOS

Serves 6 | 1 hour +

Pile 'em high, pile 'em wide. No matter which way you stack 'em, these nachos will have you oohing, aahing, and delightedly dipping. Crunchy tortilla chips are lavishly dressed with Yellow Split Pea Nacho Cheese (page 120), Sunflower // Walnut Taco Crumbles (page 302), pico de gallo, guacamole, black beans, and Quick Pickled Jalapeños (page 197) before being drizzled with tangy Cashew Sour Cream (page 303). Best yet? This tall stack of nachos has been known to win over meat lovers and plant lovers alike.

1 recipe Yellow Split Pea Nacho Cheese (page 120)*

1 recipe Cashew Sour Cream (page 303)*

1 recipe Sunflower // Walnut Taco Crumbles (page 302)*

QUICK PICO DE GALLO

2 cups grape tomatoes, quartered

1/4–1/2 small red onion, finely diced

1/4 cup chopped fresh cilantro or to taste

Sea salt

SPEEDY GUACAMOLE

1 ripe avocado, halved, pitted, and peeled

1 clove garlic, minced

Juice of 1/2–1 lime

1/4 cup fresh cilantro, stemmed and chopped (optional)

Sea salt

NACHO BASE AND TOPPINGS

4–6 servings sturdy tortilla chips

1 (15-ounce) can black beans, drained and rinsed

1/4 cup Quick Pickled Jalapeños (page 197) (optional)

4 scallions, trimmed and thinly sliced (optional)

Sliced black olives (optional)

Start by preparing the Yellow Split Pea Nacho Cheese, Cashew Sour Cream, and Sunflower // Walnut Taco Crumbles.

For the Quick Pico de Gallo

In a small bowl, stir together the tomatoes, red onion, and cilantro. Season with sea salt to taste.

For the Speedy Guacamole

Add the avocado, garlic, and lime juice to a medium bowl and use the back of a fork to thoroughly mash. Stir in the cilantro (if using), and season with sea salt to taste.

To Assemble

On a large serving platter or baking tray, spread out a layer of tortilla chips and top with the nacho cheese, taco crumbles, pico de gallo, and black beans. Repeat, creating two or three layers. Drizzle with the sour cream and garnish with the jalapeños, scallions, and black olives, if desired. Serve alongside the guacamole.

No Nuts? No Problem | *To keep this nut-free, use a nut-free plant-based milk in the* Yellow Split Pea Nacho Cheese, *omit the* Cashew Sour Cream, *and opt for the* Sunflower Taco Crumbles.

No Soy? No Problem | *To keep this soy-free, use coconut aminos instead of reduced-sodium tamari in the* Sunflower // Walnut Taco Crumbles.

Makes 3 cups | 1 hour or less

With its zesty nacho flavor, pop of protein, and natural orange glow to boot, this nacho cheese is made from whole foods and spices, and it's surprisingly nacho-y. Think ballpark nacho cheese but more delicious, more nutritious, and completely crap-free. It's great served as a dip to sink your favorite tortilla chips into; however, if you're feeling fancy, drizzle it over layers upon layers of Pile 'Em High Epic Plant-Powered Nachos (page 119).

1/2 cup uncooked yellow split peas, thoroughly rinsed

2 cups water

1 cup peeled and small-diced (1/3-inch cubes) Yukon gold potato (about 1 medium)

1 clove garlic, smashed and peeled

1/2 cup unsweetened almond milk*

1/2 cup nutritional yeast flakes

1/4 cup drained and roughly chopped jarred roasted red peppers*

1 tablespoon plus 1 teaspoon fresh lemon juice

1–1 1/2 teaspoons smoked paprika

1 teaspoon apple cider vinegar

3/4–1 teaspoon sea salt or more to taste

A few generous dashes of hot sauce (optional)

Add the split peas to a medium saucepan with the water and bring to a boil over high heat. Decrease the heat to medium-low, cover, and simmer for 40 minutes to 1 hour, or until the split peas are *very* tender and mushy. Strain off excess water. *Note:* Split peas vary greatly in their cooking time, but you want them to be nearly fall-apart tender so that they blend up velvety and smooth. If they're undercooked, your nacho cheese will have a subtle grit to it, and no one wants that.

While the split peas are cooking, steam the diced potato and garlic in a steamer or steamer basket for 20–30 minutes, or until fall-apart tender. (Avoid steaming in the microwave because it will dry out the potato.) Shake off excess water that accumulated while steaming.

Add the cooked split peas, potatoes, and garlic to a high-speed blender along with the almond milk, nutritional yeast, roasted red peppers, lemon juice, paprika, apple cider vinegar, sea salt, and hot sauce (if using). Blend on low for 10 seconds to get everything moving, increase the speed to high, and then continue to blend for 3 minutes, or until completely smooth. You want to blend long enough to bring out the starches in the potato, as this will help create a velvety texture.

Transfer to a serving bowl and serve alongside your favorite tortilla chips for dipping.

This dip is best enjoyed warm; however, leftovers can be refrigerated for up to 4 days in an airtight container and reheated.

No Nuts? No Problem | *To keep this nut-free, simply swap out the unsweetened almond milk for a nut-free plant-based milk, such as unsweetened soy milk or unsweetened rice milk.*

Roasting Your Own Peppers? | *If you opt to use homemade roasted red peppers, be sure to peel and seed them before chopping.*

Leftovers? | *To reheat, add the chilled cheese to a saucepan and whisk constantly over medium-low heat until warmed through. If needed, whisk in more unsweetened plant-based milk, 1 tablespoon at a time, to thin.*

BEET BALLS WITH SPICY TAHINI-GINGER SAUCE

Makes 22 beet balls | 1 hour +

Gimme a beet! When I thought up this recipe idea, I had no idea if I'd be able to make the texture work or if the flavors would make sense, but it's turned out to be one of my favorite recipes in the book. These beet balls are packed to their ruby-hued edges with micronutrients and infused with the bright, zesty flavors of scallion, cilantro, Sriracha, and ginger. The tahini–ginger sauce is nutty and savory with a touch of sweetness and a slow-warming kick of heat that pairs perfectly with the beet balls. This is an appetizer that can be dressed up or down depending on the occasion, and it's been known to earn high praises from even the most beet-averse.

BEET BALLS

1 cup low-sodium vegetable broth

10 ounces small cremini or button mushrooms, stemmed

2/3 cup raw shelled sunflower seeds

1/2 cup old-fashioned rolled oats

12 ounces fresh beets, peeled and roughly chopped (about 2 medium beets)

1 medium carrot, peeled and roughly chopped (about 1/2 cup)

1/3 cup packed fresh cilantro, stemmed, plus more for garnishing

3 scallions, trimmed and roughly chopped

2 cloves garlic, smashed and peeled

2 tablespoons flaxseed meal (ground flaxseed)

1 1/2 tablespoons Sriracha sauce

1 1/2 tablespoons reduced-sodium tamari*

1 1/2 tablespoons fresh lime juice

1 teaspoon minced fresh ginger

For the Beet Balls

Preheat the oven to 350°F. Line a large baking tray with parchment paper.

Add the vegetable broth and mushrooms to a large skillet over medium heat. Cover and cook for 10 minutes, or until the mushrooms are tender. Strain off the vegetable broth and reserve for another use or discard.

Meanwhile, add the sunflower seeds and rolled oats to a food processor. Process for 30 seconds, or until a coarse meal forms (the texture should resemble panko bread crumbs). Transfer to a large mixing bowl.

To the food processor, add the cooked mushrooms, beets, carrots, cilantro, scallions, garlic, flaxseed, Sriracha, tamari, lime juice, and ginger. Pulse several times and then process for 20–30 seconds, or until the vegetables are finely minced (be careful not to purée). Transfer to the mixing bowl with the oat and sunflower meal and stir to combine. The mixture will be quite damp.

Scoop out 2 tablespoons of the beet mixture, gently shape into a ball, and place on the lined baking tray. Repeat, leaving 1 inch of space between each beet ball. You should have about 22 beet balls.

Bake for 45–50 minutes, or until the beet balls are firm-tender to the touch and the bottoms are deep golden brown. Remove from the oven and allow the beet balls to cool on the pan for 10 minutes before serving.

For the Spicy Tahini-Ginger Sauce

In a small serving bowl, vigorously whisk together the tahini, tamari, lime juice, Sriracha, sesame oil, apple cider vinegar, maple syrup, garlic, and ginger until emulsified. Refrigerate until ready to serve.

(continued on next page)

SPICY TAHINI-GINGER SAUCE

1/4 cup runny tahini

2 tablespoons reduced-sodium tamari*

2 tablespoons fresh lime juice

1 tablespoon Sriracha sauce

1 tablespoon toasted sesame oil

1 tablespoon apple cider vinegar

1 tablespoon pure maple syrup

2 cloves garlic, minced

1 teaspoon minced fresh ginger

To Serve

For a casual gathering, serve the beet balls on a platter alongside the sauce and garnish with fresh cilantro. For a fancier affair, serve as individual appetizers: plate the beet balls (2 or 3 per plate), drizzle with the sauce, and garnish with fresh cilantro.

Store leftovers in the refrigerator for up to 4 days.

No Soy? No Problem | *To keep this soy-free, simply swap out the reduced-sodium tamari for coconut aminos.*

SOUPS + SALADS

SOUPS
Dreamy Tomato Bisque with Grilled Cheesy Polenta Croutons 127
Creamy Cauliflower + Turmeric Soup with Smoky Shiitake Bacon 130
Carrot + Coriander Bisque 133

SALADS
Shaved Jicama Ceviche Salad with Avocado, Mango,
Pomegranate + Pistachios 134
Marinated Kale Salad with Cherries, Green Apples + Candied Pecans 137
Fava Bean Salad with Lemony "Parmesan" Vinaigrette 138
Buckwheat, Green Apple, Cranberry + Avocado Salad 141
Roasted Cauliflower Salad with Tahini-Cilantro Vinaigrette 142
Pretty in Pink Quinoa Confetti Salad 145
Sorghum + Heirloom Cherry Tomato Salad with Basil Vinaigrette 146
Arugula, Pomegranate, Raisin, Avocado + Sunflower Seed Salad 148

I, Ashley Melillo, do solemnly swear that this chapter is free from bland, lackluster soups and wimpy, flavorless salads. Far from it, in fact. Rather, it's bursting with soothing soups that warm from head to toe and vibrant, swoon-worthy salads that satisfy.

And if my oath isn't enough to cast aside any preconceived vegan soup and salad notions, then I'll gladly clear the way and let the recipes do the talking. But before I go, allow me to point you in the right direction . . .

If you're looking for a salad that screams "summertime garden fresh!" then flip to page 146 and give that Sorghum + Heirloom Cherry Tomato Salad with Basil Vinaigrette a whirl. If rich winter foods have left your taste buds feeling heavy, pop on over to page 134 to reawaken your senses with the Shaved Jicama Ceviche Salad with Avocado, Mango, Pomegranate + Pistachios (my personal favorite). Perhaps you're looking to impress a crowd with a side salad that wows? For that scenario, I recommend the Roasted Cauliflower Salad with Tahini-Cilantro Vinaigrette on page 142. Or maybe, just maybe, you're looking for a classic soup with an epic twist. In that case, you'll want to head directly to page 127 and whip up a batch of Dreamy Tomato Bisque with Grilled Cheesy Polenta Croutons.

DREAMY TOMATO BISQUE WITH GRILLED CHEESY POLENTA CROUTONS

Serves 6 | 1 hour +

This tomato bisque gets its rich and dreamy texture from puréed cauliflower and nutritional yeast. Red bell pepper, garlic, and a variety of spices create layers of flavor that will keep you coming back for spoonful after spoonful. It's the perfect meal to warm your heart during lunch or dinner. It wouldn't be right to offer up a tomato soup recipe without some form of grilled cheese, and this time the grilled cheese gets a bite-size, plant-powered makeover. Polenta is sliced and stuffed with gooey Cashew Cheddar Cheese (page 305) before being grilled to crisp and salty perfection. Finding these grilled cheese croutons floating amid creamy tomato bisque is a bit like finding gold nuggets in a field of rubies; something that was already fantastic is made all the more wonderful.

DREAMY TOMATO BISQUE

3 tablespoons cold-pressed olive oil, plus more for garnishing

1 large yellow onion, diced (about 2 cups)

4 cloves garlic, minced

2 (28-ounce) cans unsalted whole peeled tomatoes in juice

1 small head cauliflower, cut into small florets (about 4 cups)

1 cup drained and roughly chopped jarred roasted red peppers

1 teaspoon dried oregano

1 teaspoon dried basil

Pinch of crushed red pepper flakes (optional)

1 1/2 teaspoons sea salt or to taste

1/4 cup nutritional yeast flakes

1/2–1 cup filtered water, if needed to thin soup

Fresh basil, chopped (optional)

For the Dreamy Tomato Bisque

Heat the olive oil in a large stockpot over medium heat. Add the onion and garlic and cook for 6 minutes, or until soft and translucent.

Add the canned tomatoes with their juice, cauliflower, roasted red peppers, oregano, basil, red pepper flakes (if using), and sea salt. Ensure that the cauliflower chunks are submerged in the canned tomatoes' liquid as much as possible (at first it will seem like there is too much cauliflower). Bring the mixture to a boil. Decrease the heat, cover, and vigorously simmer for 25 minutes, or until the cauliflower is fork-tender, stirring occasionally.

Turn off the heat and use an immersion blender* to purée the soup for 6–8 minutes, or until as smooth as possible. Add the nutritional yeast and more sea salt (I usually add another 1/2 teaspoon) and briefly blend again to incorporate.

Then, cover and simmer on low for another 10–15 minutes, stirring occasionally. If the soup is thicker than desired, whisk in the 1/2–1 cup water to thin.

For the Grilled Cheesy Polenta Croutons (Optional)

Slice off the rounded ends of the polenta. Stand it up on one end and carefully slice down its length, forming 6 long, 1/4-inch-thick slices. Lightly brush one side of each slice with olive oil and season with sea salt and black pepper.

Prepare the Cashew Cheddar Cheese.

(continued on next page)

GRILLED CHEESY POLENTA CROUTONS (OPTIONAL)*

1 (18-ounce) package precooked organic polenta

2–3 tablespoons olive oil, divided

Sea salt and freshly ground black pepper

1 recipe Cashew Cheddar Cheese (page 305)

Heat a well-seasoned skillet over medium-high heat. Place 3 of the polenta slices oiled-side down on the skillet. Sear for 6–8 minutes, or until the bottom of the polenta begins to pull away from the skillet and takes on a deep golden color. Then, spoon a thick layer of the cheese onto each slice, and top with the 3 remaining polenta slices (oiled side up), being careful not to squeeze out too much of the cheddar. Gently flip and grill for another 6–8 minutes, or until the polenta begins to pull away from the pan and is a rich golden color.

Remove from the heat, cool for 5 minutes, and slice into 1-inch squares.

Reheat the skillet over medium heat. Add about 1 tablespoon of the olive oil, then add the sliced croutons and cook until golden brown on all sides, gently flipping as needed (6–8 minutes).

To Assemble

Ladle the soup into bowls. Drizzle with olive oil and top with the polenta croutons and chopped fresh basil, if desired.

Refrigerate the leftover soup, covered, for up to 4 days or freeze for up to 1 month. The croutons are best when fresh.

No Grains or Nuts? No Problem | *To keep this dish grain- and nut-free, simply omit the croutons.*

No Immersion Blender? | *If you don't have an immersion blender, carefully ladle the soup into a blender in small batches and blend until smooth. Be very careful as the soup will be hot.*

CREAMY CAULIFLOWER + TURMERIC SOUP WITH SMOKY SHIITAKE BACON

Serves 4–6 | 1 hour or less

This soup garners its golden hue from ground turmeric, a root-derived spice with a mild flavor and potent anti-inflammatory properties. As cauliflower is *also* an anti-inflammatory and detoxifying agent, this soup offers quite the kick of body benefits. Plus, it's rich and creamy thanks to the addition of raw cashews and Yukon gold potatoes.

This silky soup is finished with flecks of fresh herbs and a generous sprinkling of crisp shiitake "bacon." I know, I know. Turning mushrooms into bacon sounds a little unbelievable, but at least I haven't gone completely hippie on you . . . yet. *". . . and for my next trick, I'll transform kale into cookies!"* I kid, I kid. But seriously, I've witnessed both vegans and bacon lovers fall in love with this plant-powered version. But no need to take my word for it, get cooking and you'll see for yourself just how scrumptious this veggie version can be.

1 recipe Shiitake Bacon (page 298)

CREAMY CAULIFLOWER + TURMERIC SOUP

2 tablespoons cold-pressed olive oil

1 1/2 teaspoons ground turmeric

1 teaspoon smoked paprika

1 teaspoon ground coriander

2 1/2–3 teaspoons sea salt, divided

1 large yellow onion, diced (about 2 cups)

2 medium shallots, finely diced (about 1/2 cup)

2 cloves garlic, minced

6 cups low-sodium vegetable broth

1 large head cauliflower, cut into florets (about 6 cups)

1 medium Yukon gold potato, peeled and diced (about 1 1/2 cups)

1/3 cup raw cashews

2 tablespoons apple cider vinegar or white wine vinegar

GARNISH

1/4 cup chopped fresh chives

1/4 cup fresh cilantro, stemmed

Start by making the Shiitake Bacon.

For the Creamy Cauliflower + Turmeric Soup

In a large stockpot, stir together the olive oil, turmeric, paprika, coriander, and 1/2 teaspoon of the sea salt over medium heat. Cook for 1–2 minutes to bloom the spices, stirring frequently. Add the onion, shallots, and garlic, and sauté for 6 minutes, or until soft and translucent, stirring occasionally.

Add the vegetable broth, cauliflower, potato, and cashews. Increase the heat to high and bring to a boil. Then, decrease the heat to medium-low, cover, and simmer for 20–25 minutes, or until the vegetables are tender and easily break apart when pierced with a fork.

Turn off the heat. Use an immersion blender* to purée the soup for 5 minutes, or until very smooth and creamy. Season with the remaining 2–2 1/2 teaspoons sea salt or to taste, and stir in the apple cider vinegar.

To Assemble

Ladle the soup into bowls, top with a generous mound of shiitake bacon, and garnish with the chives and cilantro.

Refrigerate leftovers, covered, for up to 4 days or freeze for up to 1 month.

No Immersion Blender? | *If you don't have an immersion blender, carefully ladle the soup into a blender in small batches and blend until smooth. Be very careful as the soup will be hot.*

CARROT + CORIANDER BISQUE

This soup is effortlessly special, demanding little in the way of ingredients and attention, yet surprising and delighting the senses nonetheless. Something about it is also incredibly soothing, and I find that enjoying a warm bowl of it for lunch brings a sense of peace and calm to a busy day. Plus, it's even tastier on the second and third day, so there's much to be gained from preparing it ahead of time. A rich, silky base of blended carrots and potatoes is balanced by the bright acidity of orange juice and the subtle warmth of fresh ginger. This soup is made just a touch lovelier with a sprinkling of fresh cilantro and juicy pomegranate seeds, but you can absolutely omit them if you want to minimize ingredients.

CARROT + CORIANDER BISQUE

1 tablespoon virgin coconut oil

1 medium yellow onion, diced (about 1 1/2 cups)

4 cups low-sodium vegetable broth

3 cups peeled and diced carrots (about 5 medium carrots)

2 cups peeled and diced Yukon gold potatoes (about 2 medium potatoes)

1 cup fresh or 100 percent pure orange juice, plus more if desired

2 teaspoons peeled and minced fresh ginger

1 teaspoon ground coriander

1 cup loosely packed fresh cilantro, stemmed

1–1 1/2 teaspoons sea salt or to taste

OPTIONAL GARNISHES

Fresh cilantro, stemmed

Pomegranate seeds

For the Carrot + Coriander Bisque

Heat the coconut oil in a large stockpot over medium heat. Add the onion and sauté for 6 minutes, or until soft and just beginning to turn golden brown and caramelized.

Stir in the vegetable broth, carrots, potatoes, orange juice, ginger, and coriander. Bring to a boil, decrease the heat, and simmer, covered, for 35–40 minutes, or until the carrots and potatoes are very tender, stirring occasionally.

Remove from the heat and stir in the cilantro and sea salt. Use an immersion blender* to carefully blend the mixture until smooth (about 4–6 minutes). It's okay if tiny flecks of cilantro are still visible, but you want to get it as silky smooth as possible.

Taste and season with more sea salt if desired. For an added pop of brightness, stir in another tablespoon or two of orange juice.

To Assemble

Ladle into bowls and garnish with more cilantro and pomegranate seeds, if desired.

Refrigerate leftovers, covered, for up to 4 days or freeze for up to 1 month.

No Immersion Blender? | *If you don't have an immersion blender, carefully ladle the soup into a blender in small batches and blend until smooth. Be very careful as the soup will be hot.*

SHAVED JICAMA CEVICHE SALAD WITH AVOCADO, MANGO, POMEGRANATE + PISTACHIOS

Serves 4 | 30 minutes or less

This might sound a little loony, but if I were to choose one salad to nosh on for the rest of my days, this would be it. Between its bright rainbow of colors and lively, zestful flavors, this salad makes for a truly joyful eating experience. Plus, it's a cinch to throw together, which increases its awesome factor by a point or two. This would make a lovely side dish to pair with the Crispy Cauliflower Tacos on page 175. But honestly, it's bold and satisfying enough to stand all on its own.

CITRUS VINAIGRETTE

1/4 cup fresh cilantro, stemmed and chopped

1/4 cup fresh lime juice

2 tablespoons fresh orange juice

2 tablespoons cold-pressed olive oil

1 clove garlic, minced

1/4 teaspoon sea salt

SHAVED JICAMA CEVICHE SALAD

1 medium jicama root (about 4 inches in diameter), peeled and halved

1 medium mango, peeled, pitted, and finely diced (about 1 cup)

1 small red onion, halved and very thinly sliced (about 1/3 cup)

1/2 cup pomegranate seeds

1 firm-ripe avocado, halved, pitted, peeled, and diced

TOPPINGS

1/3 cup shelled and toasted pistachios, roughly chopped*

Small handful fresh cilantro, stemmed (optional)

For the Citrus Vinaigrette

In a small mixing bowl, vigorously whisk together the cilantro, lime juice, orange juice, olive oil, garlic, and sea salt. Refrigerate until ready to assemble.

For the Shaved Jicama Ceviche Salad

Use a vegetable peeler or mandoline (be careful!) to shave each half of the jicama into thin pieces.

Add the shaved jicama, mango, red onion, pomegranate seeds, and avocado to a large serving bowl. Pour the citrus vinaigrette over the top and gently toss to coat.

To Serve

Divide the salad among bowls or plates and sprinkle with the chopped pistachios and cilantro (if using).

Keepin' It Raw? No Problem | *To keep this dish raw, opt for raw shelled pistachios or omit.*

No Nuts? No Problem | *To keep this dish nut-free, simply omit the pistachios.*

MARINATED KALE SALAD WITH
CHERRIES, GREEN APPLES + CANDIED PECANS

Kale salads don't have to be rabbit food. When done right, they're absolutely worthy of being craved. So how does one take a kale salad from grassy to sassy? Great question. Keep these four simple steps in mind.

Step one is to thoroughly wash the kale. Rinse and repeat, rinse and repeat, rinse and repeat. Then, pat it dry or give it a whirl around a salad spinner. A sandy, gritty, potentially buggy—gross, but true—kale salad is not fab at all, it's disgusting. And it's exactly the kind of thing that infuses a person with kale-hate, so wash your kale like you'd wash your hair after a four-day, shower-free camping trip (minus the soap, of course).

Step two is to dress it well. Kale is not the place for skimpy, wimpy dressings; I'm looking at you, fat-free [fill in the blank]. Healthy fats and an acid plus a touch of sweetness and herbs/garlic/spices/liquid seasonings/sea salt equals a proper dressing in general, but especially for a kale salad.

Step three is where the kale magic happens. Roll up your sleeves, get your (clean) hands in that bowl, and massage your flavorful dressing into the kale for at least 2 minutes. The acidity of the dressing combined with a Popeye-strength massage breaks down the tough, chewy, and fibrous walls of the kale.

And finally, step four: make it rain . . . Add toppings to boost flavor and texture. Think crunchy (nuts and seeds), juicy and chewy (fresh or dried fruit), and creamy (sliced avocado).

CANDIED PECANS

1/3 cup raw pecans

2 teaspoons coconut sugar

1 teaspoon virgin coconut oil, melted

MARINATED KALE SALAD

1 large bunch curly kale, thoroughly washed, patted dry, and stemmed

2 1/2 tablespoons apple cider vinegar

1 1/2 tablespoons natural almond butter

1 tablespoon reduced-sodium tamari*

1 tablespoon pure maple syrup

1 cup fresh sweet cherries, pitted and halved*

1 small green apple, cored and cut into matchsticks

For the Candied Pecans

Preheat the oven to 325°F. Line a small baking tray with parchment paper.

In a small bowl, combine the pecans, coconut sugar, and melted coconut oil and toss to coat.

Spread the pecans on the lined baking tray and bake for 8–10 minutes, or until golden brown and fragrant. Let cool.

For the Marinated Kale Salad

Tear the kale into bite-size pieces and transfer to a large mixing bowl.

In a small mixing bowl, whisk together the apple cider vinegar, almond butter, tamari, and maple syrup until emulsified. Pour as much of the dressing as desired over the kale, roll up your sleeves, and use your hands to massage the dressing into the kale for 2–3 minutes, or until the leaves begin to soften. The more you massage the kale, the more tender and flavorful it will become. Add the cherries and green apple and toss to coat.

Divide the salad among serving bowls and top with the candied pecans.

No Soy? No Problem | *To keep this soy-free, swap out the reduced-sodium tamari for coconut aminos.*

Can't Find Fresh Cherries? | *Use 1/3–1/2 cup dried tart cherries instead.*

Serves 2–4 | 30 minutes or less

In July of 2011, Dan and I had the most delicious, veggie-filled lunch at ABC Kitchen while vacationing in New York City. If you haven't been, allow me to paint a picture for you. The restaurant itself has an earthy yet ethereal vibe. Each dinner plate is different yet presents as if it were part of a cohesive unit, and the silverware looks as if it were retrieved from your grand-mother's collection of fine flatware. The tables, chairs, bar, and walls make the color white look brilliantly warm, and the crowd is effortlessly chic. The olive oil tastes as if it's come from olives pressed, just once, through a sieve in the back, and the salt is literally freshly shaven from gigantic salt crystals before it's brought to your table. Somebody pinch me! Is this real life?

ABC Kitchen is also home to one of the most memorable dressings I've ever tasted: a tangy lime and Parmesan vinaigrette that made my then-vegetarian knees buckle and inspired this plant-based, lemony version. Although the ingredient list is vastly different than the original, the flavor profile of this lemony "Parmesan" vinaigrette was inspired by that special lunch. It was a huge hit with my awesome recipe testers, none of whom were vegetarian or vegan at the time (although a few have since transitioned!), and many of them admitted to eating it by the spoonful or licking the food processor clean. I guess you could say this dressing is good on just about anything, but for this particular salad, it's drizzled over shelled fava beans, baby arugula, and fresh herbs. If you can't find fava beans, use shelled edamame instead (see note).

LEMONY "PARMESAN" VINAIGRETTE

3 tablespoons nutritional yeast flakes

2 tablespoons raw almonds*

1/2 teaspoon sea salt

3 tablespoons filtered water

1 tablespoon champagne vinegar

2 teaspoons fresh lemon juice

1/8 teaspoon freshly ground black pepper, plus more for seasoning

FAVA BEAN SALAD

3 cups fresh or frozen shelled fava beans*

5 ounces baby arugula (about 4 heaping cups)

2 tablespoons chopped chives

2 teaspoons chopped flat-leaf parsley (optional)

For the Lemony "Parmesan" Vinaigrette

Add the nutritional yeast, almonds, and sea salt to a small food processor or high-speed blender and process or blend for 1 minute, or until the tex-ture resembles a coarse meal. Add the water, champagne vinegar, lemon juice, and black pepper, and process or blend until emulsified. Transfer to an airtight jar and refrigerate until ready to assemble.

For the Fava Bean Salad

Bring a large pot of salted water to a boil. Create an ice bath by combin-ing a few cups ice and cool water in a large bowl. Set aside.

Add the shelled fava beans to the boiling water and cook for 1 minute. Use a large slotted spoon to quickly transfer the fava beans to the ice bath to halt cooking. Once they are cool, use the slotted spoon to transfer them to a large bowl, shaking off excess water. Peel the thin, waxy shell from the beans one at a time, and use a paper towel to gently pat dry.

In a large serving bowl, combine the fava beans, arugula, chives, and pars-ley (if using). Drizzle as much of the dressing over the salad as desired, toss to coat, season with freshly ground black pepper (if desired), and serve immediately.

No Nuts? No Problem | *To keep this nut-free, swap out the raw almonds for raw shelled sunflower seeds.*

Don't Fret over Fava | *If you can't find fava beans, substitute shelled edamame. Boil the edamame just as you would the fava beans and start assembling. (There's no waxy shell to worry about peeling, so you can skip that step altogether.)*

BUCKWHEAT, GREEN APPLE, CRANBERRY + AVOCADO SALAD

Serves 4–6 | 30 minutes or less

This salad might sound fussy and frou-frou, but it's surprisingly humble and hearty. Nutrient-packed raw buckwheat groats are cooked until tender and tossed in a bright, lemony vinaigrette. Green apples, peppery greens, cranberries, and pepitas are folded in to balance sweet and savory notes, and the final touch is a garnish of creamy avocado. Each ingredient offers a punch of vitamins and minerals, resulting in a salad that lends both good vibes and a boost of energy.

BUCKWHEAT SALAD

1 cup raw buckwheat groats

2 cups water

1 medium Granny Smith apple, cored and cut into matchsticks

2 cups baby arugula, watercress, or other peppery green, leaves and tender stems only

1/3–1/2 cup dried cranberries

1/4 cup raw pepitas

SIMPLE LEMON VINAIGRETTE

3–5 tablespoons fresh lemon juice, divided (juice of about 2 lemons)

2 tablespoons cold-pressed olive oil

1–2 teaspoons pure maple syrup

1 teaspoon Dijon mustard

1 clove garlic, minced (optional)

1/4–1/2 teaspoon sea salt, plus more for seasoning

Freshly ground black pepper, plus more for seasoning

TOPPING

1 medium avocado, halved, pitted, peeled, and sliced

For the Buckwheat Salad

Add the buckwheat groats to a fine-mesh strainer and thoroughly rinse with cold water. In a medium saucepan, combine the rinsed buckwheat and water. Bring to a boil, decrease the heat, and simmer, uncovered, for 10 minutes, or until tender, stirring occasionally to prevent burning. Strain and rinse with cold water until the water runs clear.

Transfer the cooked buckwheat to a large nonreactive (i.e., nonmetallic) serving bowl along with the apple, greens, cranberries, and pepitas.

For the Simple Lemon Vinaigrette

In a small bowl, vigorously whisk together 3 tablespoons of the lemon juice, olive oil, maple syrup, Dijon mustard, garlic (if using), sea salt, and black pepper to taste.

To Assemble

Pour the vinaigrette over the salad and toss to coat. If desired, add the remaining 2 tablespoons lemon juice to the salad to brighten the flavors, and liberally season with sea salt and black pepper.

Divide among plates and top with the sliced avocado.

ROASTED CAULIFLOWER SALAD WITH TAHINI-CILANTRO VINAIGRETTE

Serves 4–6 | 45 minutes or less

Given the abundant number of cauliflower recipes in this book, it might seem peculiar that I don't particularly enjoy raw cauliflower. I find the pungent cruciferous flavor to be a bit off-putting. However, give me a bowl of cooked cauliflower rice or a pile of roasted florets, and it's a completely different story. With a bit of heat, that pungent flavor is tamed, leaving an irresistible subtle sweetness in its wake.

For this particular dish, the cauliflower is roasted until tender and tossed in a tangy tahini-cilantro vinaigrette. Pair it with Crispy Cauliflower Tacos (page 175) for a double whammy of cauliflower, or enjoy it all on its own for a light summer lunch. It tastes even better the second day, after the flavors have had a chance to mingle with one another, so feel free to make it a day in advance to simplify your day-of prep.

ROASTED CAULIFLOWER

2 medium heads cauliflower, trimmed and cut into small florets

2 tablespoons virgin coconut oil, melted

1/2 teaspoon sea salt

Freshly ground black pepper

TAHINI-CILANTRO VINAIGRETTE

1/3 cup finely chopped fresh cilantro, plus more for garnishing

1/4 cup cold-pressed olive oil

2 tablespoons fresh lime juice

1 1/2 tablespoons apple cider vinegar

1 tablespoon tahini

1 teaspoon pure maple syrup

1 clove garlic, minced

1/4 teaspoon sea salt

Freshly ground black pepper

For the Roasted Cauliflower

Preheat the oven to 425°F. Line a large baking tray with parchment paper.

Transfer the cauliflower to the lined baking tray. Drizzle with the coconut oil, season with the sea salt and black pepper to taste, toss to coat, and spread the florets out into an even layer over the pan.

Roast for 25–30 minutes, or until the edges of the cauliflower are light golden brown. Let cool slightly. Transfer to a large serving bowl.

For the Tahini-Cilantro Vinaigrette

In a small bowl, vigorously whisk together the cilantro, olive oil, lime juice, apple cider vinegar, tahini, maple syrup, garlic, sea salt, and black pepper to taste.

Pour the vinaigrette over the roasted cauliflower and toss to coat. Taste and adjust the seasonings, adding more sea salt, black pepper, and fresh cilantro if desired.

PRETTY IN PINK QUINOA CONFETTI SALAD

Serves 4–6 | 30 minutes or less

This slightly sweet, crisp, and refreshing dish reminds me of a hearty, jazzed-up fruit salad. It makes the perfect light and hydrating summer lunch and also works great as a side salad for a summer gathering or picnic. Watermelon, strawberries, radishes, and sugar snap peas are small-diced and tossed with quinoa and fresh basil before being dressed with a simple lime vinaigrette. The combination of watermelon, strawberries, and quinoa might seem a bit unusual, but I think they complement one another in the best of ways. My awesome recipe testers reported being pleasantly surprised by just how much they loved this salad's vibrant colors and unexpected array of flavors and textures.

QUINOA CONFETTI SALAD

1 cup uncooked quinoa

1 3/4 cups water

8 radishes, trimmed and thinly sliced (optional)

1 heaping cup fresh strawberries, hulled and diced

1 heaping cup fresh watermelon chunks, cut into small cubes

1 cup sugar snap peas, trimmed and diced

1/4 cup fresh basil leaves, thinly sliced

LIME VINAIGRETTE

3 tablespoons fresh lime juice

2 tablespoons cold-pressed olive oil

2 tablespoons pure maple syrup

1 tablespoon runny tahini

1 clove garlic, minced

1/4 teaspoon sea salt

Freshly ground black pepper

For the Quinoa Confetti Salad

Thoroughly rinse the quinoa in a fine-mesh sieve or colander. Bring the water to a boil in a medium saucepan. Add the quinoa, return to a boil, and cook over medium heat for 12 minutes, uncovered, or until the quinoa has absorbed most of the water, stirring occasionally. Remove from the heat, fluff with a fork, cover, and let stand for 5 minutes.

Transfer the cooked quinoa to a large nonreactive (i.e., nonmetallic) serving bowl along with the radishes (if using), strawberries, watermelon, sugar snap peas, and basil.

For the Lime Vinaigrette

In a small mixing bowl, vigorously whisk together the lime juice, olive oil, maple syrup, tahini, garlic, sea salt, and black pepper to taste.

Pour the vinaigrette over the salad and toss to coat. Refrigerate leftovers in an airtight container for up to 3 days.

SORGHUM + HEIRLOOM CHERRY TOMATO SALAD WITH BASIL VINAIGRETTE

Serves 4–6 | 1 hour or less

This salad highlights my two late-summer favorites: juicy tomatoes and fresh basil. The tomatoes are nestled amid a bed of nutty sorghum, and the basil is blended with a small handful of ingredients to yield a vinaigrette with an herbaceous pop of green.

You're probably wondering what in the world sorghum is—I know, not the most enchanting name you've ever heard, right? I'm with you. But I have a feeling you and sorghum are going to get along swimmingly. It's a slightly chewy, mild-flavored, and affordable ancient grain. It's wonderful in salads because it doesn't clump together like most grains, and it's naturally gluten-free.

SORGHUM + HEIRLOOM CHERRY TOMATO SALAD

1 cup uncooked sorghum, thoroughly rinsed*

3 cups water

1/4 cup pine nuts (optional)

3 cups heirloom or standard cherry tomatoes, halved

1/4–1/2 small red onion, thinly sliced

BASIL VINAIGRETTE

1 cup tightly packed fresh basil leaves, stemmed

1 clove garlic, peeled

3 tablespoons cold-pressed olive oil

1 tablespoon champagne vinegar

1/2 teaspoon sea salt or to taste

1/4 teaspoon crushed red pepper flakes

Freshly ground black pepper, to taste

For the Sorghum + Heirloom Cherry Tomato Salad

In a medium pot, combine the rinsed sorghum and water over medium-high heat. Bring to a boil, cover, and decrease the heat to medium-low. Simmer for 45–55 minutes, or until the sorghum is tender yet still has a slight chewiness to it. Strain off excess water and fluff with a fork.

Toast the pine nuts (if using) in a large skillet over medium-low heat for 3–5 minutes, stirring occasionally. When they're flecked with golden spots, they're ready.

Transfer the cooked sorghum and toasted pine nuts to a large, nonreactive (i.e., nonmetallic) serving bowl along with the cherry tomatoes and red onion.

For the Basil Vinaigrette

Add all the vinaigrette ingredients to a food processor and process until emulsified. The basil should be very finely chopped.

To Assemble

Pour the vinaigrette over the salad and toss to coat. Season with sea salt and freshly ground black pepper to taste.

Refrigerate leftovers in an airtight container for up to 3 days.

Can't Find Sorghum? | *If you can't find sorghum, substitute brown rice, quinoa, or millet and prepare according to package directions.*

ARUGULA, POMEGRANATE, RAISIN, AVOCADO + SUNFLOWER SEED SALAD

Serves 2–3 | 15 minutes or less

If you're coming off a weekend, week, or month of too much indulgence, this is your salad—satisfying, powerful, and refreshing. It's minimally dressed with little more than a generous spritz of fresh lime juice, sea salt, and black pepper. The lime juice gently wilts the arugula, and the flavors and textures from the pomegranate seeds, raisins, and creamy avocado combine to create a surprisingly satisfying salad. There's an option to include a light drizzle of olive oil if you're feeling it; however, it's one of the few salads I actually prefer without it. This is my go-to light dinner when I'm feeling sapped of energy. It's easy to digest and packed with antioxidants, mineral-rich greens, and healthy fats.

5 ounces baby arugula or a mix of baby arugula and baby spinach

3/4 cup pomegranate seeds (seeds from about 1 large pomegranate)

1/2 cup raisins or to taste

1/4 cup raw shelled sunflower seeds

1–2 limes, halved

Sea salt and freshly ground black pepper

Light drizzle of cold-pressed olive oil (optional)*

1 ripe avocado, halved, pitted, peeled, and cubed

Add the arugula, pomegranate seeds, raisins, and sunflower seeds to a large serving bowl.

Squeeze as much of the lime juice over the greens as desired and toss to coat. Liberally season with sea salt and black pepper to taste, and drizzle with olive oil (if using). Toss again.

Let the salad stand for 5 minutes to gently wilt the greens.

Divide among bowls and top with the diced avocado. Serve immediately.

No Oil? No Problem | *To keep this oil-free, simply omit the olive oil.*

POWER BOWLS

The Classic: Spicy Cauliflower Rice, Roasted Sweet Potatoes +
Avocado Mash 153
Cooling Cucumber Noodle + Baked Falafel with Tzatziki 157
Mediterranean Millet with Lemony Hummus 159
Spicy Chile-Garlic Eggplant + Black Rice 163
Flourishing Fiesta with Taco Crumbles, Pico de Gallo,
Guacamole + Shiitake Bacon 165
Comforting BBQ Pulled Hearts of Palm, Crispy Kale +
Parmesan Polenta 167
Swift Sweet Potato Coconut Curry 171

If you were to drop me down in the Whole Foods salad bar, I'd resurface 15 minutes later with a bowl brimming with the most fabulously chaotic meal you'd ever seen. It would contain about fifteen different toppings comingled with the likes of six to eight premade dishes, completely disregarding all traditional flavor rules or geographical cuisine boundaries. Thanks to my heavy-handedness with the marinated artichoke hearts, it would also cost more than a three-course meal.

I'm not sure whether it's my indecisive nature or taste buds that bore easily, but I love meals with wide-ranging textures, flavors, and colors. This is why "Power Bowls"—aka a variety of mini dishes nestled next to one another in a bowl—are my absolute favorite. They offer a rainbow of flavors, nutrients, textures, and hues within one satisfying meal. Each element can typically be prepared in advance and the bowl itself can be assembled in a pinch, making it a great option for those bustling weekdays.

In this chapter, you'll find seven of my all-time favorite power bowls. If you're unsure where to start, The Classic (page 153) and the Flourishing Fiesta (page 165) will show you how it's done.

THE CLASSIC: SPICY CAULIFLOWER RICE, ROASTED SWEET POTATOES + AVOCADO MASH

Serves 2–4 | 45 minutes or less

Way back when, in the spring of 2015, I threw this meal together in a pinch before Dan and I settled in to watch a movie. It appeased my inattentive taste buds, but I truly thought the combination of cinnamon-spiced sweet potatoes, spicy cauliflower rice, and mashed avocado was a bit random to appeal to the masses. I even posted a photo on Facebook and gently poked fun at the odd combo. But when I was catching up on social media a few days later, I noticed the post had garnered a handful of enthusiastic requests for the recipe. There were even a few comments with kindly conveyed undertones of frustration because I hadn't shared the details of how to make my haphazardly concocted meal. I got the message and made sure to share the exact recipe on the blog the following week.

Given what a hit it's been—and that I've made it myself more times than I can count—I'm officially declaring it "The Classic" power bowl. It's a lovable hodgepodge of flavors, textures, and colors. Spicy cauliflower rice warms and entices, cinnamon-paprika sweet potatoes comfort and soothe, and creamy avocado mash unites two elements that might otherwise taste chaotic and incoherent when nestled into one bowl.

ROASTED SWEET POTATOES

2 large sweet potatoes, peeled and cut into 1-inch cubes (about 4 cups)

2 tablespoons grapeseed oil or other heat-tolerant oil

1 tablespoon ground cinnamon

1 tablespoon smoked paprika

Fine-grain sea salt

SPICY CAULIFLOWER RICE

1 medium head cauliflower, cored and cut into florets (about 6 cups)

1 tablespoon toasted sesame oil

5 scallions, trimmed and thinly sliced

1 cup cherry or grape tomatoes, quartered

2–3 tablespoons apple cider vinegar or rice vinegar

1–2 tablespoons reduced-sodium tamari*

1–2 tablespoons chile-garlic paste or Sriracha

For the Roasted Sweet Potatoes

Preheat the oven to 425°F. Line a large baking tray with parchment paper.

Place the sweet potatoes on the lined baking tray, drizzle with the oil, and sprinkle with the cinnamon, paprika, and sea salt to taste. Toss to coat.

Roast for 25–30 minutes, or until fork-tender, flipping at the 15-minute mark.

For the Spicy Cauliflower Rice

Add the cauliflower florets to the bowl of a food processor fitted with an S-blade. Pulse to finely chop into pieces roughly the size of rice grains.

Heat the sesame oil in a large wok or sauté pan over medium heat. Add the riced cauliflower, scallions, and tomatoes and cook for 8–10 minutes, or until the cauliflower softens, stirring occasionally.

In a small bowl, whisk together the apple cider vinegar, tamari, and chile-garlic paste. Pour the sauce over the cauliflower and cook for another 6–8 minutes, or until the "rice" develops a slight golden color and the liquid is absorbed, stirring frequently. Remove from the heat and stir in the chives and cilantro.

For the Avocado Mash

In a small bowl, use the back of a fork to mash together the avocado, lime juice, garlic, and sea salt to taste.

(continued on next page)

1/4 cup chopped chives

1/4 cup chopped fresh cilantro

AVOCADO MASH

1 ripe avocado, halved, pitted, and peeled

1 tablespoon fresh lime juice or to taste

1 clove garlic, minced

Sea salt, to taste

To Assemble

Spoon the sweet potatoes and cauliflower into bowls, snuggling them alongside one another. Top with a generous dollop of the avocado mash.

Refrigerate the leftover cauliflower rice and sweet potatoes in separate airtight containers for up to 3 days. The avocado mash is best when fresh.

No Soy? No Problem | *To keep this dish soy-free, swap out the reduced-sodium tamari for coconut aminos.*

COOLING CUCUMBER NOODLE + BAKED FALAFEL WITH TZATZIKI

Serves 4 | 1 hour +

Savory oven-baked falafel are balanced by tangy purple cabbage and red pepper slaw, cucumber noodles, and tzatziki sauce. The falafel bake up crisp and golden on the outside, yet tender and moist on the inside, and they're packed to their edges with micronutrient goodness. This is my go-to when I'm craving a summer meal that's simultaneously hearty and refreshing. Left to their own devices, the slaw and cucumber noodles would be too light to satiate, while the falafel would be too dense to counteract the steamy summer heat. But together, this dynamic trio becomes a plant-powered force of nourishment and cool summer vibes.

BAKED FALAFEL

1/3 cup old-fashioned rolled oats

1 (15-ounce) can chickpeas, drained and thoroughly rinsed

2 heaping cups stemmed and roughly chopped curly kale

1/4 cup loosely packed fresh cilantro, stemmed

1/4 cup loosely packed flat-leaf parsley, stemmed

2 small shallots, roughly chopped

2 cloves garlic, roughly chopped

2 tablespoons shelled hemp seeds

2 tablespoons tahini

1 tablespoon fresh lemon juice

1 teaspoon smoked paprika

1 teaspoon ground coriander

3/4 teaspoon ground cumin

1/2 teaspoon sea salt or to taste

TANGY PURPLE CABBAGE + RED PEPPER TAHINI SLAW

3 cups shredded purple cabbage (about 1/2 small head)

1 red bell pepper, cored, seeded, and julienned

For the Baked Falafel

Preheat the oven to 375°F. Line a large baking tray with parchment paper.

In a food processor, process the rolled oats for 1 minute, or until a coarse flour develops. Transfer to a large mixing bowl and set aside.

Add the remaining falafel ingredients to the food processor and pulse 30–40 times to coarsely chop and mix. The mixture should be finely chopped but still have some texture. Transfer to the bowl with the oat flour, and use a large wooden spoon to mix well.

Scoop out a scant 2 tablespoons of the falafel dough, form into a patty, and place on the lined baking tray. Repeat with the remaining dough. You should have 12 patties.

Bake for 15 minutes, gently flip each patty, and bake for another 10–15 minutes, or until the exteriors are crisp and golden. Remove from the oven and let cool slightly before serving.

For the Tangy Purple Cabbage + Red Pepper Tahini Slaw

Meanwhile, add the purple cabbage, red pepper, and cilantro to a large nonreactive (i.e., nonmetallic) mixing bowl.

In a small mixing bowl, vigorously whisk together the tahini, apple cider vinegar, maple syrup, and sea salt until emulsified. Pour it over the slaw and toss to coat.

For the Tzatziki Sauce

Prepare the Tzatziki Sauce and refrigerate until ready to serve.

(continued on next page)

1/3 cup loosely packed fresh cilantro, stemmed and finely chopped

2 tablespoons tahini

2 tablespoons apple cider vinegar

1/2 teaspoon pure maple syrup

1/4 teaspoon sea salt or to taste

TZATZIKI SAUCE

1 recipe Tzatziki Sauce (page 303)*

COOLING CUCUMBER NOODLES

1 large hothouse or English cucumber, ends trimmed

For the Cooling Cucumber Noodles

Use a spiralizer to spiralize the cucumber into noodles. Alternatively, use a vegetable peeler to shave the cucumber lengthwise into long, ribbonlike strips.

To Assemble

Divide the cucumber noodles, slaw, and falafel patties among bowls. Drizzle the cucumber noodles and falafel with the tzatziki sauce. Serve immediately.

Refrigerate leftovers in separate airtight containers for up to 3 days.

No Nuts? No Problem | *To keep this dish nut-free, use shelled hemp seeds instead of cashews to make the Tzatziki Sauce.*

Comforting + Cozy Remix | *Bump up the comfort factor by taking this dish from bowl to bread—pita bread, that is. Tuck the falafel, cucumber noodles, and slaw into a warm pita pocket, drizzle with the tzatziki, and sink your teeth in. Crunch.*

Serves 4 | 45 minutes or less

Cooked millet (or quinoa if you prefer) is tossed with oodles of Mediterranean veggies and drizzled with a red wine vinaigrette before being nestled into a bowl alongside a generous dollop of Lemony Hummus (page 304) and grilled pita bread.

This is a personal favorite of mine, and it was a favorite among recipe testers, too. To quote my dedicated recipe tester and friend Emily, "It was so good . . . I made it for dinner and am taking it for lunches for the rest of the week, and I'm honestly already so excited for lunch tomorrow!" And my clever sister-in-law, Amy, had the brilliant idea to scoop it into warm pita pockets to serve as a sandwich. So if you want to take it from bowl to handheld, spoon the millet into a warm pita pocket and dollop with the hummus.

MEDITERRANEAN MILLET

1 cup uncooked millet*

2 cups filtered water

1/2 teaspoon sea salt

2 medium tomatoes, diced

1 cup diced cucumber (about 1/2 medium cucumber)

1/4 small red onion, thinly sliced

1/3 cup oil-packed sun-dried tomatoes, drained and roughly chopped

1/4 cup kalamata olives, halved and pitted (optional)

1/4 cup fresh flat-leaf parsley or basil, chopped

1/4 cup pine nuts or sunflower seeds

HERBED RED WINE VINAIGRETTE

1/4 cup cold-pressed olive oil

3 tablespoons red wine vinegar

1 clove garlic, peeled

1/2 teaspoon dried oregano

(continued on next page)

For the Mediterranean Millet

Add the millet to a large, dry saucepan and toast over medium heat for 3–5 minutes, or until golden and fragrant. Stir in the water and sea salt and increase the heat to high. The water may sputter, so be careful as you're pouring. Once the liquid is boiling, decrease the heat to low, cover, and simmer for 15 minutes, or until most of the water is absorbed. Remove from the heat and keep covered for 10 minutes, or until the millet absorbs the remaining liquid. Fluff with a fork.

Transfer the cooked millet to a large mixing bowl along with the tomatoes, cucumber, red onion, sun-dried tomatoes, kalamata olives (if using), parsley, and pine nuts. Set aside.

For the Herbed Red Wine Vinaigrette

Add the olive oil, red wine vinegar, garlic, oregano, basil, mustard, sea salt, and black pepper to a high-speed blender and blend until emulsified.

Pour the vinaigrette over the millet and toss to coat.

To Serve

Divide the millet, hummus, and pita wedges among bowls.

Refrigerate leftovers in separate airtight containers for up to 3 days.

1/2 teaspoon dried basil

1/2 teaspoon Dijon mustard

1/4 teaspoon sea salt

Freshly ground black pepper

FOR SERVING

1 recipe Lemony Hummus (page 304) or hummus of choice

2 pita breads, cut into sixths*

Can't Find Millet? | *If you can't find millet, use quinoa instead. Thoroughly rinse 1 cup uncooked quinoa in a sieve or fine-mesh colander. Bring 1 3/4 cups water to a boil in a heavy 2-quart saucepan. Stir in the quinoa and sea salt, return to a boil, and cook, uncovered, over medium heat for 12 minutes, or until the quinoa has absorbed most of the water. Remove from the heat, fluff with a fork, cover, and let stand for 5 minutes before combining with the other salad components.*

No Gluten? No Problem | *To keep this gluten-free, opt for gluten-free pita bread or omit.*

SPICY CHILE-GARLIC EGGPLANT + BLACK RICE

Serves 4 | 1 hour +

I know . . . eggplant. Womp, womp. Hear me out on this one. Eggplant can be spongy, flavorless, and off-putting if it's not handled correctly, but after five years of cooking it and trying many techniques, I've learned how to successfully tame an eggplant. Smaller varieties are easier to work with because they don't require an hour-long, salt-induced sweat session like traditional globe eggplant does. For this dish, I recommend using Chinese eggplant, but you can also use Japanese eggplant if you stumble upon it first. You'll dry sauté the eggplant to soften it, and *then* add a flavor-packed chile-garlic sauce. Dry sautéing takes the guesswork out of eggplant and mitigates the risk of over-oiling. This saucy, tender, and flavorful eggplant is served alongside nutty black rice.

CILANTRO-LIME BLACK RICE

1 cup uncooked black pearl rice or short-grain black rice

1 3/4 cups filtered water

1/4 cup chopped fresh cilantro

1 1/2 tablespoons fresh lime juice

1/4–1/2 teaspoon sea salt

SPICY CHILE-GARLIC EGGPLANT

1/4 cup cool filtered water

1 teaspoon arrowroot starch

3–4 cloves garlic, minced

2 scallions, trimmed and thinly sliced

1 red chile pepper, seeded and minced

2 tablespoons balsamic vinegar

1 1/2 tablespoons reduced-sodium tamari*

1 teaspoon peeled and minced fresh ginger root

1 teaspoon toasted sesame oil

1 teaspoon pure maple syrup

18 ounces Chinese eggplant, trimmed and cut into 1/2-inch-thick rounds

2 tablespoons chopped fresh cilantro

1 small lime, halved

For the Cilantro-Lime Black Rice

Pour the black rice into a sieve or fine-mesh colander and thoroughly rinse until the water runs clear. In a medium saucepan, bring the black rice and filtered water to a boil over medium-high heat. Cover, decrease the heat to low, and simmer for 35–45 minutes, or until the rice is tender and most of the water is absorbed. Remove from the heat and let stand for 10 minutes, covered. Stir in the cilantro, lime juice, and sea salt.

For the Spicy Chile-Garlic Eggplant

Prepare the eggplant when the rice has about 15 minutes of simmer time remaining. In a medium bowl, whisk together the water and arrowroot until dissolved. Then, whisk in the garlic, scallions, chile, balsamic vinegar, tamari, ginger, sesame oil, and maple syrup. Place the bowl within reach of the stove.

Heat a large wok or sauté pan over medium-high heat for 1–2 minutes. Once the pan is hot, add the sliced eggplant and dry sauté for 6–10 minutes, or until softened and the white flesh is flecked with a rich golden hue, stirring occasionally at first but with greater frequency in the last few minutes. The eggplant should be tender but not mushy.

Decrease the heat to medium and pour the sauce over the eggplant. Sauté for another 2–3 minutes, or until the sauce thickens and is absorbed by the eggplant. Turn off the heat. Stir in the cilantro, and spritz with as much lime juice as desired.

To Assemble

Spoon the rice and eggplant into bowls. Serve warm. Refrigerate leftovers in separate airtight containers for up to 3 days.

No Soy? No Problem | *To keep this soy-free, swap out the reduced-sodium tamari for coconut aminos.*

FLOURISHING FIESTA WITH TACO CRUMBLES, PICO DE GALLO, GUACAMOLE + SHIITAKE BACON

Serves 4 | 1 hour or less

This power bowl has got it going on. It offers the deeply satisfying heartiness of a burrito, the fresh crunch and zesty spices of a taco salad, and the nutrient range of a vibrant vegetable patch. A colorful pinwheel of cilantro-flecked brown rice, taco crumbles, pico de gallo, guacamole, greens, and purple cabbage is liberally drizzled with a cilantro-lime crema. And if you can imagine all of that plus the magnificent finishing touch of smoky shiitake bacon, then you're beginning to understand why this is one of my favorite meals ever. It's frequently in my weekly recipe lineup, often making consecutive weeknight appearances.

A word to the dainty salad eaters: this might not be your cup of lettuce. When building your meals solely around plants, you've typically got to go big or you'll go hungry. Cast your salad stereotypes aside, grab your roomiest bowls, and let's get chopping.

CILANTRO-LIME BROWN RICE

1 cup uncooked short-grain brown rice

2 cups water

1/3 cup chopped fresh cilantro or to taste

Juice of 1/2–1 lime

Sea salt

FLOURISHING FIESTA TOPPINGS

1 recipe Shiitake Bacon (page 298)

1 recipe Cilantro-Lime Crema (page 302)*

1 recipe Sunflower // Walnut Taco Crumbles (page 302)*

2 scallions, trimmed and thinly sliced

Quick Pickled Jalapeños (optional) (page 197)

Lime wedges (optional)

Hot sauce (optional)

(continued on next page)

For the Cilantro-Lime Brown Rice

Pour the rice into a sieve or colander and thoroughly rinse until the water runs clear. In a medium saucepan, bring the brown rice and the 2 cups water to a boil over medium-high heat. Stir once, cover, and decrease the heat to low. Simmer for 40–50 minutes, or until the rice is tender and most of the water is absorbed.

Remove from the heat and let stand for 10 minutes, covered. Gently fluff with a fork, and stir in the cilantro, lime juice, and sea salt to taste.

For the Flourishing Fiesta Toppings

Make the Shiitake Bacon, Cilantro-Lime Crema, and Sunflower // Walnut Taco Crumbles. Prepare the scallions and other toppings (if using) and set aside.

For the Quick Pico de Gallo

In a small bowl, stir together the tomatoes, red onion, and cilantro. Season with sea salt to taste.

For the Speedy Guacamole

Add the avocado, garlic, and lime juice to a medium bowl and use the back of a fork to thoroughly mash. Season with sea salt to taste.

To Assemble

Divide the romaine, arugula, purple cabbage (if using), rice, taco crumbles, pico de gallo, guacamole, scallions, and jalapeños (if using) among bowls. Generously drizzle with the cilantro-lime crema and sprinkle with the shiitake bacon. Serve with lime wedges and hot sauce if desired.

QUICK PICO DE GALLO

2 cups grape tomatoes, halved or quartered

1/4–1/2 small red onion, finely diced

1/4 cup chopped fresh cilantro or to taste

Sea salt

SPEEDY GUACAMOLE

2 small ripe avocados, halved, pitted, and peeled

1–2 cloves garlic, minced

Juice of 1 lime or to taste

Sea salt

BASE

2 small heads romaine, chopped

Several handfuls baby arugula

2 cups thinly sliced purple cabbage (optional)

No Nuts? No Problem | *To keep this nut-free, use shelled hemp seeds to make the* Cilantro-Lime Crema *and opt for the* Sunflower Taco Crumbles.

No Soy? No Problem | *To keep this soy-free, use coconut aminos instead of reduced-sodium tamari in the* Sunflower // Walnut Taco Crumbles.

Craving Something Warm? | *Swap out the* Sunflower // Walnut Taco Crumbles *for warm spiced chickpeas. Drain and rinse 1 (15-ounce) can of chickpeas. Add them to a large skillet and season to taste with the same spices used for the taco crumbles. Cook over medium-low heat for 6–8 minutes, or until warmed through and golden brown.*

COMFORTING BBQ PULLED HEARTS OF PALM, CRISPY KALE + PARMESAN POLENTA

Serves 4 | 45 minutes or less

This dish transcends the seasons: in hot weather, the barbecue flavors beckon; in chilly temperatures, the Parmesan polenta makes for hearty comfort food. If you're unfamiliar with hearts of palm, they're a tender white vegetable harvested from the innermost stalk of certain palm trees. These long, tubular stalks have a flavor similar to artichoke hearts and their slightly crisp exterior gives way to a soft, stringy interior. In this recipe, they're simmered in barbecue sauce until tender and shredded, soaking in oodles of flavor and taking on a texture that's incredibly similar to pulled meat. They're spooned over a creamy bed of polenta that's been seasoned with Nut // Seed Parmesan Cheese (page 299), and the final touch is a handful of perfectly crisp kale. Gotta squeeze in those greens.

COMFORTING BBQ PULLED HEARTS OF PALM

3/4 cup 10-Minute Sweet + Tangy BBQ Sauce (page 300) or BBQ sauce of choice*

1/2 cup filtered water

1 (14.5-ounce) can hearts of palm, drained

CRISPY KALE

1 bunch curly kale, washed, stemmed, torn into large pieces, and patted dry

1 1/2 tablespoons cold-pressed olive oil

Sea salt and freshly ground black pepper

PARMESAN POLENTA

3 1/2 cups filtered water

1 teaspoon sea salt, plus more if needed

1 cup uncooked polenta (coarse cornmeal)

1/4 cup Nut // Seed Parmesan Cheese (page 299)*

For the Comforting BBQ Pulled Hearts of Palm

In a large sauté pan, whisk together the BBQ sauce and water. Add the hearts of palm and bring to a boil over medium-high heat. Decrease the heat to medium-low, cover, and simmer for 15 minutes, or until the hearts of palm are tender, stirring occasionally.

Use two forks to thoroughly pull apart and shred the hearts of palm. Continue to simmer with the lid off for another 5 minutes, or until most of the sauce has been absorbed, stirring frequently.

For the Crispy Kale

While the hearts of palm are simmering, preheat the oven to 350°F and line two large baking trays with parchment paper.

Divide the kale between the lined baking trays and drizzle with the olive oil. Gently massage the oil into the kale and spread the leaves out in a single layer across each pan.

Roast for 15 minutes, or until crisp. Season with sea salt and freshly ground black pepper to taste.

For the Parmesan Polenta

In a large saucepan over high heat, bring the water and sea salt to a rolling boil.

(continued on next page)

Slowly add the polenta while whisking continuously. Be careful not to add too much at once or you'll end up with lumpy polenta. Continue to whisk until smooth. Decrease the heat to low and simmer for 10 minutes, or until tender, whisking frequently.

Turn off the heat and whisk in the Nut // Seed Parmesan Cheese. Taste and season with more sea salt, if desired.

To Assemble

Spoon the polenta into bowls. Top with the BBQ pulled hearts of palm and kale. Serve immediately. Refrigerate leftovers.

Give Your BBQ Sauce a Once-Over | *If you're avoiding refined sugars, scan the ingredients as you're selecting your barbecue sauce and adjust accordingly. Or save yourself the hassle of label scanning and make my* 10-Minute Sweet + Tangy BBQ Sauce.

No Soy? No Problem | *To keep this dish soy-free, make the* 10-Minute Sweet + Tangy BBQ Sauce *and use coconut aminos instead of reduced-sodium tamari.*

No Nuts? No Problem | *To keep this dish nut-free, opt for a seed-based Parmesan.*

SWIFT SWEET POTATO COCONUT CURRY

Serves 4 | 30 minutes or less

Late fall and winter draw out some of my fiercest sweet potato cravings, and Dan's cravings seem to have a similar rhythm. Thus, our fall and winter dinners tend to bounce back and forth between this dish and The Classic power bowl (page 153). This sweet potato coconut curry is truly swift, requiring just 30 minutes from start to finish. Sweet potatoes are simmered in a rich, spice-laced coconut broth until they begin to break down, forming a thick and creamy curry. It's finished with a sprinkling of scallions, fresh cilantro, and raisins before being served with a side of warm brown rice or quinoa.

1 tablespoon curry powder

1 teaspoon sea salt

1/2 teaspoon ground coriander

1/4 teaspoon ground ginger

1/8 teaspoon ground turmeric

1 medium yellow onion, finely diced (about 1 cup)

1 cup filtered water, divided

1 (14-ounce) can full-fat coconut milk

2 large sweet potatoes, peeled and cut into 1/2-inch cubes (about 4 cups)

3 scallions, trimmed and thinly sliced

1/3 cup raisins (optional)

1/4 cup fresh cilantro, stemmed and chopped

4 cups cooked brown rice or quinoa, for serving (optional)*

1 lime, cut into wedges, for spritzing (optional)

Toast the curry powder, sea salt, coriander, ginger, and turmeric in a medium stockpot over medium heat for 30 seconds, stirring constantly.

Add the yellow onion and 1/3 cup of the water, and cook for 5 minutes, or until the onion is soft and translucent, stirring frequently.

Whisk in the coconut milk and the remaining 2/3·cup water, and bring to a boil.

Add the sweet potatoes, decrease the heat to medium-low, cover, and rapidly simmer for 10–15 minutes, or until the sweet potatoes are fork-tender, stirring occasionally.

Stir in the scallions, raisins (if using), and cilantro, and continue to simmer, uncovered, for 5 minutes, or until the sweet potatoes begin to break down into the sauce, stirring frequently. Remove from the heat.

Spoon the curry into bowls and serve with warm brown rice and lime wedges, if desired.

No Grains? No Problem | *To keep this grain-free, opt for quinoa, a grain-like seed, instead of brown rice.*

SANDWICHES, TACOS + PIZZA

Crispy Cauliflower Tacos with Tangy Slaw + Avocado Crema 175

White Pizza with Garlic-Herb Oil, Mozzarella + Puffy Potato Crust 179

SuperSeeded Pesto Pizza with Rainbow Veggies, Mozzarella +
Sweet Potato Crust 180

Mushroom-Lentil Sliders with Herbed Hemp Aioli 183

Shaved Carrot Reuben with Special Sauce + Swiss Cheese 185

Sloppy Shiitakes with Tangy Rainbow Slaw 189

"Meatball" Marinara Sub with Basil Aioli 191

Baked Yellow Split Pea Burgers with Tzatziki Sauce 195

Garlic-Mushroom Tacos with Quick Pickled Jalapeños +
Chipotle-Tomato Crema 197

BBQ Pulled Jackfruit with Cashew Cheddar Cheese +
Seeded Ranch Dressing 201

There's a small, family-owned Italian deli named Frantonio's that my family has frequented for the last twenty years. It's home to one of my all-time favorite sandwiches, the "Vegi Amore," which I fell in love with more than a decade ago. The Vegi Amore is a combination of roasted red peppers, artichoke hearts, basil, lettuce, and juicy tomato slices piled high on a toasted Italian roll and drizzled with some of the best olive oil I've ever tasted. It's a simple sandwich that packs a punch of freshness. And it proves that veggies can hold their own between two slices of bread provided they're well paired and lovingly seasoned. I haven't attempted to recreate the Vegi Amore (when something is perfect, there's no need to tinker), but it has served as a source of inspiration for many of the hand-held bites on my blog and in this book.

In addition to sandwiches, this chapter includes tacos and pizza and burgers, too! And these plant-centered handheld meals are designed to please even the more veggie-averse palates. Want to ditch the meat but just can't seem to kick that summertime craving for BBQ pulled pork? Try the BBQ Pulled Jackfruit with Cashew Cheddar Cheese + Seeded Ranch Dressing on page 201. Or perhaps you're looking to pull your Reuben-loving Great-Aunt Hilda over to the plant-passionate side? In that case, you'll need the assistance of the Shaved Carrot Reuben with Special Sauce + Swiss Cheese on page 185. If you're looking to spice up a week-night with a speedy, flavor-packed meal, whip up a batch of the Garlic-Mushroom Tacos with Quick Pickled Jalapeños + Chipotle-Tomato Crema on page 197. And you simply must check out the pizza recipes on pages 179 and 180. With veggie-based crusts and a field of delectable toppings, these pizzas will nourish your body and delight your taste buds one slice at a time.

CRISPY CAULIFLOWER TACOS WITH
TANGY SLAW + AVOCADO CREMA

Makes 12 tacos | 1 hour or less

Crunchy, tangy, crisp, creamy, citrusy, vibrant, delicious. I've said it before, and I feel compelled to say it again: these tacos are speaking my food-love language, and I just can't quit them. This recipe quickly staked its claim as one of the most adored on my blog, and it's been known to win the affection of everyone from meat-loving adults to cauliflower-fearing kids. Battered, seasoned, and baked crispy cauliflower florets are tucked into warm corn tortillas, topped with a tangy purple cabbage slaw, and drizzled with avocado cream. The final touch is a splash of fresh lime juice, and then it's time to bite, savor, and repeat.

CRISPY CAULIFLOWER

1 cup old-fashioned rolled oats

2 tablespoons chopped fresh cilantro

2 teaspoons chili powder

1 teaspoon fine-grain sea salt

1 teaspoon smoked paprika

1/2 teaspoon ground cumin

1/4 teaspoon garlic powder

1/4 teaspoon ground turmeric (optional)

1/8 teaspoon cayenne pepper

1 1/4 cups unsweetened almond milk*

3/4 cup brown rice flour

1 tablespoon fresh lime juice

1 small or 1/2 large head cauliflower, cut into bite-size florets

TANGY SLAW

2 cups thinly sliced purple cabbage

1/4 cup fresh lime juice

1 tablespoon apple cider vinegar

1/2 tablespoon pure maple syrup (or other liquid sweetener)

1/4 teaspoon fine-grain sea salt

For the Crispy Cauliflower

Preheat the oven to 400°F. Line a large baking tray with parchment paper.

Add the rolled oats to a food processor. Pulse 75–80 times, or until a coarse meal forms. The texture should be similar to panko bread crumbs. Transfer to a large, shallow bowl, and whisk in the cilantro, chili powder, sea salt, paprika, cumin, garlic powder, turmeric (if using), and cayenne pepper.

In another large, shallow bowl, whisk together the almond milk, brown rice flour, and lime juice until smooth.

From left to right, line up the cauliflower florets, almond milk batter, oat crumbs, and baking tray. Place a handful of cauliflower florets into the almond milk batter, toss to coat, shake off excess batter, and transfer to the oat and spice mixture. Toss to coat and transfer to the lined baking tray. Repeat with the remaining cauliflower.

Bake for 25–30 minutes, or until crisp and light golden, tossing halfway through baking. Remove from the oven and let cool slightly.

For the Tangy Slaw

While the cauliflower is baking, add the purple cabbage, lime juice, apple cider vinegar, maple syrup, and sea salt to a medium nonreactive (i.e., nonmetallic) mixing bowl. Toss to coat and set aside, stirring occasionally.

For the Avocado Crema

Add the avocado, cilantro, lime juice, and sea salt to a food processor. Process for 3–4 minutes, or until smooth. The texture should resemble mayonnaise.

(continued on next page)

AVOCADO CREMA

1 ripe avocado, halved, pitted, and peeled

1/4 cup fresh cilantro, stemmed

2 tablespoons fresh lime juice

1/4 teaspoon fine-grain sea salt

TACOS

12 small soft corn tortillas

Fresh cilantro, stemmed

2 small limes, cut into wedges

To Assemble

Heat the tortillas, one at a time, in a small skillet over medium heat for 20–30 seconds per side. Fill each with 3–4 pieces of the cauliflower, a small handful of cabbage slaw, and a dollop of crema.

Garnish with cilantro and serve with lime wedges to spritz the tacos.

Refrigerate leftovers in separate airtight containers for up to 3 days. The Avocado Crema is best when fresh.

No Nuts? No Problem | *To keep this nut-free, swap out the unsweetened almond milk for a nut-free plant-based milk, such as unsweetened soy milk or unsweetened rice milk.*

WHITE PIZZA WITH GARLIC-HERB OIL, MOZZARELLA + PUFFY POTATO CRUST

Serves 2 | 1 hour +

I'm not sure if it's my Chicago roots or my carb-craving ways, but there are few foods I love more than pizza. Although I no longer participate in the ceaseless debate over best Chicago deep-dish (for the record, my vote always went to Gino's East), I've found plenty of ways to foster my pizza adoration since going vegan. And although store-bought vegan cheeses and premade pizza dough work great in a pinch, I've even found ways to up the nutritional perks. Because when you love pizza as much as I do, you've gotta make those slices count.

This pizza is simple yet so incredibly satisfying. Puffy Potato Pizza Crust (page 295) is liberally brushed with garlic-herb oil, dotted with gooey homemade mozzarella cheese, and topped with fresh, peppery greens. Chicago pizzerias, try to keep pace with these plant-powered pizza strides, will you?

PIZZA BASE

1 recipe Puffy Potato Pizza Crust, baked (page 295)*

GARLIC-HERB OIL

2 tablespoons cold-pressed olive oil

2 cloves garlic, minced

2 teaspoons chopped fresh rosemary leaves

1/8–1/4 teaspoon crushed red pepper flakes

1/4 teaspoon sea salt

TOPPINGS

1 recipe Cashew // Hemp Seed Mozzarella Cheese (page 305)*

Handful baby arugula or other peppery baby greens

For the Pizza Base

Start by preparing and baking the Puffy Potato Pizza Crust. After baking, leave the oven heated to 400°F.

For the Garlic-Herb Oil

Meanwhile, heat the olive oil, garlic, rosemary, red pepper flakes, and sea salt in a small sauté pan over medium heat for 2 minutes, or until it begins to rapidly simmer. Decrease the heat to low and lightly simmer for 2–4 minutes, or until the rosemary's vibrant green hue fades to soft golden-green, stirring frequently and being careful not to burn the garlic. Remove from the heat and cool slightly.

For the Toppings

Prepare the Cashew // Hemp Seed Mozzarella Cheese.

To Assemble

Brush the baked pizza crust with the garlic-herb oil and top with tablespoonfuls of the mozzarella. Bake for 5 minutes to warm the crust and toppings. Remove from the oven and garnish with the arugula. Slice and serve immediately.

Leftovers will keep in the refrigerator for up to 3 days.

No Nuts? No Problem | *To keep this nut-free, use sunflower flour in the crust instead of almond flour and opt for* Hemp Seed Mozzarella Cheese.

Leftovers? | *Second-day pizza can be just as good as pizza from day one. And no, we're not talking about cold pizza for breakfast, although if that's your jam, no judgment here! To reheat it, preheat the oven to 400°F. Then, arrange the pizza slices on a small baking tray and bake for 8–10 minutes, or until warmed through with crisp edges.*

SUPERSEEDED PESTO PIZZA WITH RAINBOW VEGGIES, MOZZARELLA + SWEET POTATO CRUST

Serves 2 | 1 hour +

You might recognize this rainbow-hued pizza from the cover. With jewel-toned veggies strewn across a bright orange crust that's been generously slathered with spring-green pesto, there's much to adore about its appearance. But this pizza's delightfulness runs more than surface-deep. Its fresh, vibrant toppings are perfectly complemented by its savory and deeply satisfying crust. And it's delectability is made all the more wonderful by the fact that each and every slice is brimming with vitamin- and mineral-rich vegetables, so you can have your health and eat pizza, too.

PIZZA BASE

1 recipe Sweet Potato Pizza Crust, baked (page 296)*

TOPPINGS

1 bunch scallions or spring onions, trimmed

Cold-pressed olive oil

Sea salt and freshly ground black pepper

1/4–1/3 cup SuperSeed Pesto (page 297)

1 recipe Cashew // Hemp Seed Mozzarella Cheese (page 305)*

1/3 cup drained and thinly sliced jarred roasted yellow peppers

Handful baby arugula or other peppery baby greens

Thinly sliced radicchio (optional)

Small handful fresh basil leaves, thinly sliced

For the Pizza Base

Start by preparing and baking the Sweet Potato Pizza Crust. After baking, leave the oven heated to 400°F.

For the Toppings

Line a small rimmed baking pan with parchment paper.

Spread the scallions on the lined pan and lightly drizzle with olive oil. Use your hands to massage the oil into the scallions. Season with sea salt and black pepper. Roast for 18–24 minutes, or until tender and just beginning to turn golden brown.

Meanwhile, prepare the SuperSeed Pesto and Cashew // Hemp Seed Mozzarella Cheese.

To Assemble

Slather the baked pizza crust with as much of the pesto as desired and arrange the roasted scallions on top. Top with tablespoonfuls of the mozzarella, and garnish with the roasted yellow peppers, arugula, radicchio (if using), and basil.

Slice and serve immediately.

Leftovers will keep in the refrigerator for up to 3 days.

No Nuts? No Problem | *To keep this nut-free, use sunflower flour in the crust instead of almond flour and opt for* Hemp Seed Mozzarella Cheese.

Leftovers? | *Second-day pizza can be just as good as pizza from day one. And no, we're not talking about cold pizza for breakfast, although if that's your jam, no judgment here! To reheat it, preheat the oven to 400°F. Then, arrange the pizza slices on a small baking tray and bake for 8–10 minutes, or until warmed through with crisp edges.*

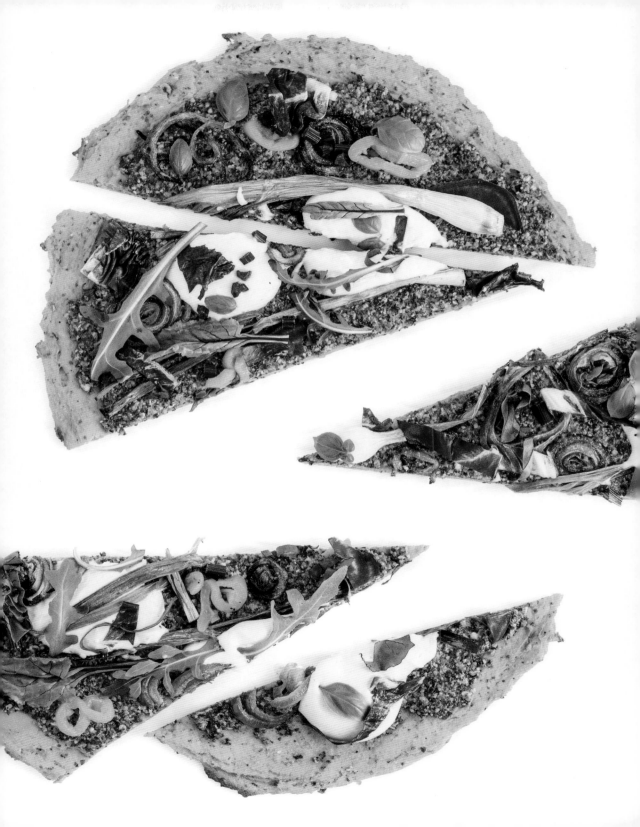

Makes 12 sliders | 1 hour +

These sliders are petite, bite-sized, and miniature on the outside and hearty, meaty, and mighty on the inside. Don't judge a book by its cover or a burger by its size. The mushroom-lentil patties are lightly pan-fried to yield golden-brown, seared exteriors and tender interiors. Then, they're tucked away into slider rolls along with a handful of arugula and a drizzle of zesty herbed aioli.

MUSHROOM-LENTIL PATTIES

1/2 cup uncooked green lentils, thoroughly rinsed

1/4 cup raw shelled sunflower seeds

2 1/2 cups plus 2 tablespoons filtered water, divided

1 tablespoon flaxseed meal (ground flaxseed)

1 tablespoon cold-pressed olive oil

3 medium shallots, finely diced (2/3 cup)

3 cloves garlic, minced

10 ounces cremini or baby bella mushrooms, stemmed and finely diced

1 tablespoon balsamic vinegar

1 tablespoon reduced-sodium tamari*

1/2 teaspoon dried oregano

1/4 teaspoon dried thyme

1/2 cup oat flour

1/4 cup old-fashioned rolled oats

1/2–3/4 teaspoon fine-grain sea salt

Freshly ground black pepper

2 tablespoons heat-tolerant oil, such as refined sunflower oil or grapeseed oil

For the Mushroom-Lentil Patties

In a medium saucepan, combine the lentils, sunflower seeds, and 2 1/2 cups of the water over medium-high heat. Bring to a boil, decrease the heat, and simmer, uncovered, for 20–25 minutes, or until the lentils are tender but not mushy. Strain off excess water, transfer to a large mixing bowl, and use the back of a fork to coarsely mash about half of the lentils.

In a small bowl, whisk together the flaxseed meal and the remaining 2 tablespoons water. Set aside to thicken.

Meanwhile, heat the olive oil in a large skillet over medium-low heat. Add the shallots and garlic and cook for 4–5 minutes, or until translucent, stirring occasionally.

Add the mushrooms, balsamic vinegar, tamari, oregano, and thyme and cook for another 10–12 minutes, or until the mushrooms are tender and most of the liquid has cooked off, stirring occasionally. Transfer to the mixing bowl with the lentil mixture. Add the flaxseed mixture, oat flour, rolled oats, sea salt, and black pepper to taste; stir to combine.

Line a small pan with parchment paper. Lightly grease a 1/4-cup measuring cup, and use it to scoop up a scant 1/4 cup (about 3 tablespoons) of the slider mixture. Form into a patty that is about 3/4 inch thick and 2 inches in diameter and transfer to the lined pan. Repeat with the remaining mixture. You should have 12 patties.

Refrigerate for at least 1 hour to set the patties before cooking.

When you're ready to cook the patties, line a large dinner plate with a few paper towels and place it within reach of the stove.

Heat 1 tablespoon of the heat-tolerant oil in a large skillet over medium heat until it begins to thin out and spread across the pan.

(continued on next page)

HERBED HEMP AIOLI

1/2 cup shelled hemp seeds

1/4 cup plus 2 tablespoons filtered water

1/4 cup roughly chopped chives

1/4 cup fresh cilantro, stemmed

3 tablespoons white wine vinegar or apple cider vinegar

2 cloves garlic, peeled

1/2 teaspoon sea salt or to taste

SLIDER BASE AND TOPPING

1 recipe Puffy Spelt + Potato Slider Rolls (page 293) or 12 store-bought slider rolls*

Baby arugula

Add half of the slider patties to the pan, being careful not to overcrowd. Cook for 2–3 minutes, flip the patties, and cook for another 2–3 minutes, or until golden brown and firm to the touch. Transfer to the paper towel–lined plate until ready to assemble. Add the remaining 1 tablespoon oil to the skillet, if necessary, and cook the remaining sliders.

For the Herbed Hemp Aioli

Add all the aioli ingredients to a blender and blend for 1–2 minutes, or until smooth, stopping to scrape down the sides as needed. Refrigerate until ready to assemble.

To Assemble

Slice the slider rolls in half, place a tiny handful of arugula on the bottom of each bun, place the patty on top, and drizzle with the aioli. Serve immediately.

Refrigerate leftovers in separate airtight containers for up to 3 days.

No Soy? No Problem | *To keep this dish soy-free, swap the reduced-sodium tamari for coconut aminos.*

No Gluten? No Problem | *To keep this dish gluten-free, use store-bought gluten-free slider rolls.*

Protein Powerhouse | *The aioli is both flavor-packed and nutritionally efficient thanks to the hemp seeds. Just 3 tablespoons of these tiny but mighty seeds offer 10 grams of plant-based protein!*

Spicy Sriracha Aioli | *To spice up these sliders, swap out the Herbed Hemp Aioli for this zesty Sriracha version. Better yet, make both so that you and your dinner mates can top as you please! In a blender, combine 1/2 cup shelled hemp seeds, 1/4 cup filtered water, 2 1/2 tablespoons Sriracha, 1 1/2 tablespoons reduced-sodium tamari, 1 tablespoon fresh lime juice, 1 tablespoon apple cider vinegar, and 1–2 peeled cloves garlic. Blend on high until smooth, stopping to scrape down the sides as needed. Keep refrigerated.*

Makes 4 sandwiches | 45 minutes or less

It's time to think outside the meat substitute box. Carrots have played second fiddle and side dish for far too long, and now it's their turn to steal the show. In this veggie-centric twist on a classic Reuben, carrots are placed at center ~~stage~~ sandwich, demonstrating the depths of their versatility, wit, and popular appeal. With a little love and creativity, they're transformed into something altogether meaty and satisfying, proving that it's possible to eat close to the earth without sacrificing the flavors, textures, or meals of memories past.

Carrots are shaved lengthwise into long ribbons and simmered in a sauce spiked with classic corned beef and pastrami spices. Then, they're piled high on toasted rye bread and topped with melted Cashew // Hemp Seed Swiss Cheese (page 304), a delicious sauce, and sauerkraut. This is a sandwich that will leave your face messy, your body nourished, and your heart satisfied.

SHAVED CARROTS

4 large carrots, peeled and trimmed

1/4 cup filtered water

2–3 tablespoons reduced-sodium tamari or to taste*

2 tablespoons apple cider vinegar

1/4 teaspoon freshly ground black pepper

1/4 teaspoon ground allspice

1/4 teaspoon ground cloves

1/4 teaspoon ground cardamom

1/4 teaspoon ground cinnamon

1/4 teaspoon crushed red pepper flakes (optional)

SPECIAL SAUCE

1/2 cup filtered water

1/4 cup shelled hemp seeds

2 tablespoons oil-packed sun-dried tomatoes, drained

1 1/2 tablespoons apple cider vinegar

1/2 tablespoon Sriracha

1 teaspoon smoked paprika

1 clove garlic, peeled

1/4 teaspoon sea salt or to taste

3 tablespoons finely chopped dill pickles (optional)

For the Shaved Carrots

Use a wide vegetable peeler or mandoline to carefully shave the carrots, lengthwise, into long, ribbonlike strips. You'll need about 4 loosely packed cups of shaved carrots.

In a small bowl, whisk together the water, tamari, vinegar, black pepper, allspice, cloves, cardamom, cinnamon, and red pepper flakes (if using).

Heat a large sauté pan over medium heat. Once the pan is hot, add the carrots and liquid spice mixture. Cover and simmer for 10–12 minutes, or until the carrots are firm-tender and most of the liquid has been absorbed, stirring occasionally at first but with greater frequency during the last few minutes.

Remove from the heat and let cool slightly.

For the Special Sauce

Meanwhile, in a high-speed blender, combine all the sauce ingredients except for the pickles and blend until smooth, stopping to scrape down the sides to encourage blending. If needed, add more water, 1 tablespoon at a time, to thin.

Stir in the pickles (if using) and refrigerate until ready to assemble.

To Assemble

Prepare the Cashew // Hemp Seed Swiss Cheese.

(continued on next page)

SANDWICH BASE AND TOPPINGS

1 recipe Cashew // Hemp Seed Swiss Cheese (page 304)*

8 slices rye bread, toasted*

1 cup sauerkraut

Top 4 slices of the toasted rye bread each with a mound of the shaved carrots, 1/4 cup sauerkraut, a dollop of Swiss cheese, and a drizzle of sauce. Cover with the remaining slices of bread, slice each sandwich in half, and serve immediately.

No Soy? No Problem | *To keep this dish soy-free, swap out the reduced-sodium tamari for coconut aminos.*

No Nuts? No Problem | *To keep this dish nut-free, opt for* Hemp Seed Swiss Cheese.

No Gluten? No Problem | *To keep this dish gluten-free, swap out the rye for your favorite gluten-free bread.*

Makes 4–6 sandwiches | 45 minutes or less

Roll up your sleeves, prepare your napkins, and arm your tablecloths with place mats: it's time to get deliciously sloppy.

This plant-powered remix of a sloppy joe sandwich leans on a base of sliced shiitakes and cremini mushrooms. The mushrooms are coated in spices and simmered in barbecue sauce until they're tender and super saucy. Then, they're piled high on Puffy Spelt + Potato Buns (page 293) and topped with crunchy rainbow slaw, balancing comfort with a pop of freshness.

SLOPPY SHIITAKES

10 ounces cremini mushrooms, stemmed and diced

8 ounces shiitake mushrooms, stemmed and thinly sliced

1 1/2 tablespoons smoked paprika

1 tablespoon coconut sugar

1 teaspoon onion powder

3/4 teaspoon ground cumin

1/2 teaspoon garlic powder

1/4 teaspoon fine-grain sea salt or to taste

1 tablespoon cold-pressed olive oil

2 cloves garlic, minced

1/2 cup 10-Minute Sweet + Tangy BBQ Sauce (page 300) or favorite barbecue sauce*

1/4 cup filtered water

TANGY RAINBOW SLAW

2 cups shredded green or purple cabbage (or a mix of both)

1 medium carrot, peeled and cut into matchsticks

2 scallions, trimmed and cut into matchsticks

1/4 cup shelled hemp seeds*

1/4 cup filtered water

1/4 cup loosely packed fresh cilantro, stemmed

(continued on next page)

For the Sloppy Shiitakes

Add the mushrooms to a large mixing bowl.

In a small mixing bowl, whisk together the smoked paprika, coconut sugar, onion powder, cumin, garlic powder, and sea salt. Sprinkle the spice mixture over the mushrooms and toss to coat.

Add the olive oil and garlic to a large skillet and cook over medium-low heat for 30 seconds, or until fragrant. Add the seasoned mushrooms and cook for 5 minutes, or until the mushrooms just begin to wilt and soften, stirring occasionally.

Whisk together the barbecue sauce and water; pour over the mushrooms and stir to incorporate.

Cover and simmer for 15–20 minutes, or until the mushrooms are tender and the sauce is thick and bubbly, stirring occasionally. Remove from the heat and season with more sea salt, if desired.

For the Tangy Rainbow Slaw

Meanwhile, add the cabbage, carrot, and scallions to a medium nonreactive (i.e., nonmetallic) mixing bowl.

In a high-speed blender, combine the hemp seeds, water, cilantro, lime juice, garlic, apple cider vinegar, and sea salt. Blend on high for 1–2 minutes, or until smooth; pour over the cabbage mixture and toss to coat.

To Assemble

Spoon a generous heap of the mushrooms onto each of the toasted buns and top with the slaw. Serve immediately.

Refrigerate leftovers in separate airtight containers for up to 3 days.

1 tablespoon plus 1 teaspoon
fresh lime juice

1 clove garlic, smashed and
peeled

1 teaspoon apple cider vinegar or
white wine vinegar

1/4 teaspoon sea salt or to taste

SANDWICH BASE

4–6 Puffy Spelt + Potato Buns
(page 293) or buns of choice, split
and toasted*

Give Your BBQ Sauce a Once-Over | *If you're avoiding refined sugars, scan the ingredients as you're selecting your barbecue sauce and adjust accordingly—many brands contain processed sugars. Or save yourself the hassle of label scanning and make my* 10-Minute Sweet + Tangy BBQ Sauce.

No Soy? No Problem | *To keep this dish soy-free, make the* 10-Minute Sweet + Tangy BBQ Sauce *and use coconut aminos instead of reduced-sodium tamari.*

Can't Find Hemp Seeds? | *If you can't find hemp seeds, use raw cashews instead.*

No Gluten? No Problem | *Use your favorite gluten-free buns to keep these sandwiches gluten-free.*

Makes 4 sandwiches | 1 hour +

Cauliflower and sun-dried tomatoes are finely grated and cooked with zesty Italian spices, taking on a surprisingly meaty look before being formed into "meatballs" and baked. Then they're nestled into sub rolls and drizzled with warm marinara and a quick and easy basil aioli. These plant-powered "meatballs" are soft and tender rather than firm and chewy like soy- or wheat-based meatless meatballs, so they meld into the sandwich bread in the best of ways. They do require a bit of time, love, and care to make; however, they can be made ahead of time, frozen, and thawed for a quick weeknight meal.

CAULIFLOWER + SUN-DRIED TOMATO "MEATBALLS"

4 ounces dry-packed, no-salt-added sun-dried tomatoes (about 1 1/2 cups)

1 medium head cauliflower, cored and cut into small florets (about 6 cups)

1 tablespoon cold-pressed olive oil

1 small yellow onion, finely diced (about 1/2 cup)

2 cloves garlic, minced

1 teaspoon dried basil

1/2–3/4 teaspoon sea salt or to taste

1/2 teaspoon dried oregano

1/4 teaspoon crushed red pepper flakes

1/4 teaspoon crushed fennel seed (optional)

1 tablespoon chia seeds

2 tablespoons filtered water

1 tablespoon oat flour

1 tablespoon balsamic vinegar

BASIL AIOLI

1/2 cup raw cashews or shelled hemp seeds*

1/3 cup filtered water

1/3 cup packed basil leaves

2 tablespoons apple cider vinegar or white wine vinegar

For the Cauliflower + Sun-Dried Tomato "Meatballs"

Preheat the oven to 400°F. Line a small baking tray with parchment paper.

Soak the sun-dried tomatoes in hot water for 15 minutes to soften. Drain.

Meanwhile, add the cauliflower florets to the bowl of a food processor fitted with the S-blade and pulse until finely grated. Add the sun-dried tomatoes and pulse until the tomatoes are finely chopped and the cauliflower takes on a burnt-orange hue.

Heat the olive oil in a large sauté pan over medium heat. Add the onion and garlic and sauté for 3 minutes, or until just beginning to soften.

Stir in the grated cauliflower mixture along with the basil, sea salt, oregano, red pepper flakes, and fennel seed (if using). Cook for 15–18 minutes, or until browned and just beginning to separate into large crumbles, stirring every few minutes. Remove from the heat and let cool slightly.

Meanwhile, whisk together the chia seeds and water in a small bowl. Set aside for 5–10 minutes to thicken.

Add the chia mixture, oat flour, and balsamic vinegar to the cauliflower mixture and stir to incorporate. Scoop out a scant 1/4 cup of the mixture, form and compact into a ball, and place on the lined baking tray. Repeat with the remaining mixture. You should have 12 "meatballs."

Bake for 16–20 minutes, or until the meatballs feel set to the touch and the bottoms are a rich golden-brown hue. Remove from the oven.

For the Basil Aioli

While the "meatballs" bake, add all the aioli ingredients to a high-speed blender and blend on high until smooth. Refrigerate until ready to assemble.

(continued on next page)

2 cloves garlic, smashed and peeled

1/4 teaspoon sea salt or to taste

SUB BASE AND TOPPINGS

1 recipe Cashew // Hemp Seed Mozzarella Cheese (optional, page 305)*

4 sprouted or multigrain sub rolls*

1 cup marinara sauce, warmed

Handful baby arugula

To Assemble

Prepare the Cashew // Hemp Seed Mozzarella Cheese (if using).

If your sub rolls are thick, use a spoon to scoop out some of the inner bread to thin the rolls. This trick makes flavors pop by bringing balance to a sandwich that would otherwise be dominated by bread. Toast, if desired.

Stuff each roll with 3 "meatballs," slather with the warm marinara, drizzle with the aioli, and top with the mozzarella (if using) and arugula. Serve immediately.

Be Kind to Your Blender | *If you're not using a high-speed blender (e.g., Vitamix or Blendtec), soak the cashews in water for 2 hours or boil them for 10 minutes to soften before blending.*

No Nuts? No Problem | *To keep these sandwiches nut-free, use hemp seeds instead of cashews to make the aioli and mozzarella (if using).*

No Gluten? No Problem | *To keep these sandwiches gluten-free, use your favorite gluten-free sub rolls.*

Spaghetti Remix | *Serve the "meatballs" over spaghetti squash or brown rice spaghetti with warm marinara and* Nut // Seed Parmesan Cheese *(page 299).*

Makes 6 burgers | 1 hour +

Exactly one second after I snapped this photo, this three-story tower of burgers leaned like Pisa and toppled before I could do a thing about it. A cucumber slice found its edge and went rolling across the table with freakish composure, tzatziki splattered, and I frantically previewed the single photo I'd managed to snap to ensure it wasn't a blurry mess. You can pile your protein-packed split pea burgers high and outfit them with veggies and tzatziki sauce, but you certainly can't tame them. It was a good reminder that when things literally fall to pieces, we'd best heed the advice of a cucumber and roll with it.

BAKED YELLOW SPLIT PEA BURGERS

3/4 cup uncooked yellow split peas, thoroughly rinsed

3/4 cup uncooked short-grain brown rice, thoroughly rinsed

1 tablespoon cold-pressed olive oil, plus more for greasing

1 small yellow onion, finely diced (about 1 cup)

4 scallions, trimmed and thinly sliced

1 teaspoon ground cumin

1/2 teaspoon ground coriander

1/4 teaspoon ground turmeric (optional)

1 tablespoon flaxseed meal (ground flaxseed)

2 tablespoons filtered water

1/2 cup oat flour

2 tablespoons apple cider vinegar

1 1/4 teaspoons fine-grain sea salt

Freshly ground black pepper

BURGER BASE AND TOPPINGS

1 recipe Tzatziki Sauce (page 303)*

6 Puffy Spelt + Potato Buns (page 293) or buns of choice*

2 medium vine-ripened tomatoes, thinly sliced

1 small cucumber, thinly sliced

For the Baked Yellow Split Pea Burgers

Combine the split peas, brown rice, and plenty of water (about 5 cups) in a large saucepan over medium-high heat. Bring to a boil, cover, and decrease the heat to medium-low. Simmer for 40–55 minutes, or until the split peas are very tender. Add more water to keep the peas submerged while cooking, if needed. Use a sieve or fine-mesh colander to strain off the excess water.

Meanwhile, heat the olive oil in a large sauté pan over medium-low heat. Add the onion, scallions, cumin, coriander, and turmeric (if using), and cook for 8 minutes or until the onions are soft and light golden brown. Remove from the heat.

In a small mixing bowl, whisk together the flaxseed meal and filtered water. Set aside for 5–10 minutes to thicken.

Transfer the cooked split pea mixture to a large mixing bowl and use the back of a fork to roughly mash about half of the peas. Then, add the cooked onion mixture, flaxseed mixture, oat flour, apple cider vinegar, sea salt, and black pepper to taste. Stir well to combine. The mixture should be very moist.

Preheat the oven to 375°F. Line a large baking tray with parchment paper and grease a 1/2-cup measuring cup with olive oil.

Use the measuring cup to scoop out a 1/2 cup of the mixture. Form into a patty that is 1 inch thick and approximately 3 inches in diameter, and transfer to the lined baking tray. (The dough will be sticky and difficult to work with, so take your time.) Repeat with the remaining mixture. You should have 6 patties.

Bake for 12 minutes, use a metal spatula to gently flip each patty, and bake for another 10–14 minutes, or until both sides are light golden in color. Be careful not to overbake. Remove from the oven and let cool slightly.

(continued on next page)

To Assemble

Prepare the Tzatziki Sauce.

Stuff each bun with a yellow split pea patty. Top with the tomato and cucumber slices, and generously drizzle with the tzatziki sauce. Serve immediately.

Refrigerate leftovers in separate containers for up to 3 days.

No Nuts? No Problem | *To keep this dish nut-free, use shelled hemp seeds to make the* Tzatziki Sauce.

No Gluten? No Problem | *To keep this dish gluten-free, use your favorite gluten-free buns.*

GARLIC-MUSHROOM TACOS WITH
QUICK PICKLED JALAPEÑOS + CHIPOTLE-TOMATO CREMA

Makes 8 tacos | 30 minutes or less

The key to rich, flavorful mushrooms with a meaty bite is dry sautéing them before adding any liquid or seasonings. This might seem like it opposes cooking logic, but lend me a minute or two of your complete and utter trust. Mushrooms contain a hefty amount of water that is ultimately released during cooking, and when they're given the opportunity to cook solely in their own liquid, their flavor intensifies rather than becoming muted by other liquids, oils, etc. Once they're cooked, you'll add just the tiniest bit of olive oil, a generous sprinkle of minced garlic, and some sea salt. Peace out, soggy mushroom tacos.

Those flavorful mushrooms get tucked into warm corn tortillas with diced onion and cilantro before being drizzled with a slightly smoky, subtly spicy tomato crema. The final touch is a garnish of quick pickled jalapeños.

QUICK PICKLED JALAPEÑOS

1 cup apple cider vinegar

1/2 teaspoon sea salt

3 medium jalapeños, trimmed, halved lengthwise, seeded, and thinly sliced

GARLIC-MUSHROOM FILLING

20 ounces cremini or button mushrooms, brushed or wiped clean and halved or quartered depending on size

1/2 tablespoon cold-pressed olive oil

3 cloves garlic, minced

1/2 teaspoon sea salt or to taste

CHIPOTLE-TOMATO CREMA

1/2 cup raw cashews or shelled hemp seeds*

1/2 cup filtered water

1/4 cup canned fire-roasted crushed tomatoes

1 tablespoon finely diced chipotle pepper in adobo sauce or more to taste

1 clove garlic, peeled

For the Quick Pickled Jalapeños

In a large airtight jar, vigorously whisk together the vinegar and sea salt until the salt dissolves.

Add the jalapeños, secure the lid, and give it a few shakes. Refrigerate until ready to serve.

For the Garlic-Mushroom Filling

Heat a large pan over high heat.

Once the pan is hot, add the mushrooms, decrease the heat to medium-high, and cook for 6 minutes, or until there is just the tiniest amount of mushroom liquid remaining and they have a deep, golden-brown glisten to them, nudging them around the pan as needed to prevent burning. It will initially seem like the mushrooms might burn, but this is about the point when they will release their liquid.

Decrease the heat to medium-low and add the olive oil, garlic, and sea salt. Cook for another 2 minutes, or until the garlic scent mellows, stirring frequently.

For the Chipotle-Tomato Crema

Add the cashews and filtered water to a high-speed blender and blend on high for 2 minutes, or until completely smooth, stopping to scrape down the sides as needed. Then, add the fire-roasted tomatoes, chipotle pepper, garlic, apple cider vinegar, and sea salt, and blend for another 1–2 minutes, or until smooth.

(continued on next page)

1/2 tablespoon apple cider vinegar

3/4 teaspoon sea salt or to taste

TACOS

8 small corn tortillas, warmed

1 small yellow onion, finely diced

Fresh cilantro, stemmed (optional)

2 small limes, quartered

To Assemble

Scoop a bit of the mushroom filling into each tortilla and drizzle with the crema. Top with the pickled jalapeños, diced yellow onion, and cilantro (if using). Serve warm, garnished with the lime wedges (to spritz).

Refrigerate leftovers in separate airtight containers for up to 3 days.

Be Kind to Your Blender | *If you're not using a high-speed blender (e.g., Vitamix or Blendtec), soak the cashews in water for 2 hours or boil them for 10 minutes to soften before blending.*

No Nuts? No Problem | *To keep this dish nut-free, use shelled hemp seeds to make the crema.*

BBQ PULLED JACKFRUIT WITH CASHEW CHEDDAR CHEESE + SEEDED RANCH DRESSING

Makes 4 sandwiches | 1 hour or less

This is a dolled-up version of a recipe for BBQ pulled jackfruit sandwiches that I shared on the Blissful Basil blog back in July 2013. Although most of the extra fixings are optional, I recommend going big with this sandwich, because gooey cheddar cheese and creamy ranch dressing that taste like a dream *and* pack a punch of micronutrients are too good to pass up. So, slather on the toppings, drench your jackfruit in BBQ sauce, and grab one of those adorable red-and-white checked napkins. It's time to eat.

BBQ PULLED JACKFRUIT

1 (20-ounce) can young green jackfruit in water or brine*

1 tablespoon coconut sugar

1 tablespoon chili powder

1/2 teaspoon garlic powder

1/8 teaspoon cayenne pepper (optional)

1/2 cup 10-Minute Sweet + Tangy BBQ Sauce (page 300) or barbecue sauce of choice*

1/4 cup filtered water

SEEDED RANCH DRESSING

1/4 cup shelled hemp seeds or raw pepitas

1/4 cup filtered water

1 scallion, trimmed and cut in half

1 clove garlic, peeled

1–2 teaspoons apple cider vinegar

1/4 teaspoon onion powder

1/4 teaspoon sea salt or to taste

Freshly ground black pepper

SANDWICHES

1 recipe Cashew // Hemp Seed Cheddar Cheese (page 305)*

For the BBQ Pulled Jackfruit

In a colander, drain and rinse the jackfruit. Trim away the tough triangular tip from each piece of jackfruit, reserving only the soft, stringy flesh. If you spot any round, bulblike seeds, you can either leave them (they're edible) or remove and discard them.

In a medium mixing bowl, whisk together the coconut sugar, chili powder, garlic powder, and cayenne pepper (if using). Add the jackfruit pieces and toss to coat.

Heat a large sauté pan over medium heat. Once the pan is hot, add the seasoned jackfruit and sauté for 2–3 minutes, stirring occasionally.

Whisk together the barbecue sauce and water. Pour it over the jackfruit, decrease the heat to low, cover, and simmer for 15–20 minutes, or until the jackfruit is tender, stirring occasionally.

Uncover the pan and use two forks to thoroughly shred the jackfruit. Continue to simmer, uncovered, for another 5 minutes, or until the barbecue sauce is absorbed, stirring frequently.

For the Seeded Ranch Dressing

Prepare the seeded ranch dressing while the jackfruit is cooking.

In a high-speed bender, combine all the dressing ingredients and blend on high for 2 minutes, or until smooth, adding more water, 1 tablespoon at a time, if needed to thin. Refrigerate until ready to assemble.

To Assemble

Prepare the Cashew // Hemp Seed Cheddar Cheese

(continued on next page)

4 Puffy Spelt + Potato Buns (page 293) or other sandwich buns, sliced*

1/2 small red onion, thinly sliced

1/4 cup loosely packed fresh cilantro, stemmed

Divide the BBQ jackfruit among the rolls, spoon on the cheddar, and drizzle with the dressing. Top with the sliced red onions and cilantro. Serve immediately.

Can't Find Jackfruit? | *Use 2 (14-ounce) cans hearts of palm instead and skip the trimming step.*

Give Your BBQ Sauce a Once-Over | *If you're avoiding refined sugars, scan the ingredients as you're selecting your barbecue sauce and adjust accordingly—many brands contain processed sugars. Or save yourself the hassle of label scanning and make my* 10-Minute Sweet + Tangy BBQ Sauce.

No Soy? No Problem | *To keep this dish soy-free, make the* 10-Minute Sweet + Tangy BBQ Sauce *and use coconut aminos instead of reduced-sodium tamari.*

No Nuts? No Problem | *To keep this nut-free, opt for the* Hemp Seed Cheddar Cheese.

No Gluten? No Problem | *To keep this dish gluten-free, use your favorite gluten-free buns.*

PASTA + NOODLES

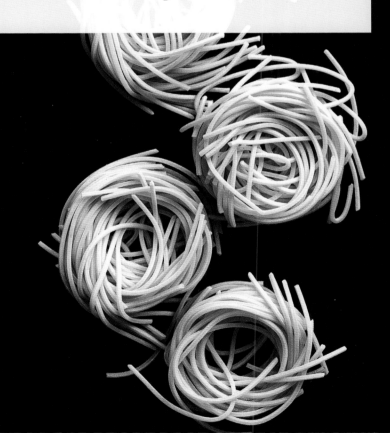

Kale, Artichoke + Leek Mac 'n' Cheese with Herbed Oat Crumbs 205

Roasted Mushroom, Cilantro + Walnut Pesto Pasta 208

Triple Noodle Power Pad Thai 211

Burst Heirloom Tomato + SuperSeed Pesto Pasta 212

Cashew e Pepe 215

Velvety Mac 'n' Yellow Split Pea Cheese 216

Baked Mostaccioli with Walnut Bolognese + Cashew Mozzarella 219

I have a theory that my brain holds on to memories of eating pasta more strongly than memories of pasta-less meals. Psychologically speaking, emotionally charged, positive experiences create "stickier" memories than those eliciting indifference, so perhaps it's my undying love for pasta that's allowed these memories to prevail. Whatever the reason, a quick mention of pasta is enough to bring a timeline of fond memories to mind . . .

I remember a childhood mac-'n'-cheese food fight with my brother Brad in which I victoriously hurled a Velveeta-coated shell at him with such precision that it clung to his eyelid for a solid two seconds. Other than his pride, he was completely unscathed, and we both laughed so hard we cried. Other memories that leap to mind are a family dinner digging into my mom's fettuccine Alfredo, and consuming heaps of chilled deli pasta while boating with my dad and stepmom the summer before eighth grade. Oh yes, and a romantic evening in Rome when Dan and I enjoyed the most magical "raviolo" at a tiny, family-run trattoria.

Given my pasta theory, it will probably come as no surprise that I've grown attached to each and every dish in this chapter, but I'm especially fond of the Roasted Mushroom, Cilantro + Walnut Pesto Pasta (page 208) and the Cashew e Pepe (page 215). And for the love of all things pasta, you simply cannot miss the Baked Mostaccioli with Walnut Bolognese + Cashew Mozzarella on page 219. I hope these recipes lay the foundation for your own pasta memories to take hold.

KALE, ARTICHOKE + LEEK MAC 'N' CHEESE WITH HERBED OAT CRUMBS

Serves 4–6 | 1 hour or less

If you're looking to sneak some veggies and other goodness into your mac 'n' cheese, look no further. This mac 'n' cheese might be dressed in more mature adult clothes, but it's just as satisfying and cheesy as the childhood favorite. Sautéed kale, artichokes, garlic, and leeks are woven throughout warm elbow pasta before being coated in a rich, gooey white cheddar sauce. To take this already comforting dish to a dream-worthy level of delectability, finish it with a flavorful field of toasted herbed oat crumbs.

HERBED OAT CRUMBS (OPTIONAL BUT RECOMMENDED)

1/2 cup old-fashioned rolled oats

1/2 teaspoon sea salt

1/4 teaspoon dried basil

1/4 teaspoon dried parsley

1/4 teaspoon dried thyme

1/4 teaspoon garlic powder

1/4 teaspoon crushed red pepper flakes (optional)

Freshly ground black pepper

1 tablespoon cold-pressed olive oil

KALE, ARTICHOKE, AND LEEK MACARONI

12 ounces uncooked brown rice elbow macaroni or rigatoni

2 tablespoons cold-pressed olive oil

4 cloves garlic, minced

2 leeks, thoroughly washed, trimmed, halved lengthwise, and thinly sliced*

1 small bunch curly kale, washed, stemmed, and thoroughly chopped (about 4 heaping cups)

1/4 teaspoon sea salt

1 (14-ounce) can artichoke hearts, drained and roughly chopped

For the Herbed Oat Crumbs (Optional but Recommended)

Start by making the herbed oat crumbs (if using).

In a food processor, combine the oats, sea salt, basil, parsley, thyme, garlic powder, red pepper flakes (if using), and black pepper to taste. Process for 30 seconds, or until you have coarse, panko-like crumbs.

Heat the olive oil in a large skillet over medium-low heat. Add the oat crumbs and pan-toast for 6–8 minutes, or until golden brown, stirring occasionally. Remove from the heat and set aside.

For the Kale, Artichoke, and Leek Macaroni

Bring a large pot of salted water to a boil. Add the pasta and cook until al dente according to package directions. Drain, reserving 1 cup of the pasta water, and return the cooked pasta to the pot.

Meanwhile, add the olive oil, garlic, and leeks to a large sauté pan over medium-low heat. Sauté for 4 minutes, or until the leeks are just beginning to soften, stirring frequently.

Stir in the kale and sea salt and cook for another 8 minutes, or until the kale is very tender and wilted but still has a vibrant green hue to it, stirring occasionally. Remove from the heat and stir in the artichokes.

For the White Cheddar Cheese Sauce

While the kale is cooking, add the soaked cashews, filtered water, nutritional yeast, arrowroot, apple cider vinegar, sea salt, and smoked paprika (if using) to a high-speed blender. Blend on high for 2–3 minutes, or until completely smooth.

(continued on next page)

WHITE CHEDDAR CHEESE SAUCE

2/3 cup raw cashews, soaked in boiling water for 10 minutes and drained (to soften)*

1 1/3 cups filtered water

1/4 cup nutritional yeast flakes

2 tablespoons arrowroot starch

2 tablespoons apple cider vinegar

1 teaspoon sea salt, plus more to taste

1/2–1 teaspoon smoked paprika (optional for smoky flavor)

Once the pasta and kale mixture are ready, transfer the cheese mixture to a medium saucepan. Whisk constantly over medium heat for 5 minutes, or until very thick and just shy of stretchy. Remove from the heat. Arrowroot loses its thickening power if overheated, so be attentive to it.

To Assemble

Add the sautéed kale mixture and the cheese sauce to the pot with the pasta and toss to thoroughly coat. If needed, add pasta water, a few tablespoons at a time, to thin the sauce. Season with more sea salt, if desired (I usually add another 1/4 teaspoon).

Spoon the macaroni into a large serving dish, and sprinkle the top with the herbed oat crumbs (if using). Scoop into bowls and serve warm.

Refrigerate leftovers, covered, for up to 4 days.

Can't Find Leeks? | *Leeks can be tricky to find when they're not in season, but the mac 'n' cheese making must go on, so feel free to substitute two large shallots in their place. Thinly slice the shallots into rounds and follow the cooking instructions just as you would for the leeks.*

No Nuts? No Problem | *To keep this dish nut-free, swap out the raw cashews for shelled hemp seeds and skip the soaking.*

Serves 4 | 30 minutes or less

This is my favorite pesto recipe of all time. There, I said it. I have this fear that it will be overlooked given that it's not the prettiest pesto ever to be seen. Although those brown and neutral hues literally pale in comparison to the bright, vibrant green of more traditional pesto, I promise you it's worth your time and ingredients. Need more convincing? It was a high-ranked favorite among recipe testers with feedback such as, "The pesto . . . my goodness, I could eat that on a cracker by itself!" And another noting, "This is so, so, so good!!"

Mushrooms and garlic are roasted before being pulsed to pesto perfection. Their rich, savory flavors are balanced by the brightness of lime juice and the freshness of cilantro. And those red pepper flakes? Well, they offer a small pop of heat to keep you on your toes; however, feel free to omit if you're sensitive to spice.

12 ounces uncooked brown rice rigatoni, fettuccini, or lasagna noodles

1 pound baby bella or cremini mushrooms, stemmed and quartered

6 cloves garlic, smashed and peeled

4 tablespoons cold-pressed olive oil, divided

1/2 cup raw walnut pieces

1/2 cup fresh cilantro, stemmed, plus more for garnishing

2 tablespoons fresh lime juice, plus more to taste

3/4 teaspoon fine-grain sea salt, plus more to taste

1/2 teaspoon crushed red pepper flakes, plus more to taste

Preheat the oven to 400°F. Line both a large baking pan and a small baking pan with parchment paper.

Bring a large pot of salted water to a boil. Add the pasta and cook until al dente according to package directions. Drain, reserving 1 cup of the pasta water, and return the cooked pasta to the pot.

Meanwhile, spread the mushrooms and garlic on the large lined pan, drizzle with 1 tablespoon of the olive oil, toss to coat, and roast for 15–18 minutes, or until tender, golden brown, and slightly wrinkled. Reserve approximately 1/2 cup of the roasted mushrooms for garnishing the pasta (the rest will be used to make the pesto).

Spread the walnuts on the small lined pan and toast in the oven for 5–6 minutes, or until fragrant.

In a food processor, combine the roasted mushrooms and garlic, remaining 3 tablespoons olive oil, toasted walnuts, cilantro, lime juice, sea salt, and red pepper flakes. Pulse 45–50 times, or until the mushrooms are finely minced and the texture resembles a coarse pesto.

Spoon the pesto over the pasta and toss to coat, adding the pasta water a few tablespoons at a time as needed to thin the sauce.

Divide the pasta among bowls. Top with the reserved roasted mushrooms. Spritz with more fresh lime juice and garnish with more cilantro, red pepper flakes, and sea salt, if desired.

Refrigerate leftovers in an airtight container for up to 3 days.

Get Vibrant | *Walnuts are packed with vitamin E—hellooo, shiny hair and glowing skin—anti-inflammatory tannins, and omega-3s.*

TRIPLE NOODLE POWER PAD THAI

Serves 2 | 30 minutes or less

Oodles of raw zucchini, jicama, and carrot noodles are tossed in a nutty, tangy, and slightly sweet tahini-lime dressing and topped with a rainbow of vegetables and a trio of seeds. This is a simple, light, and refreshing meal that teeters between salad and noodle territory. If you want to increase the heartiness of this dish, substitute 6–8 ounces of rice noodles for the raw vegetable noodles. Simply cook the noodles until al dente, toss them in the dressing, and top with the vegetables and seeds.

RAW VEGETABLE NOODLES

2 medium zucchini, trimmed

1 medium jicama root, peeled, or 1 large seedless hothouse or "English" cucumber, trimmed and peeled

1 large carrot, trimmed and peeled

TAHINI-LIME DRESSING

1/4 cup runny tahini

2 tablespoons fresh lime juice

1 1/2 tablespoons reduced-sodium tamari*

1 tablespoon toasted sesame oil

1 tablespoon pure maple syrup

1 tablespoon apple cider vinegar

2 cloves garlic, minced

TOPPINGS

1 cup thinly sliced purple cabbage

1 small red bell pepper, cored, seeded, and julienned

4 scallions, trimmed and sliced into matchsticks

1/4 cup fresh cilantro, stemmed and chopped

2 tablespoons raw shelled sunflower seeds

1 tablespoon shelled hemp seeds

1 tablespoon sesame seeds

1 small lime, cut into wedges

For the Raw Vegetable Noodles

Use a spiralizer to spiralize the vegetables into noodles. Alternatively, use a vegetable peeler to shave the vegetables into long, ribbonlike strips.

For the Tahini-Lime Dressing

In a small mixing bowl, vigorously whisk together the tahini, lime juice, tamari, sesame oil, maple syrup, apple cider vinegar, and garlic until emulsified.

To Assemble

Divide the noodles between 2 bowls. Drizzle with as much of the dressing as desired, and top with the purple cabbage, red pepper, scallions, cilantro, and a generous sprinkling of the seeds (sunflower, hemp, and sesame). Garnish with the lime wedges.

No Soy? No Problem | *To keep this dish soy-free, swap out the reduced-sodium tamari for coconut aminos.*

Serves 4 | 30 minutes or less

There's an honesty to Italian food that I've always admired. A dish is brought to life by heart rather than experience, making the finished product a sort of barometer for the soul. Ingredients are treated with care and respect, and the focus is on highlighting the beauty of each, allowing it to shine individually while also becoming an integral part of something much bigger than itself. Simple yet complex, comforting yet vibrant, and modest yet elevated—Italian fare embodies these charming dichotomies that make it altogether irresistible.

  This pasta is a perfect example of those tiny contradictions; it's simple to make yet the flavors are complex; it comforts like a cozy winter stew yet brims with vibrant, garden-fresh hues; and it's humble yet somehow incredibly special. I hope this dish finds as special a place in your heart as it has in mine.

SUPERSEED PESTO PASTA

12 ounces uncooked brown rice rigatoni, penne, or fusilli

1 recipe SuperSeed Pesto (page 297)

BURST HEIRLOOM TOMATOES

2 tablespoons cold-pressed olive oil

3 cloves garlic, smashed, peeled, and roughly chopped

1 teaspoon dried oregano

1 teaspoon dried basil

1/2 teaspoon dried parsley

1/4 teaspoon crushed red pepper flakes (optional)

4 heaping cups heirloom or standard cherry tomatoes

Pinch of sea salt, plus more to taste

Handful fresh basil, thinly sliced

For the SuperSeed Pesto Pasta

Bring a large pot of salted water to a boil. Add the pasta and cook until al dente according to package directions. Drain, reserving 1 cup of the pasta water, and return the cooked pasta to the pot.

Meanwhile, make the SuperSeed Pesto and refrigerate until ready to assemble.

For the Burst Heirloom Tomatoes

Heat the olive oil in a large sauté pan over medium-low heat until it begins to thin out and coat the pan. Add the garlic, oregano, basil, parsley, and red pepper flakes (if using) and briefly cook until fragrant, approximately 1 minute.

Add the cherry tomatoes and a pinch of sea salt, and increase the heat to medium-high. Use a large wooden spoon to occasionally nudge the tomatoes and garlic around the pan to prevent burning, and watch out for the hot oil and juices as the tomatoes burst. Cook for 6–12 minutes, or until the tomatoes burst open, begin to wrinkle, and develop a light golden hue at their edges. Remove from the heat and stir in the fresh basil.

To Assemble

Spoon the pesto over the pasta and toss to coat, adding the pasta water a few tablespoons at a time as needed to thin the sauce. Taste and season with more sea salt, if desired.

Divide the pasta among bowls and top with the burst tomatoes. Refrigerate leftovers in separate airtight containers for up to 3 days.

Remix It | *The pesto and burst tomatoes also make a vibrant, flavorful crostini topping. Simply slather crusty pieces of toasted baguette with the pesto and top with the burst cherry tomatoes. Perfection.*

CASHEW E PEPE

Serves 4–6 | 1 hour +

Traditionally referred to as Cacio e Pepe (or Cheese and Pepper), this plant-based version swaps the *cacio* for cashews. But the *pepe*? She's all there. Before going vegan, I enjoyed traditional Cacio e Pepe on three occasions: once in New York City, once at home, and once in Rome. Each experience left a lasting impression on my taste buds, and the memories tugged at my apron tails every time I contemplated going the purely plant-based route. I'm happy to say that this cashew version is just as memorable as the others, and it's one of my favorite recipes in this book. It's a plant-powerful victory. Peppery Italian pasta for all!

PASTA

1 pound uncooked gluten-free or regular spaghetti, tonnarelli, perciatelli, or bucatini pasta*

GRATED CASHEW CHEESE

1/4 cup raw cashews

2 tablespoons nutritional yeast flakes

1/2 teaspoon sea salt

CASHEW CREAM

1/2 cup filtered water

1/3 cup raw cashews, soaked in water for 2 hours, drained

1/4 teaspoon sea salt

PEPE

1 teaspoon freshly ground black pepper, plus more for garnishing

For the Pasta

Bring a large pot of salted water to a boil. Add the pasta and cook until it's just shy of al dente. (You'll finish cooking it in the pan, so you want it to have a bite to it at this point.) Drain, reserving 2 cups of the pasta water.

For the Grated Cashew Cheese

Meanwhile, add the raw cashews, nutritional yeast, and sea salt to a food processor, and process for 1 minute, or until the mixture resembles finely grated cheese.

For the Cashew Cream

Add the filtered water, soaked raw cashews, and sea salt to a high-speed blender and blend on high for 2 minutes, or until the mixture resembles heavy cream. Place within reach of the stove.

For the Pepe and To Assemble

Once the pasta has been cooked and drained, add the black pepper to a large sauté pan over medium heat. Dry toast for 1 minute, or until fragrant, swirling the pan around to prevent burning. Add the cashew cream and 1 cup of the reserved pasta water and whisk until smooth. Bring it to a simmer. Then, add the cooked pasta and toss to coat. Simmer for 2 minutes, or until the pasta is al dente and the sauce thickens slightly.

Remove from the heat and stir in the grated cashew cheese. You want the sauce to cling to the pasta without dripping off of it. If absolutely needed, add more pasta water, 1 tablespoon at a time, if the pasta seems too dry.

Divide the pasta among bowls. Season to taste with more freshly ground black pepper and sea salt, if desired. Serve immediately.

No Gluten? No Problem | *To keep this dish gluten-free, opt for a gluten-free pasta, such as brown rice pasta or corn pasta.*

Garlic Remix | *If you're a garlic lover, add 2–3 cloves minced garlic to the skillet along with the cashew cream for a garlicky rendition of this comforting pasta.*

Serves 4–6 | 1 hour +

There are about a million recipes for vegan mac 'n' cheese, but this one is different from all the others. Most recipes rely on anywhere from 1–4 cups of raw cashews for the base of the sauce; however, this one doesn't have a single cashew in sight, making the ingredients much less expensive. And unlike other cashew-free, plant-tastic cheese sauces, this one is made with yellow split peas, which add a rich texture, hearty flavor, and punch of protein. Thanks to the split peas and nutritional yeast, one batch of this velvety cheese sauce boasts an impressive 60 grams of plant-based protein. The next time someone asks you where vegans get their protein from, you'll have the most enticing answer ever: "mac 'n' cheese!"

1/2 cup uncooked yellow split peas, thoroughly rinsed

2 cups water

1 cup peeled and small-diced (1/3-inch cubes) Yukon gold or yellow potato (about 1 medium)

1/3 cup diced yellow onion

2 cloves garlic, smashed and peeled

1 pound uncooked brown rice elbow macaroni, shells, fusilli, or rigatoni

1/2 cup unsweetened almond milk*

1/2 cup nutritional yeast flakes

2 tablespoons fresh lemon juice

1 tablespoon reduced-sodium tamari*

1 teaspoon apple cider vinegar

1 teaspoon smoked paprika

3/4 teaspoon fine-grain sea salt, plus more to taste

Freshly ground black pepper

Combine the split peas and water in a large saucepan over high heat. Bring to a boil, cover, and decrease the heat to medium-low. Simmer for 40 minutes to 1 hour, or until the split peas are very tender and mushy. Strain off excess water. Note: Split peas vary greatly in their cooking time, but you want them to be nearly fall-apart tender so that they blend up velvety and smooth. If they're undercooked, your cheese sauce will have a subtle grit to it, and no one wants that.

While the split peas are cooking, steam the potato, onion, and garlic in a steamer or steamer basket for 20–30 minutes, or until fall-apart tender. (Avoid steaming in the microwave because it will dry out the potato.) Shake off excess water that accumulated while steaming.

Meanwhile, bring a large pot of generously salted water to a boil. Add the pasta and cook until al dente according to package directions. Drain and return the cooked pasta to the pot.

Add the cooked split peas and steamed potato mixture to a high-speed blender along with the almond milk, nutritional yeast, lemon juice, tamari, apple cider vinegar, paprika, and sea salt. Blend on low speed for 10 seconds to get everything moving, increase the speed to high, and continue to blend for 2–3 minutes, or until velvety and smooth.

Pour the cheese sauce over the pasta and toss to coat. It will initially seem like there is too much sauce, but the pasta will grab onto it as you stir.

Generously season with sea salt and freshly ground black pepper to taste. Serve warm. Refrigerate leftovers in an airtight container for up to 4 days.

No Nuts? No Problem | *To keep this dish nut-free, simply swap out the unsweetened almond milk for a nut-free plant-based milk, such as unsweetened soy milk or unsweetened rice milk.*

No Soy? No Problem | *To keep this dish soy-free, swap out the reduced-sodium tamari for coconut aminos.*

BAKED MOSTACCIOLI WITH WALNUT BOLOGNESE + CASHEW MOZZARELLA

Serves 8 | 1 hour +

This dish is hearty, comforting, and perfect for chilly weather. It's one of my all-time favorites and was highly praised by recipe testers, too. In fact, one tester's non-vegan Italian husband declared it his "favorite pasta ever." I did a little dance when I read that feedback! This pasta is best when enjoyed fresh from the oven, but you can absolutely refrigerate/freeze it (it'll just be a bit drier after reheating, as most baked pastas are). You can also prep it ahead of time and hold off on baking until just before serving.

WALNUT BOLOGNESE

2 cups raw walnut pieces*

3 ounces soft, no-salt-added dry-packed sun-dried tomatoes (about 1/3 cup)

3 cloves garlic, smashed and peeled

1 1/2 teaspoons sea salt or to taste

1 teaspoon onion powder

1 teaspoon dried oregano

1 teaspoon dried basil

1 teaspoon dried parsley

1 teaspoon smoked paprika

1/2 teaspoon crushed fennel seed

1/4 teaspoon crushed red pepper flakes or to taste

1/8 teaspoon freshly ground black pepper or to taste

2 tablespoons cold-pressed olive oil, plus more for greasing

2 (14.5-ounce) cans diced tomatoes

1 (15-ounce) can tomato sauce

1 (6-ounce) can tomato paste

3/4 cup filtered water

BAKED MOSTACCIOLI

1 cup raw cashews*

1 1/3 cups filtered water

For the Walnut Bolognese

To a food processor, add the walnuts, sun-dried tomatoes, garlic, sea salt, onion powder, oregano, basil, parsley, paprika, fennel seed, red pepper flakes, and black pepper. Pulse 30 times, or until finely chopped and crumbly.

Heat the olive oil in a large stockpot over medium-low heat. Add the walnut mixture and sauté for 5 minutes, or until the herbs are wafting a rich, toasted scent, stirring frequently.

Stir in the diced tomatoes, tomato sauce, tomato paste, and filtered water. Decrease the heat to low and simmer, partially covered, for 30 minutes, stirring occasionally. Taste and season with more sea salt, if needed to balance the tang of the sun-dried tomatoes.

For the Baked Mostaccioli

While the Bolognese is simmering, preheat the oven to 350°F, bring a large pot of salted water to a boil, and lightly grease a large, deep baking dish with olive oil.

While you wait for the water to boil, prepare the mozzarella sauce. Add the cashews, water, nutritional yeast, arrowroot, vinegar, and sea salt to a high-speed blender, and blend on high until completely smooth. Set aside.

Add the pasta to the pot of boiling water, and cook until al dente according to package directions. Drain and transfer the cooked pasta to the stockpot with the finished walnut Bolognese; stir to evenly coat. Transfer to the prepared baking dish and cover with foil.

Bake for 25 minutes, or until the bolognese is bubbling.

(continued on next page)

2 tablespoons nutritional yeast flakes

2 tablespoons arrowroot starch

2 tablespoons apple cider vinegar or white wine vinegar

1 teaspoon sea salt or to taste

1 pound uncooked brown rice mostaccioli, penne, or rigatoni

Chopped fresh parsley (optional)

1 recipe Nut // Seed Parmesan Cheese (page 299)*

Remove the foil from the baking dish, drizzle the mostaccioli with half of the mozzarella sauce, and gently stir a few times to cut the sauce into the pasta. Then, drizzle the remaining mozzarella sauce across the surface of the mostaccioli, return the dish to the oven, and bake, uncovered, for 10 minutes, or until the mozzarella sauce thickens slightly.

Remove from the oven and sprinkle with fresh parsley (if using) and as much of the Parmesan as desired. Serve warm.

Refrigerate leftovers for up to 4 days or freeze for up to 1 month.

No Nuts? No Problem | *To make this dish nut-free, use raw shelled sunflower seeds instead of walnuts, shelled hemp seeds instead of cashews, and opt for a seed-based Parmesan.*

Be Kind to Your Blender | *If you're not using a high-speed blender (e.g., Vitamix or Blendtec), soak the cashews in water for 2 hours or boil them for 10 minutes to soften before blending.*

VEGGIE-CENTRIC MAINS

Creamy Garlic-Mushroom Risotto 223

Baked Chiles Rellenos with Homemade Mozzarella + Salsa Roja 227

Cauliflower Chorizo Stuffed Cabbage Rolls with Cilantro-Lime Crema 229

Crispy Oat-Crusted Cauliflower Steaks with Homemade
Mozzarella + Marinara 233

Fresh Corn Polenta with Garlicky Mushroom Confit 235

Pulled Hearts of Palm Tamales with Chipotle Crema +
Pineapple Pico de Gallo 239

Easy Does It Sunday Evening Chili 243

Most of the salads, soups, sandwiches, pizzas, tacos, and pastas in this book are intended to hold their own as a satisfying meal. But in addition to those options, I wanted to create a chapter of veggie-centered main courses that are just as worthy of gracing your dinner table for a special occasion as they are for a casual weeknight meal. In the recipes that follow, vegetables become the cornerstone of typically meat- or cheese-reliant dishes without sacrificing an ounce of flavor, heartiness, or craveability. With a little love, a dash of playful creativity, and just enough seasoning, vegetables are brought to life and prove that plant-based eating is about the abundance of what is added rather than the scarcity of what is missing.

If you're cooking for comfort, you'll love the Crispy Oat-Crusted Cauliflower Steaks with Homemade Mozzarella + Marinara on page 233. For a small dinner party or date night in, you'd be remiss to skip over the Creamy Garlic-Mushroom Risotto on page 223. If you want to switch on your taste buds with a dynamic medley of flavors, flip directly to page 229 and get to work on the Cauliflower Chorizo Stuffed Cabbage Rolls with Cilantro-Lime Crema. Or perhaps it's Sunday and you're after a hassle-free meal to nosh on while burning through back-to-back episodes of your favorite Netflix series. In that case, go for the Easy Does It Sunday Evening Chili on page 243.

CREAMY GARLIC-MUSHROOM RISOTTO

Serves 2 as an entrée or 4 as a side dish | 1 hour or less

Oh, do I have a story for you. In 2006 I was back at home living with my mom, Celeste, and stepdad, Mike, during a gap between college and real life. Throughout the summer I had been cooking for my parents as a way to thank them for putting a roof over my head, and Mike—having roots in the restaurant industry—had taught me how to make a perfectly creamy risotto topped with sautéed mushrooms. He emphasized the basic rules of risotto: start with shallots and butter or olive oil; toast the Arborio rice until mostly translucent to soften the grain; and above all else, stir the risotto *constantly*. Given its luxurious texture, it's often assumed that risotto is packed with butter and cream, but it's actually the starches released while stirring that make it so wonderfully silky.

One evening as I added the first ladle of broth to the Arborio rice, I received the usual reminder from Mike as he headed outside: "From here on out, keep stirring." Less than a minute later, I heard screaming and Mike came running back through the kitchen in a panic. He was in a state of shock, rambling that my mom had tripped, cut her leg, and needed to go to the hospital. Just as I dropped the spoon into the risotto pan and turned to run to my mom's aid, his ramblings transformed into a very clear, concise demand: "Just stir the f--king risotto!!!" At that point, I figured either 1) he was crazier than I thought when it came to his risotto rules, or 2) this was his way of distracting me during a slightly traumatic event. With hindsight on my side, I'm confident it was a bit of both. Nearly four hours and 60 stitches later, my mom was okay. That night, we noshed on reheated risotto while giggling about Mike's infamous catchphrase. Moral of the story: stir that risotto no matter what.

This is a plant-based version of that tried-and-true classic I first learned how to make. Cashew cream is woven throughout the finished risotto, and mushrooms are dry sautéed before being seasoned with a bit of olive oil, garlic, and parsley.

GARLICKY MUSHROOMS

1 pound cremini or button mushrooms, brushed or wiped clean and thickly sliced

1/2 tablespoon cold-pressed olive oil

Small handful flat-leaf parsley, chopped

2 cloves garlic, minced

1/4 teaspoon sea salt or to taste

CASHEW CREAM (OPTIONAL BUT RECOMMENDED)

1/3 cup raw cashews*

1/3 cup filtered water

For the Garlicky Mushrooms

You'll want to make the mushrooms first, because it's impossible to successfully multitask once the risotto gets started.

Heat a large sauté pan over high heat. Once the pan is hot, add the mushrooms, decrease the heat to medium-high, and cook for 6 minutes, or until there is just the tiniest amount of mushroom liquid remaining and they have a deep, golden-brown glisten to them, nudging them around the pan as needed to prevent burning. It will initially seem like the mushrooms might burn but this is about the point when they will release their liquid.

Decrease the heat to medium-low and add the olive oil, parsley, garlic, and sea salt. Cook, stirring frequently, for another 2 minutes, or until the garlic scent mellows and the parsley wilts. Remove from the heat and set aside.

For the Cashew Cream (Optional but Recommended)

Add the cashews and filtered water to a high-speed blender, and blend on high until completely smooth and creamy. Place within reach of the stove.

(continued on next page)

RISOTTO

4 cups low-sodium vegetable broth

2 cups filtered water

1 1/2 tablespoons cold-pressed olive oil

2 medium shallots, minced (about 1/2 cup)

2 cloves garlic, minced

1 cup uncooked Arborio rice

1/2 cup room-temperature dry white wine

1/2 tablespoon fresh lemon juice

1–1 1/2 teaspoons sea salt or to taste

Freshly ground black pepper

For the Risotto

Heat the vegetable broth and water in a large stockpot over low heat until hot and simmering. It's important to keep the broth hot throughout the cooking process.

Add the olive oil, shallots, and garlic to another large sauté pan and cook over medium-low heat for 2–4 minutes, or until the shallots are just starting to soften, stirring occasionally.

Okay, from here on out, no straying from the stove. Grab your favorite wooden spoon and get comfortable.

Add the Arborio rice to the pan and toast, stirring constantly, for 4 minutes, or until the rice is pale golden and mostly translucent with just a small fleck of white in the center of the grain. Take your time with this step as it's important to break down the wall of the grain so that it can absorb liquid as it cooks.

Add the white wine and cook for 2 minutes, or until the liquid is almost absorbed, stirring constantly.

Increase the heat to medium, and use a ladle to add approximately 1/2 cup of the hot vegetable broth to the pan. Use figure-eight motions to stir the rice constantly as it absorbs the broth. When nearly all of the broth has been absorbed, add another 1/2 cup broth.

Repeat this process, adding broth, stirring constantly, and never leaving the pan, until the risotto is thick, creamy, and tender. You might not need to use all of the broth, so test for doneness. This typically takes 20–25 minutes.

Turn off the heat and stir in the cashew cream (if using), lemon juice, sea salt, and black pepper to taste.

Divide the risotto among bowls and top with the mushrooms.

Be Kind to Your Blender | *If you're not using a high-speed blender (e.g., Vitamix or Blendtec), soak the cashews in water for 2 hours or boil them for 10 minutes to soften before blending.*

No Nuts? No Problem | *To keep this dish nut-free, simply omit the Cashew Cream.*

BAKED CHILES RELLENOS WITH HOMEMADE MOZZARELLA + SALSA ROJA

Makes 4 chiles + 2 cups salsa | 1 hour +

Before I went vegan, chiles rellenos was a favorite of mine. Traditionally, the dish involves battering cheese-stuffed poblano peppers in an egg white mixture, frying them, and nestling them over a bed of warm salsa roja. However, for this purely plant-based version, the poblano peppers are charred over an open flame and peeled before being stuffed with a gooey cashew mozzarella and coated in an oat crust. They're baked until crisp and golden and served over a warm five-ingredient salsa. Personally, I think these improve on the original in both flavor and nutritional oomph.

I recommend purchasing the largest poblano peppers you can find—they're much easier to work with and will accommodate more of that tasty mozzarella. This is a fairly time-intensive recipe because of the charring and baking, but each step is in service of making the ultimate chiles rellenos. Thus, what you put forth in time will be repaid in flavor.

CHILES RELLENOS

4 large poblano chile peppers

1 cup old-fashioned rolled oats

3/4 teaspoon sea salt

1/2 teaspoon dried oregano

1/4 teaspoon crushed red pepper flakes

1–2 batches Cashew // Hemp Seed Mozzarella Cheese (page 305), as needed to stuff the peppers*

8 toothpicks

SALSA ROJA

8 ripe plum tomatoes (about 28 ounces), cored

1/2 medium yellow onion, peeled and quartered

4 cloves garlic, smashed and peeled

1/4 cup fresh cilantro, stemmed

1/2 teaspoon sea salt or to taste

For the Chiles Rellenos

Turn 4 gas burners on high and place a pepper directly onto each burner grate over the open flame.* Use heat-safe tongs to rotate the peppers every 3–4 minutes until blistered and blackened on all sides. Transfer to a medium bowl and tightly cover with foil to steam. Let stand for 10 minutes, or until softened.

Meanwhile, preheat the oven to 400°F. Line a small baking tray with parchment paper.

Add the oats, sea salt, oregano, and red pepper flakes to a food processor and process for 30 seconds, or until the oats resemble coarse bread crumbs. Transfer to a shallow baking dish.

Next, prepare the Cashew // Hemp Seed Mozzarella Cheese and set aside. Depending on the size of your poblano peppers, you'll need either 1 or 2 batches.

Once the peppers have softened, carefully peel away the charred skin from each. Do not rinse; it's okay if there are a few lingering flecks of blackened skin.

Place the peppers on a cutting board and use a paring knife to make a 1-inch slit, widthwise, just below the stem of each pepper, slicing through the top layer only and leaving the stem intact. Then, beginning at the center of the slit, slice lengthwise down each pepper, cutting through the top layer only. Gently open the flaps of each pepper like you're opening a tiny book. Scrape out and discard the seeds and membranes.

(continued on next page)

Stuff each pepper with the mozzarella, being careful not to overfill (if the mozzarella has thickened too much to easily scoop, vigorously whisk in 1 tablespoon filtered water to thin). Fold in the flaps and weave 2 toothpicks vertically down the seam of each pepper to secure.

One at a time, place the peppers in the oat crumbs and use your hands to sprinkle the oats on the top and sides to coat. If needed, lightly brush the peppers with water to help the oats stick. Transfer to the lined baking tray, seam-side up.

Bake for 20 minutes, carefully flip the peppers seam-side down, and bake for another 15–20 minutes, or until the oat crumbs take on just the slightest golden hue and feel crisp to the touch.

For the Salsa Roja

Make the salsa roja while the chiles are baking. Add all the salsa ingredients to a blender and purée.

Transfer to a large saucepan and bring to a boil over medium-high heat. Decrease the heat to low and simmer, uncovered, for 10–15 minutes, or until reduced and thickened into a sauce, stirring occasionally.

To Assemble

Spoon a generous amount of salsa over each plate. Carefully remove the toothpicks from the chiles, and place the peppers, seam-side down, on top of the salsa. Serve immediately.

No Nuts? No Problem | *To keep this nut-free, opt for* Hemp Seed Mozzarella Cheese.

Afraid of Working over an Open Flame? Use your Broiler! | *Instead of charring the peppers over your stove, place the peppers on a small baking tray and char them under a broiler, rotating every few minutes.*

Repurpose It | *The* Salsa Roja *can be used as a classic salsa with other snacks. Simply chill it and serve with tortilla chips.*

CAULIFLOWER CHORIZO STUFFED CABBAGE ROLLS WITH CILANTRO-LIME CREMA

Serves 4 (2 rolls per serving) | 1 hour +

If you think Shiitake Bacon (page 298) is crazy, you're really going to think cauliflower chorizo is crazy. The idea to use grated cauliflower and sun-dried tomatoes as the foundation for a plant-based chorizo popped into my head midway through my afternoon yoga routine. I figured it was unlikely to actually work, but I gave it a shot anyway (I love a good cooking challenge). The finished product was surprisingly chorizo-like, so I shared the recipe in a blog post for breakfast tacos, and it quickly became a reader favorite.

Unlike in most meat-free chorizo, there isn't a processed ingredient or tofu crumble to be found in this recipe. Just two veggies and lots of spices—ten, to be exact. That spice-laden "chorizo" is rolled up in blanched cabbage leaves along with a mixture of peppers and onions. The rolls are finished with a generous drizzle of Cilantro-Lime Crema (page 302) that brightens and melds the flavors in the most wonderful way.

CAULIFLOWER CHORIZO STUFFED CABBAGE ROLLS

8 large savoy cabbage leaves

1 extra-large or 2 small heads cauliflower, cored and cut into florets (8–10 cups)

3/4 cup oil-packed sun-dried tomatoes (about one 8.5-ounce jar), oil drained

1 1/2 tablespoons smoked paprika

2 1/4 teaspoons garlic powder

1 1/2 teaspoons ground coriander

1 1/2 teaspoons dried oregano

1 1/4 teaspoons sea salt or to taste, plus more for seasoning as needed

3/4 teaspoon ground cumin

3/4 teaspoon ground turmeric

3/4 teaspoon dried thyme

1/4 teaspoon cayenne pepper

1/4 teaspoon ground cinnamon

2 1/2 tablespoons cold-pressed olive oil, divided

For the Cauliflower Chorizo Stuffed Cabbage Rolls

Bring a large pot of salted water to a boil. Lay a clean kitchen towel on a flat work surface.

Shave or cut away the tough, knobby portion of the stem from the back of each cabbage leaf. Then, add 2–3 cabbage leaves to the boiling water, cook for 1–2 minutes or until softened and pliable, and transfer to the kitchen towel to dry. Repeat with the remaining cabbage leaves.

Add the cauliflower florets to the bowl of a food processor fitted with the S-blade and pulse until finely grated. If necessary, grate in batches, returning all the grated cauliflower to the food processor before the next step.

Pack the drained sun-dried tomatoes into a measuring cup and press to strain off any lingering oil. Add them to the food processor with the grated cauliflower, and pulse until the tomatoes are finely chopped and the cauliflower takes on a light orange hue, stopping to scrape down the sides as needed.

In a large mixing bowl, whisk together the paprika, garlic powder, coriander, oregano, sea salt, cumin, turmeric, thyme, cayenne pepper, and cinnamon. Add the grated cauliflower mixture, and use your hands to massage the spices into the cauliflower mixture.

Heat 1 1/2 tablespoons of the olive oil in a large sauté pan over medium heat.

(continued on next page)

2 poblano peppers, seeded and sliced into 1/3-inch-thick strips

1 medium yellow onion, sliced into 1/3-inch-thick rounds

TOPPINGS

1 recipe Cilantro-Lime Crema (page 302)*

Fresh cilantro, stemmed

Chopped purple cabbage, for a pop of color (optional)

1 lime, cut into wedges

Add the cauliflower mixture to the pan and cook for 30–40 minutes, stirring occasionally during the first 20–25 minutes and frequently during the last 10–15 minutes. If needed, decrease the heat to medium-low to prevent burning. The "chorizo" is ready once the mixture is crumbly and browned but still moist.

While the "chorizo" is cooking, heat the remaining 1 tablespoon olive oil in another large sauté pan over medium heat. Add the peppers, onion, and a pinch of sea salt, and sauté for 18–20 minutes, or until softened and just beginning to turn golden brown at the edges, stirring occasionally.

For the Toppings and To Assemble

Prepare the Cilantro-Lime Crema

Stuff each cabbage leaf with about 1/3 cup of the chorizo mixture and 1/4 cup of the pepper and onion mixture. Fold in the sides and roll away from your body to create a burrito-like wrap. Repeat with the remaining cabbage leaves. You should have 8 rolls.

Divide the cabbage rolls among plates. Drizzle with the Cilantro-Lime Crema, and garnish with the cilantro, purple cabbage (if using), and lime wedges.

Refrigerate leftovers in separate airtight containers for up to 3 days.

No Nuts? No Problem | *To keep this nut-free, use shelled hemp seeds to make the* Cilantro-Lime Crema.

CRISPY OAT-CRUSTED CAULIFLOWER STEAKS WITH HOMEMADE MOZZARELLA + MARINARA

Serves 4 | 1 hour +

This baked, vegan, and gluten-free take on chicken (or eggplant) Parmesan is a comforting crowd-pleaser. It hits the spot just like its battered, breaded, and fried predecessors minus the unwanted I-need-a-nap lethargy that typically follows. Cauliflower steaks are battered and coated in an oat and herb crust before being baked until crisp, slathered with gooey mozzarella, and embraced by a warm bed of marinara. Forget the fryer, let the chickens roam freely, and arm your crisper drawers with cauliflower; this vegetable-remixed classic is about to take your taste buds by storm.

2 large heads cauliflower, outer leaves removed

1 1/2 cups old-fashioned rolled oats

1 1/2 teaspoons dried basil

1 1/2 teaspoons dried oregano

1–1 1/2 teaspoons fine-grain sea salt

3/4 teaspoon garlic powder

3/4 teaspoon onion powder

1/4 teaspoon crushed red pepper flakes or to taste

1 cup unsweetened almond milk*

3/4 cup brown rice flour

1 1/2 tablespoons fresh lemon juice

1 recipe Cashew // Hemp Seed Mozzarella Cheese (page 305)*

3 cups jarred marinara sauce, warmed*

Fresh basil, thinly sliced

Preheat the oven to 400°F. Line a large baking sheet with parchment paper.

One at a time, carefully stand each head of cauliflower on its stem and use a sharp knife to cut it in half down the center. Then, cut as many 3/4-inch-thick cauliflower steaks from the center of each half as you can. You'll want at least 2 from each head of cauliflower for a total of 4, but preferably more, if possible.

Add the rolled oats to a food processor and process for 30 seconds, or until a coarse meal forms. You want a texture similar to panko bread crumbs. Transfer to a large, shallow bowl, and whisk in the basil, oregano, sea salt, garlic powder, onion powder, and red pepper flakes.

In another large, shallow bowl, whisk together the almond milk, brown rice flour, and lemon juice until smooth.

From left to right, line up the cauliflower steaks, almond milk batter, herbed oat crumbs, and baking sheet.

One at a time, dip the cauliflower steaks into the almond milk batter, toss to coat, shake off excess batter, and transfer to the oat and herb mixture. Carefully toss until evenly coated and transfer to the lined baking sheet. Repeat with the remaining cauliflower steaks.

Bake for 20 minutes, carefully flip each cauliflower steak, and bake for another 15–20 minutes, or until crisp and light golden.

Meanwhile, prepare the Cashew // Hemp Seed Mozzarella Cheese.

To Assemble

Once the cauliflower steaks have finished baking, remove the parchment paper from beneath them and heat the broiler on high.

(continued on next page)

Spoon a few tablespoons of the mozzarella onto each cauliflower steak, gently spreading it out over the surface, and broil for 2–4 minutes, or until the cheese is golden brown and bubbly.

Spoon a generous amount of marinara over each plate. Place the cauliflower steaks on top of the marinara and garnish with the fresh basil. Serve immediately.

No Nuts? No Problem | *To keep this nut-free, swap out the unsweetened almond milk for a nut-free plant-based milk, such as unsweetened soy milk or unsweetened rice milk, and opt for* Hemp Seed Mozzarella Cheese.

Give Your Marinara Sauce a Once-Over | *If you're avoiding refined sugars or oil, scan the ingredients as you're selecting your sauce and adjust accordingly.*

Leftover Cauliflower Florets? | *Reserve the extra florets from the sides of the cauliflower for another recipe, such as* The Classic *power bowl (page 153).*

Ultra-Hearty Remix | *To up the heartiness factor, serve the cauliflower over cooked brown-rice pasta that's been tossed with warm marinara.*

Serves 4 | 1 hour or less

This is easily one of the most decadent and luxurious dishes in this book, and it's perfect for a special occasion. The polenta is made with fresh corn rather than dried corn grits, and its perfect creaminess and sweet corn flavor will make you question why you'd ever go back to using the bagged stuff. It's also surprisingly simple to make—quickly process fresh sweet corn in a food processor and simmer with a drizzle of olive oil, water, and sea salt. That's it.

While the polenta simmers, you'll make the garlicky mushroom confit. This sounds a bit complicated and fussy, but I promise it's not much trouble at all. Confit is simply a method of cooking that involves poaching something in oil while maintaining a 170°F temperature. In this case, mushrooms are poached in olive oil along with garlic and herbs. The mushrooms are served using a slotted spoon to drain off the vast majority of the oil. However, if you're hesitant to use the confit method or don't have an instant-read cooking thermometer to ensure the consistent temperature needed, consult the note below the recipe for an alternative.

FRESH CORN POLENTA

8 ears sweet corn, shucked and silks removed

1 tablespoon cold-pressed olive oil

1 cup filtered water

1/2–3/4 teaspoon sea salt or to taste

GARLICKY MUSHROOM CONFIT

1 pound assorted mushrooms (shiitake, oyster, chanterelles, cremini, morels, etc.), brushed or wiped clean

1 cup mild-flavored cold-pressed olive oil, divided*

10 cloves garlic, peeled and halved

4 sprigs thyme

3 sprigs rosemary

Sea salt and freshly ground black pepper

FINISHING TOUCHES

1 lemon, halved (optional)

Several slices hearty gluten-free or seeded bread, toasted (optional)

For the Fresh Corn Polenta

Slice off the knobby handle on each ear of corn. One at a time, stand the ears up in a large shallow bowl. Use a knife to carefully slice vertically down the ear of corn to release the kernels and milky liquid. Repeat with all 8 ears of corn.

Transfer the kernels and milky liquid to a food processor, and process for 10–15 seconds, or until the texture resembles coarse grits. The kernels should be thoroughly chopped but not puréed.

Heat the olive oil in a large sauté pan over medium-low heat. Stir in the corn mixture, water, and sea salt.

Bring to a rapid simmer. Then, decrease the heat to low and cook, uncovered, for 15–20 minutes, or until thick and creamy, stirring every few minutes. Season with more sea salt, if desired.

For the Garlicky Mushroom Confit

Prepare the mushrooms. If the stems are tender (e.g., oyster), simply trim them; however, if they're woody and tough (e.g., shiitake), remove and discard them.

Add the mushrooms and 1/4 cup of the olive oil to a large saucepan over medium heat and cook, stirring occasionally for 5 minutes, or until the mushrooms are just beginning to soften.

(continued on next page)

Add the remaining 3/4 cup olive oil, garlic, thyme, and rosemary, and ensure that the mushrooms are mostly submerged. Insert an instant-read cooking thermometer into the oil.

Gently heat the oil to 170°F and continue poaching the mushrooms for 8 minutes, or until tender, adjusting the heat to maintain a temperature that is as close to 170°F as possible. It's okay if the temperature bobs up and down a bit, just be sure to keep it above 160°F and below 200°F.

Remove from the heat and transfer the mushrooms, oil, and herbs to a serving bowl. Generously season with sea salt and black pepper.

To Serve

Divide the polenta among bowls or plates, and use a slotted spoon to top with the mushrooms, leaving the garlic and herbs behind and straining off excess olive oil. Spritz with fresh lemon juice and season with a bit more sea salt and black pepper, if desired.

Serve warm with slices of toasted bread (if using).

Not Up to Confit? | *Substitute 2 cups low-sodium vegetable broth for the olive oil to poach the mushrooms. Start by cooking the mushrooms in 1/4 cup of the broth and then add the remaining 1 3/4 cups broth when you add the garlic and herbs. Just keep in mind that the texture of the mushrooms won't be quite as firm or meaty with this method.*

PULLED HEARTS OF PALM TAMALES WITH
CHIPOTLE CREMA + PINEAPPLE PICO DE GALLO

Makes 30 small tamales | 1 hour +

Tamales require a bit of prep and a hefty steam time, *but* you'll note this recipe is designed to make a big batch. That means by investing the effort now, you can enjoy tamales throughout the week. They freeze and quickly reheat as needed for speedy weeknight meals. But there is one crucial caveat: don't tackle this recipe at the last minute; set aside a calm moment and a solid hour for preparation to make the dough and wrap the tamales. Then, it's hands-off steaming for another 90 minutes. I know, 90 minutes is a *long* time, but please, please, please trust me when I say this recipe is worth it. I've had not one but *three* tamale connoisseurs declare these the best tamales they've ever eaten. And not one of them was vegan or vegetarian.

The filling, a spiced and pulled hearts of palm mixture, is stuffed into mounds of tender tamale dough. Once the tamales have endured that lengthy 90-minute steam, they're dressed up with chipotle crema and fresh pineapple salsa.

TAMALE DOUGH AND HUSKS

32 large dried corn husks*

4 1/2–5 1/2 cups low-sodium vegetable broth, as needed

4 cups masa harina (golden corn flour)

2 teaspoons aluminum-free baking powder

1 tablespoon sea salt or to taste

1 cup virgin coconut oil

PULLED HEARTS OF PALM FILLING

1 tablespoon virgin coconut oil or cold-pressed olive oil

1 medium yellow onion, diced (about 1 1/2 cups)

2 cloves garlic, minced

2 (14-ounce) cans hearts of palm, drained

1 (15-ounce) can tomato sauce

1/2 cup filtered water

1 1/2 tablespoons smoked paprika

1 tablespoon coconut sugar or pure maple syrup

For the Tamale Dough and Husks

Place the corn husks in a large baking dish and add enough boiling water to submerge them completely. If they begin to float, lay another baking dish or pan on top to keep them submerged. Soak for 30 minutes, or until soft and pliable. Once softened, remove 2 of the corn husks, tear each lengthwise into long, thin ribbons, and return to the soaking water (these will be used to tie the tamales).

Meanwhile, heat the vegetable broth in a medium saucepan over medium-low heat until it begins to simmer. Remove from the heat and set aside.

In a large mixing bowl, whisk together the masa, baking powder, and sea salt. Use a pastry cutter or fork to cut the coconut oil into the masa until you have small, pea-size crumbles.

Measure out 4 1/2 cups of the hot broth and slowly add it to the masa while stirring. Stir until just combined. If the dough appears dry, add more hot broth, 1/4 cup at a time, until the texture resembles thick, spongy polenta or damp sand. Let the dough rest for 30 minutes.

For the Pulled Hearts of Palm Filling

While the dough is resting, prepare the filling. Heat the oil in a large sauté pan over medium heat. Add the onion and cook for 6 minutes, or until soft and translucent; add the garlic and cook for another minute, stirring occasionally.

(continued on next page)

2 teaspoons chili powder

1/2–1 teaspoon sea salt or to taste

1/2 teaspoon ground cumin

1/4 teaspoon cayenne pepper, more or less to taste

CHIPOTLE CREMA

3/4 cup plus 2 tablespoons filtered water

3/4 cup raw cashews*

2 cloves garlic, peeled

2 tablespoons fresh lime juice

1 tablespoon smoked paprika

1/2–1 tablespoon minced chipotle pepper in adobo sauce

1/2 teaspoon sea salt or to taste

PINEAPPLE PICO DE GALLO

1 large pineapple, peeled, cored, and finely diced

1 small red onion, finely diced (about 1/2 cup)

1/3 cup fresh cilantro, stemmed and chopped

1–2 small jalapeños, seeded and minced

Juice of 1 lime or to taste

1/4 teaspoon sea salt or to taste

Stir in the hearts of palm, tomato sauce, water, smoked paprika, coconut sugar, chili powder, sea salt, cumin, and cayenne pepper. Cover and simmer, stirring occasionally for 10–15 minutes, or until the sauce is thick and bubbly and the hearts of palm are tender enough to shred.

Turn off the heat and use two forks to thoroughly shred the hearts of palm lengthwise into long strands. Then, turn the heat back on medium, cover, and cook for another 5 minutes, or until most of the liquid has been absorbed, stirring frequently. Remove from the heat and let cool slightly.

To Assemble the Tamales

Set up the steamer. Place a steaming basket within a large stockpot and fill the pot until the water rises just below the bottom of the basket.

Lay a corn husk on a clean work surface with the thin, tapering end pointing toward you. Scoop out a scant 1/4 cup of the tamale dough and spread it out into a 3 × 4-inch rectangle in the center of the husk, leaving at least a 2-inch border surrounding the dough. Spread a heaping tablespoon of the filling lengthwise down the center of the dough. Lift the two long sides of the husk and bring them together to touch so that both edges of dough pull inward and meet in the middle, forming a seam and sealing in the filling. Gently press or pinch the dough to secure the seam. Roll both sides of the corn husk in the same direction around the tamale. Then, fold the thin, pointy end of the husk upward and gently secure with a husk ribbon, forming a closed bottom. Leave the top of the husk open. Repeat with the remaining corn husks, tamale dough, and filling.

Once the tamales are formed, place them upright in the steamer so they're standing on their closed ends. Be careful not to pack them in too closely (depending on the size of your steamer, you may need to steam in batches).

Cover the pot and steam the tamales for 75–90 minutes, or until the corn husks easily peel away from the tamales, adding more boiling water to the bottom of the pot if needed to maintain a steady level of steam.

Turn off the heat and let the tamales stand in the steamer basket for 5–10 minutes to firm up before serving.

For the Chipotle Crema

Add all the crema ingredients to a high-speed blender. Blend on high for 2–4 minutes, or until completely smooth. Refrigerate until ready to serve.

For the Pineapple Pico de Gallo

In a large bowl, stir together all of the pico de gallo ingredients. Cover and refrigerate until ready to serve.

To Serve

Just before serving, remove and discard the husks. Drizzle each tamale with the crema and top with the pineapple salsa.

Refrigerate leftovers in separate airtight containers for up to 4 days or freeze for up to 1 month.

Can't Find Corn Husks? | *Use 8 × 8-inch parchment paper squares and kitchen twine instead.*

Be Kind to Your Blender | *If you're not using a high-speed blender (e.g., Vitamix or Blendtec), soak the cashews in water for 2 hours or boil them for 10 minutes to soften before blending.*

Plan, Prepare, Conquer | *The pineapple salsa and tamales freeze well, so go ahead and freeze your leftovers. Thaw the pineapple salsa in the refrigerator overnight. To reheat frozen tamales, wrap each—corn husk and all—in a damp paper towel and microwave until moist, tender, and warmed through to the filling. The crema will keep up to 3 days when refrigerated but doesn't freeze well, so you may need to prepare a fresh batch when you reheat the tamales.*

EASY DOES IT SUNDAY EVENING CHILI

Serves 6 | 1 hour +

This chili requires just 15 minutes of active prep time and then you can sit back, relax, and occasionally give it a stir. It's the perfect meal to have simmering in the background on a lazy Sunday afternoon while you binge-watch *House of Cards* (Frank Underwood, you scare me, but I just can't quit you).

This chili garners its meatiness from walnuts and sun-dried tomatoes that have been pulsed into a crumble and sautéed with onions, peppers, tomatoes, beans, and an array of spices. Balsamic vinegar and tamari deepen both the flavor and the color of the chili. The balsamic enhances the complexity of the chili's acidity and mingles with the tomatoes in the loveliest of ways, while the tamari adds an enticing umami quality. A lengthy simmer time melds the flavors together, and then it's time to serve. Spoon this chili into bowls, pile on the toppings, and serve with a hefty handful of tortilla chips for dipping!

CHILI

2 tablespoons cold-pressed olive oil or vegetable broth*

1 large yellow onion, diced

2 red bell peppers, cored, seeded, and diced

1 medium poblano pepper, cored, seeded, and diced

1 cup raw walnut pieces*

3 ounces no-salt-added, dry-packed sun-dried tomatoes

3 cloves garlic, minced

2 tablespoons chili powder

1 tablespoon smoked paprika

2 teaspoons ground cumin

1 teaspoon dried oregano

1 teaspoon sea salt or to taste

1/2 teaspoon ground coriander

2 (28-ounce) cans unsalted whole peeled tomatoes in juice

2 (15-ounce) cans kidney beans, drained and rinsed

1 (15-ounce) can black beans, drained and rinsed

1 cup filtered water

1–2 tablespoons balsamic vinegar

(*continued on next page*)

For the Chili

Heat the olive oil in a large stockpot over medium heat. Add the onion, red peppers, and poblano pepper, and sauté for 6 minutes, or until the peppers are just beginning to soften and the onions are generously flecked with golden-brown edges, stirring occasionally.

Meanwhile, add the walnuts and sun-dried tomatoes to a food processor and pulse 30 times, or until roughly minced and crumbly. Transfer to the stockpot along with the garlic, chili powder, smoked paprika, cumin, oregano, sea salt, and coriander. Decrease the heat to medium-low and sauté for 4 minutes, or until the spices are wafting a rich, toasted scent, stirring frequently.

Add the whole peeled tomatoes with juice and bring to a simmer, using a spoon to thoroughly crush them to the desired size as they heat. Add the kidney beans, black beans, and water, and continue to simmer for 5 minutes, stirring occasionally.

Then, stir in the balsamic vinegar, tamari, and maple syrup, and decrease the heat to medium-low. Partially cover, leaving the lid askew, and simmer for 30 minutes, stirring occasionally to prevent burning.

Cover completely and continue to simmer for at least another 45 minutes but preferably 1 hour or longer, stirring occasionally to prevent burning. Taste and season with more sea salt, if desired.

Ladle into bowls, layer on the toppings, and get cozy. Refrigerate leftovers up to 4 days or freeze for up to 1 month.

1 1/2 tablespoons reduced-sodium tamari*

1 tablespoon pure maple syrup or coconut sugar

RECOMMENDED TOPPINGS

Sliced avocado

Halved grape tomatoes

Thinly sliced scallions

Fresh cilantro, stemmed and chopped

Crushed tortilla chips

Cashew Sour Cream (page 303)*

No Oil? No Problem | *To keep this dish oil-free, opt for vegetable broth instead of olive oil.*

No Nuts? No Problem | *To keep this dish nut-free, use raw shelled sunflower seeds instead of walnuts and omit the* Cashew Sour Cream.

No Soy? No Problem | *To keep this dish soy-free, swap out the reduced-sodium tamari for coconut aminos.*

Leftovers? | *This chili is even better on the second day after the flavors have mingled overnight!*

SOPHISTICATED SWEETS + SIMPLE TREATS

Dessert loving is in my genes. Having sprung from a long line of dessert devotees, I have a mouth lined with sweet teeth, and my heart beats a bit faster in the presence of chocolate. Every member of my mom's family playfully claims to have a "second stomach" reserved for dessert. Sounds like an exaggeration, but if the Harty family is around, you'd best keep a watchful eye on your sweets. In the presence of a perfectly iced birthday cake, there will undoubtedly be at least one wandering finger that finds its way to the buttercream frosting and "accidentally" scrapes across the surface. It's a miracle if a cake can make it to candle time unscathed.

And while we're on the topic of desserts, I should mention that I'm not one to shame sugar or fat, and I hope you aren't either. Because if you're going to have dessert, it should be worth having. And by "worth having," I mean it should taste good. Like real good. So let's make a pact to boot the sugar-free sweeteners and fat-free syrups. If something sounds too good to be true, it probably tastes like crap or is packed with crap (or both—yikes). But with a few thoughtful swaps, we can have our delectable desserts and maybe even reap some nutritional benefits, too.

So without further ado, let's get to the grand finale: the sweet stuff. I'm particularly fond of (read: obsessed with) the Cosmically Fudgy Cacao-Tahini Brownies on page 251 as well as the Chocolate Chip Coconut Oil Cookie Bars on page 265. If you're looking for a dessert to impress a crowd, the Sweet Vanilla Chickpea Cake with Strawberry Compote + Coconut Whip (page 275) has been known to steal the hearts of many. The Seasonal Fruit Crisps on page 269 are a personal favorite of mine because they offer a fuss-free modern twist on a comforting classic. And if you're a peanut butter and chocolate fiend, the "An Ode to Ohio" Peanut Butter Cookie Dough + Caramel Buckeye Bars on page 283 are calling your name!

ENLIVENING LEMON BARS

Makes 16 bars | 1 hour +

These lemons bars taste just like traditional lemon bars, and they're made from unprocessed, whole-food ingredients. The shortbread crust is a combination of rolled oats, coconut flour, coconut oil, and maple syrup. It's buttery, rich, and the perfect complement to the tangy lemon filling. And speaking of the filling, the main ingredient is likely to surprise you. Traditionally, lemon bar filling calls for about half a dozen eggs, and vegan variations tend to rely on blended silken tofu as a substitute. However, this lemon filling is made with a base of . . . Yukon gold potatoes. Yes, potatoes! Or po-tah-toes, if that's your thing. They're steamed and blended with fresh lemon juice, coconut oil, pure maple syrup, vanilla, kala namak (for an eggy taste), a dash of turmeric, and arrowroot starch to create a thick, sink-your-teeth-in lemony filling.

CRUST

1 cup oat flour

1/4 cup coconut flour

1/8 teaspoon fine-grain sea salt

1/4 cup virgin coconut oil, melted

1/4 cup pure maple syrup

1 teaspoon pure vanilla extract

LEMON FILLING

1 cup peeled and small-cubed (1/3-inch cubes) Yukon gold potato (about 1 medium potato)

3/4 cup fresh lemon juice (about 4 large lemons)

2 tablespoons arrowroot starch, plus more for dusting

1/2 cup virgin coconut oil, melted

1/4 cup plus 1 tablespoon pure maple syrup

2 teaspoons pure vanilla extract

1/4 teaspoon kala namak (black salt) or fine-grain sea salt

1/8 teaspoon ground turmeric (optional, for color)

1–2 tablespoons fresh lemon zest (optional)

For the Crust

Preheat the oven to 350°F. Line an 8 × 8-inch metal baking pan with parchment paper. (Double-check your pan size—a 9 × 9-inch pan won't work for this recipe.)

In a large mixing bowl, whisk together the oat flour, coconut flour, and sea salt. Add the coconut oil, maple syrup, and vanilla, and stir well to combine. Let the dough rest for 5 minutes to thicken, stirring once or twice. You should have a soft, slightly spongy dough.

Scoop the dough into the lined pan, and use your fingers to press and spread it into an even layer. At first it will seem like there isn't enough, but just keep working it out toward the edges. You want a thin, evenly distributed layer. Use a fork to poke several holes over the surface to prevent bubbling.

Bake for 12–14 minutes, or until the edges are just barely turning golden and the crust feels softly set but not yet crisp. Let cool completely in the pan.

For the Lemon Filling

The potato needs to be measured precisely, so make sure you have exactly 1 cup of small-cubed potato, and steam it in a steamer or steamer basket for 20–25 minutes, or until fork-tender. (Avoid steaming in the microwave, because it will dry out the potato rather than infusing it with moisture.)

In a small mixing bowl, whisk together the lemon juice and arrowroot until the arrowroot dissolves. Set aside.

(continued on next page)

Add the steamed potato, lemon juice mixture, coconut oil, maple syrup, vanilla, kala namak, and turmeric (if using) to a high-speed blender or food processor. Blend for 2–3 minutes, or until completely smooth, stopping to scrape down the sides as needed. Add the lemon zest (if using) and pulse to incorporate.

Transfer to a large saucepan and whisk constantly over medium heat for 3–5 minutes, or until the filling thickens and becomes slightly translucent. Be careful not to overheat.

To Assemble

Pour the lemon filling over the crust. Loosely cover the pan and chill in the freezer for 3 hours. Then, transfer to the refrigerator and chill for another 3 hours, or until the filling has set well enough to slice. The filling will continue to firm up and thicken the longer the bars are refrigerated, so keep this in mind if you prefer a denser, thicker lemon filling.

Gently lift the bar out of the pan. If desired, sift a small amount of arrowroot starch over the surface to lightly dust. Slice into 16 small squares.

Return the bars to the parchment-lined pan and keep chilled. Leftovers will keep in the refrigerator for up to 1 week.

Makes 12 brownies | 1 hour or less

If these brownies could talk, I might be embarrassed by some of the things they would say. For instance, they might disclose just how many times I've made them. Pshh, it was for practical purposes, like ensuring the recipe was thoroughly tested. It's not like I'm obsessed with their dense, gooey interiors and fudge-glazed surface or anything. Or perhaps these brownies would recount, in blush-inducing detail, the kitchen dance I did after taking that first bite. (For the record, it's best described as an unpredictable mash-up of moves that starts out fresh and rapidly deteriorates into a stale throwback to the "robot" dance.) But truth be told, if these brownies *could* talk, I'd happily take the heat if it meant I could enjoy just one more bite of their chocolaty splendor.

Their fudgy, out-of-this-world texture is all thanks to tahini, and their intense chocolate flavor comes from antioxidant-rich cacao. They're sweetened with coconut sugar, an unrefined, raw sugar derived from the coconut palm tree. And the icing on these already dreamy treats? Fudgy chocolate glaze.

CACAO-TAHINI BROWNIES

1 cup coconut sugar

1/2 cup runny tahini

1 teaspoon pure vanilla extract

1 1/4 cups oat flour

1/4 cup raw cacao powder

1 1/2 teaspoons aluminum-free baking powder

1/4 teaspoon fine-grain sea salt

1/3 cup filtered water or unsweetened almond milk, plus more if needed*

CHOCOLATE FUDGE GLAZE

1/4 cup (1.3 ounces) raw cacao butter disks or roughly chopped chunks*

2 tablespoons raw cacao powder

2 tablespoons pure maple syrup

1 tablespoon unsweetened almond milk*

For the Cacao-Tahini Brownies

Preheat the oven to 350°F. Line an 8 × 8-inch square baking pan with parchment paper. (Double-check your pan size—a 9 × 9-inch pan won't work for this recipe.)

In a large mixing bowl, beat together the coconut sugar, tahini, and vanilla for 1 minute using a hand mixer with the beater attachments or a stand mixer with the paddle attachment.

In a medium mixing bowl, whisk together the oat flour, cacao powder, baking powder, and sea salt. Place the water within reach of the mixer.

With the mixer on low, slowly add the oat flour mixture to the coconut sugar mixture. Then, immediately add the water, increase to medium speed, and beat for 15 seconds, or until incorporated. The finished dough should be moist and pulled together in large mounds as it moves around the mixing bowl, not dry and broken into small crumbles. *Note*: If the dough appears dry and crumbly, add another 1–2 tablespoons filtered water or almond milk. A little liquid goes a long way in this recipe, so start with 1 tablespoon and mix again before determining whether or not a second tablespoon is needed. Adding more liquid may increase the baking time by a minute or two, so adjust as needed.

Scoop the brownie dough into the lined pan, and use your fingers or a spatula to press and spread it into an even layer. At first it will seem like there isn't enough, but just keep working it out toward the edges of the pan. You want a thin, evenly distributed layer.

(continued on next page)

Bake for 16–20 minutes, or until the edges appear slightly crackled and a toothpick inserted into the center comes out mostly clean with a few moist crumbs at the tip. Lean toward underbaking if you're questioning doneness, as this will ensure a dense, fudgy texture.

Let cool completely in the pan. In a pinch, cool at room temperature for 5 minutes and then transfer to the refrigerator to expedite the cooling process.

For the Chocolate Fudge Glaze

Once the brownies have cooled, make the chocolate glaze. Melt the cacao butter in a double boiler or bain-marie over low heat. Be careful not to overheat or it will seize and take on a gritty texture.

Remove from the heat and whisk in the cacao powder, maple syrup, and almond milk until smooth and glossy.

Pour the glaze over the brownie and tilt the pan back and forth to evenly coat the surface. Chill for 20 minutes, or until the glaze is set. Then, gently lift the brownie out of the pan and slice into 12 bars.

Return the brownies to the parchment-lined pan and loosely cover with foil. For soft, gooey brownies, store at room temperature. For dense, slightly chewy brownies, store in the refrigerator.

No Nuts? No Problem | *To keep this nut-free, opt for filtered water instead of almond milk.*

What in the World Is Cacao Butter? | *Cacao butter is the pure, crushed butter from the cocoa bean; see page 21 for details.*

Oily Brownies? | *On the first day, you'll notice that the brownies are slightly oily and delicate due to the natural oils from the tahini, but they'll firm up and absorb the oil as they rest, making them even more delicious by the second day.*

MINI BANOFFEE PIES WITH GRAHAM-CRACKER COOKIE CRUST

Makes 12 mini pies | 45 minutes or less

Banoffee pie, a popular English dessert, is a combination of toffee, bananas, whipped cream, and chocolate curls layered into a pie crust or served over crumbly biscuits. I first had banoffee pie when my uncle made it for the holidays several years ago, and it immediately became one of my favorite desserts. These miniature vegan versions involve filling homemade mini graham-cracker crusts with gooey 5-Minute Caramel Sauce (page 306), sliced bananas, and Coconut Whipped Cream (page 308) and garnishing each with a generous sprinkling of dark chocolate curls. They can be served straight from the pan as a crowd-pleasing handheld dessert, or for a bit more decadence, slice each into sixths, scatter on a plate or in a bowl, and top with more whipped cream, caramel, and chocolate curls.

SPECIAL EQUIPMENT

12 large (2 1/2-inch) parchment paper baking cups

GRAHAM-CRACKER COOKIE CRUST

1 cup coconut sugar

1/3 cup virgin coconut oil, at room temperature

1 teaspoon pure vanilla extract

1 1/2 cups oat flour

1 1/2 teaspoons aluminum-free baking powder

1/8 teaspoon fine-grain sea salt

2 tablespoons filtered water

TOPPINGS

1 recipe 5-Minute Caramel Sauce (page 306), cooled slightly*

1 recipe Coconut Whipped Cream (page 308)

1 ripe banana, peeled and thinly sliced into coins

1 (3.5-ounce) bar quality vegan dark chocolate*

For the Graham-Cracker Cookie Crust

Preheat the oven to 350°F. Line a muffin pan with the parchment paper baking cups.

In a stand mixer fitted with the paddle attachment, beat together the coconut sugar, coconut oil, and vanilla on high speed for 1 minute.

In a medium mixing bowl, whisk together the oat flour, baking powder, and sea salt. Place within reach of the mixer.

With the mixer off, add the water to the coconut sugar mixture and start beating while slowly adding the oat flour mixture. Beat for 30 seconds, or until the dough pulls together into large, moist mounds as it moves around the mixing bowl. When you first add the dry ingredients, the dough will be dry and crumbly; however, just keep beating on high—the finished dough will look and feel similar to Play-Doh. If the dough is still dry and crumbly after beating for 30 seconds, add more filtered water, 1 tablespoon at a time, and continue beating until it pulls together.

Scoop approximately 2 tablespoons of the dough into each baking cup, dividing any extra dough evenly among the 12 baking cups. Use your fingers to press the dough firmly and evenly into the bottom and 1 inch up the sides of each cup, forming a well. To quicken the process, use the bottom of a small juice glass to press the dough into the bottom and up the sides.

(continued on next page)

Bake for 10–16 minutes, or until the crusts are golden brown and a toothpick inserted into the center of one comes out mostly clean with a few moist crumbs at the tip. If you prefer a soft, chewy, cookielike crust, bake for 10–14 minutes; if you prefer a crisp, crunchy crust, bake for 14–16 minutes. They'll puff up quite a bit while baking; however, they'll fall and settle back into crust shape as they cool. Also, don't worry if there is an oily sheen to the crusts when you first remove them from the oven; the oil will be reabsorbed as they cool.

Transfer the entire pan to an oven-safe cooling rack. Let cool completely.

To Assemble

While the crusts cool, prepare the 5-Minute Caramel Sauce and the Coconut Whipped Cream.

Spoon 1 tablespoon of caramel into each cup and top with 2 or 3 banana slices, being careful not to overfill the crusts. Spoon, pipe, or drizzle a bit of whipped cream over the caramel. Use a vegetable peeler to shave as much of the dark chocolate as desired over each mound of whipped cream.

Keep chilled in the refrigerator until just before serving.

No Nuts? No Problem | *To keep these treats nut-free, use sunflower seed butter or tahini to make the* 5-Minute Caramel Sauce.

No Soy **or Refined Sugar? No Problem** | *To keep these treats soy-free and refined-sugar-free, opt for* Homemade Chocolate *(page 306).*

RAW CANNOLI BARS

Makes 12 bars | 1 hour +

"Leave the gun. Take the cannoli." —The Godfather

I've seen *The Godfather* more times than I can count. Around the time I was just starting high school, it became a New Year's Day tradition to watch the three-hour movie while consuming a comforting Italian feast with family. Although I'm not down with the violence in the film, the one thing I can agree with is the above line—taken apart from the fact that the character that made the statement had just shot someone, of course. Anger, guns, and violence? Leave it behind. Let's eat sweet Italian dessert with a plant-passionate twist instead.

CANNOLI FILLING

1 1/2 cups raw cashews

2/3 cup packed and pitted Medjool dates

1/4 cup plus 2 tablespoons filtered water

2 tablespoons fresh lemon juice

3/4 teaspoon pure almond extract

1/4 teaspoon ground cinnamon

PISTACHIO CRUST

1 cup raw shelled pistachios*

1 cup packed and pitted Medjool dates

TOPPING

2 tablespoons raw cacao nibs*

1 tablespoon crushed raw pistachios*

For the Cannoli Filling

Soak the cashews and dates in hot water for 30 minutes to soften; drain.

Add the soaked cashews and dates, filtered water, lemon juice, almond extract, and cinnamon to a food processor. Process for 6–8 minutes, or until smooth and creamy, stopping to scrape down the sides as needed. The texture should resemble a thick frosting.

For the Pistachio Crust

Line a 5 × 10-inch loaf pan with parchment paper.

Add the pistachios and dates to a food processor, pulse 10 times, and then process until the mixture begins to clump together, adding more dates if needed. It should stick together when pressed between your fingers.

Scoop the crust mixture into the lined pan and use your hands to press and compact it into an even layer.

To Assemble

Pour the filling over the crust and smooth out with a spatula. Sprinkle with the cacao nibs and chopped pistachios.

Freeze for 2 hours to set. Once set, gently lift out of the pan and slice into bars. Store the bars in the refrigerator to maintain optimal texture.

No Need to Keep It Raw? | *Feel free to substitute roasted, unsalted pistachios for the raw pistachios and chopped vegan dark chocolate for the raw cacao nibs.*

Makes 1 (16-ounce) shake or 2 (8-ounce) shakes | 15 minutes or less

This was one of the very first recipes I created for this book. The idea was inspired by one of my favorite blog recipes, Just Beet It! Red Velvet Fudge, but I was concerned something might be lost during translation from fudge to shake. I couldn't have been more wrong. Upon first sip, I literally squealed. This shake is ultra-creamy, cold, and chocolaty, and it has the deepest, prettiest red hue thanks to the addition of raw beet juice.

1/2 cup chilled coconut cream*

1/2–1 cup ice

1/4 cup fresh beet juice or 1/3 cup peeled and grated fresh beets

4 Medjool dates, pitted*

2 tablespoons raw cacao powder or 1/4 cup cocoa powder

1 teaspoon pure vanilla extract

Add all the ingredients to a high-speed blender, and blend until smooth and creamy.

What in the World Is Coconut Cream? | *Coconut cream is the thick white cream that collects at the top of a chilled can of coconut milk. To collect it: refrigerate a can of full-fat coconut milk for at least 8 hours, open the can, and scoop out the firm cream at the top, excluding the watery liquid (i.e., coconut water) at the bottom.*

Be Kind to Your Blender | *If you're not using a high-speed blender (e.g., Vitamix or Blendtec), soak the dates in hot water for 30 minutes to soften before blending.*

Makes 5 shortcakes | 1 hour or less

Tender, buttery, and zesty lemon-thyme shortcakes are stuffed with sweet, syrupy blackberry compote before receiving a generous dollop of coconut whipped cream. This reminds me of a dressy, gourmet version of strawberry shortcake with a deeper, darker berry twist. The lemon zest adds a lively zing to the comforting biscuits while the compote offers a pop of freshness and a playful purple hue. These shortcakes are perfect for a special date night at home or as the sweet end to a summer dinner party with friends.

LEMON-THYME SHORTCAKES

1 tablespoon chia seeds

2 tablespoons filtered water

3 tablespoons pure maple syrup

1 tablespoon fresh lemon juice

1 teaspoon pure vanilla extract

1 1/2 cups gluten-free old-fashioned rolled oats

1 tablespoon coconut flour

1 tablespoon aluminum-free baking powder

2 teaspoons lemon zest

1 teaspoon chopped fresh thyme

1/8 teaspoon fine-grain sea salt

1/4 cup virgin coconut oil, chilled

BLACKBERRY COMPOTE

2 cups fresh or frozen blackberries

2 tablespoons pure maple syrup

2 tablespoons filtered water

TOPPING

1 recipe Coconut Whipped Cream (page 308)

For the Lemon-Thyme Shortcakes

Preheat the oven to 400°F. Line a small baking tray with parchment paper.

In a medium spouted mixing bowl, whisk together the chia seeds and water. Let stand for 10 minutes to thicken. Then, whisk in the maple syrup, lemon juice, and vanilla. Set aside.

Add the rolled oats to a food processor and process for 4 minutes, or until a fine flour develops. Transfer to a large mixing bowl and whisk in the coconut flour, baking powder, lemon zest, thyme, and sea salt. Add the chilled coconut oil, and use your fingers to cut it into the oat flour mixture until you have small crumbles.

Add the wet ingredients and stir to incorporate.

Line a clean work surface with parchment paper and form the dough into a disk. Cover the dough with another piece of parchment paper, and use a rolling pin to roll it into a 1-inch-thick oval. Use a 3-inch round cookie cutter to punch out 5 shortcakes, rerolling the dough if needed.

Transfer the shortcakes to the lined baking tray, and bake for 10–14 minutes, or until just barely turning golden. Let cool for 2 minutes on the baking tray and then transfer to a wire cooling rack. Cool completely.

For the Blackberry Compote

Add the blackberries, maple syrup, and water to a medium saucepan over medium heat. Bring to a boil, decrease the heat, and simmer, uncovered, for 10–12 minutes, or until the blackberries break down into a sauce, stirring occasionally. Cool slightly.

To Assemble

Use a serrated knife to carefully slice the shortcakes in half. Fill each shortcake with the compote and top with the whipped cream. Serve immediately.

SNICKERDOODLE COOKIE BARS

If the pages of this book were a bit wider, I would have more aptly named these bars: "The Snickerdoodle Cookie Bars That Convinced Dan's Coworkers That Vegan Desserts Are Better Than the 'Real' Thing." Sadly, these pages aren't roomy enough to accommodate such a lavish title, but thank goodness for the luxurious space in this headnote.

These cookie bars are tender with just the right amount of sink-your-teeth-in density. Dan was quick to declare these as his all-time favorite "sweet thing" ever. I once sent him to work with a batch packed into his computer bag and when he returned home that evening he shared two memorable pieces of feedback from his coworkers. First, that everyone loved them and a few people even suggested business ideas solely centered around these bars. And second, someone offered up this price-less reaction: "I thought vegan food was supposed to be gross, why do these taste so good?!"

1 cup coconut sugar

1/3 cup virgin coconut oil

1 teaspoon pure vanilla extract

1 1/2 cups oat flour

1 teaspoon ground cinnamon

1 1/2 teaspoons aluminum-free baking powder

1/8 teaspoon fine-grain sea salt

2 tablespoons filtered water, plus more if needed

Preheat the oven to 350°F. For thicker bars, line a 9 × 5-inch loaf pan with parchment paper. For thinner bars, line an 8 × 8-inch square pan with parchment paper. (Double-check your pan size—a 9 × 9-inch pan won't work for this recipe.)

In a stand mixer fitted with the paddle attachment, beat together the coconut sugar, coconut oil, and vanilla on high speed for 1 minute.

In a medium mixing bowl, whisk together the oat flour, cinnamon, baking powder, and sea salt. Place within reach of the mixer.

With the mixer off, add the water and start beating while slowly adding the oat flour mixture. Beat for 30 seconds, or until the dough pulls together into large, moist mounds as it moves around the mixing bowl. When you first add the dry ingredients, the dough will be dry and crumbly; however, just keep beating on high—the finished dough will look and feel similar to Play-Doh. If the dough is still dry and crumbly after beating for 30 seconds, add more filtered water, 1 tablespoon at a time, and continue beating until it pulls together.

Scoop the dough into the lined pan, and use your fingers to press and spread it into an even layer. At first it will seem like there isn't enough, but just keep working it out toward the edges. You want a thin, evenly distributed layer.

Bake for 16–20 minutes, or until the edges are golden and crackled and a toothpick inserted into the center comes out mostly clean with a few moist crumbs at the tip. Be careful not to overbake. Let cool completely in the pan.

Gently lift out of the pan and slice into 12 bars. The bars will initially be oily to the touch; however, within a few hours, the oil will be reabsorbed.

Return the bars to the parchment-lined pan and loosely wrap with foil.

CHOCOLATE CHIP COCONUT OIL COOKIE BARS

Makes 12 cookie bars | 45 minutes or less

If I ever get my hands on your copy of this cookbook, you can bet your plant-passionate pennies that I'll double-dog-ear this page. These cookie bars are my favorite, favorite, FAVORITE dessert ever. I've made this recipe countless times—most often to devour alone with Dan, but we occasionally share. And on the few occasions when we've been willing to release our chocolate-flecked grip from this pan of cookies, they've received rave reviews from everyone who's been graced with their presence. If you're a chocolate chip cookie fan who's trying to figure out which dessert recipe to start with, start here. Please, start here. You won't regret it. As a matter of fact, I have a feeling you'll be dog-earing this page yourself.

1 cup coconut sugar

1/3 cup virgin coconut oil

1 teaspoon pure vanilla extract

1 1/2 cups oat flour

1 1/2 teaspoons aluminum-free baking powder

1/8 teaspoon baking soda

1/8 teaspoon fine-grain sea salt

2 tablespoons filtered water, plus more if needed

1/3–1/2 cup vegan dark chocolate chips*

Preheat the oven to 350°F. Line an 8 × 8-inch baking pan with parchment paper. (Double-check your pan size, because a 9 × 9-inch pan won't work for this recipe—your cookie bars would end up dry and crumbly instead of moist and delectable.)

In a stand mixer fitted with the paddle attachment, beat together the coconut sugar, coconut oil, and vanilla on high speed for 1 minute.

In a medium mixing bowl, whisk together the oat flour, baking powder, baking soda, and sea salt. Place within reach of the mixer.

With the mixer off, add the water and start beating while slowly adding the oat flour mixture. Beat for 30 seconds, or until the dough pulls together into large, moist mounds as it moves around the mixing bowl. When you first add the dry ingredients, the dough will be dry and crumbly; however, just keep beating on high—the finished dough will look and feel similar to Play-Doh. If the dough is still dry and crumbly after beating for 30 seconds, add more filtered water, 1 tablespoon at a time, and continue beating until it pulls together. Stir in the chocolate chips.

Scoop the dough into the lined pan, and use your fingers to press and spread it into an even layer. At first it will seem like there isn't enough, but just keep working it out toward the edges. You want a thin, evenly distributed layer.

Bake for 20–24 minutes, or until a toothpick inserted into the center comes out mostly clean with a few moist crumbs at the tip. Do not overbake. Let cool for 10 minutes in the pan; then, gently lift the bar out of the pan and place on a wire cooling rack to cool completely.

Slice into 12 bars. The bars will initially be oily to the touch; however, within a few hours, the oil will be reabsorbed. Return the bars to the parchment-lined pan and loosely wrap with foil.

No Soy? No Problem | *To keep this soy-free, use soy-free chocolate chips, such as Enjoy Life brand.*

DOUBLE-CHOCOLATE CHERRY CHUNK ICE CREAM

If you haven't tried banana ice cream, often referred to as "nice" cream or banana soft-serve, you're in for a real treat. We have the talented Gena Hamshaw of The Full Helping (www.thefullhelping.com) to thank for this frozen delight.

The key to making ultra-dreamy banana ice cream is to add as little liquid as possible while blending to maintain a thick texture. It's also important to use ripe, speckled bananas to ensure a smooth and creamy outcome (using unripe or just-ripe bananas will yield a goopy texture). This particular version is dressed up in chocolate and cherries and comes together in a speedy 15 minutes or less. Frozen bananas, cacao powder, and almond extract are whirled to cool and frosty perfection, scooped into a bowl, and topped with cherries and cacao nibs.

2 ripe and speckled bananas, peeled, sliced, and frozen

1 tablespoon raw cacao powder

1/4–1/2 teaspoon pure almond extract*

2–4 tablespoons unsweetened dried cherries or fresh cherries, chopped

1 tablespoon cacao nibs or chopped vegan dark chocolate

Add the frozen bananas, cacao powder, and almond extract to a food processor, and process until thick and creamy, stopping to scrape down the sides as needed. If absolutely necessary, add filtered water or plant-based milk, 1 tablespoon at a time, to encourage blending.

Scoop into a bowl and top with the cherries and cacao nibs. Serve immediately.

No Nuts? No Problem | *To keep this treat nut-free, swap out the almond extract for pure vanilla extract.*

SEASONAL FRUIT CRISPS: APPLE-ALMOND + BLACKBERRY-SUNFLOWER

Serves 6–8 | 1 hour +

Two fruit crisps are better than one. Keep things fresh and seasonal by enjoying Apple-Almond in the fall and winter months and Blackberry-Sunflower in the spring and summer months. These crisps involve fewer than ten ingredients and just 15 minutes of active kitchen time. Then, pop them in the oven for an hour (or less) and do your own thing while the fruit softens and the topping crisps up to golden-brown perfection. Serve them all on their own or à la mode with coconut milk ice cream and a drizzle of 5-Minute Caramel Sauce (page 306).

FALL + WINTER: APPLE-ALMOND CRISP

APPLE FILLING

4 large (2 pounds) Granny Smith or Honeycrisp apples, peeled, cored, and diced

3 tablespoons pure maple syrup

1 tablespoon fresh lemon juice

2 teaspoons arrowroot starch

3/4 teaspoon ground cinnamon

ALMOND TOPPING

1 1/2 cups old-fashioned rolled oats, divided

1/2 cup raw almonds*

1/2 teaspoon ground cinnamon

1/8 teaspoon fine-grain sea salt

1/4 cup pure maple syrup

1/4 cup virgin coconut oil, melted, plus more for greasing

Preheat the oven to 350°F. Lightly grease a medium round, oval, or rectangular 1 1/2-quart baking dish with coconut oil.

For the Apple Filling

In a large mixing bowl, combine the diced apples, maple syrup, lemon juice, arrowroot, and cinnamon. Toss to coat, and transfer to the prepared baking dish.

For the Almond Topping

Add 1/2 cup of the rolled oats and the raw almonds to a food processor and process for 15 seconds, or until a coarse meal forms. Transfer to a large mixing bowl and whisk in the remaining 1 cup rolled oats, cinnamon, and sea salt. Add the maple syrup and melted coconut oil and stir to combine.

To Assemble

Sprinkle the topping evenly over the apple filling. Bake, uncovered, for 50 minutes to 1 hour, or until the topping is deep golden brown and you can hear the liquid bubbling within the filling. Remove from the oven and cool slightly before serving.

Serve with vanilla coconut milk ice cream and a drizzle of 5-Minute Caramel Sauce (page 306), if desired.

Refrigerate leftovers, covered, for up to 4 days.

No Nuts? No Problem | *To keep this crisp nut-free, swap the almonds for raw shelled sunflower seeds.*

(continued on next page)

BLACKBERRY FILLING

4 pints (2 pounds, 4 ounces) fresh blackberries

1/4–1/3 cup pure maple syrup, depending on sweetness of blackberries

1 tablespoon arrowroot starch

1/4 teaspoon ground cardamom

SUNFLOWER TOPPING

1 1/2 cups old-fashioned rolled oats, divided

1/2 cup raw shelled sunflower seeds

1/4 teaspoon ground cardamom

1/8 teaspoon fine-grain sea salt

1/4 cup pure maple syrup

1/4 cup virgin coconut oil, melted, plus more for greasing

Preheat the oven to 350°F. Lightly grease a medium round, oval, or rectangular 1 1/2-quart baking dish with coconut oil.

For the Blackberry Filling

In a large mixing bowl, combine the blackberries, maple syrup, arrowroot, and cardamom. Toss to coat, and transfer to the prepared baking dish.

For the Sunflower Topping

Add 1/2 cup of the rolled oats and the raw sunflower seeds to a food processor and process for 15 seconds, or until a coarse meal forms. Transfer to a large mixing bowl and whisk in the remaining 1 cup rolled oats, cardamom, and sea salt. Add the maple syrup and melted coconut oil and stir to combine.

To Assemble

Sprinkle the topping evenly over the blackberry filling. Bake, uncovered, for 50 minutes to 1 hour, or until the topping is deep golden brown and you can hear the liquid bubbling within the filling. Remove from the oven and cool slightly before serving.

Serve with vanilla coconut milk ice cream and a drizzle of 5-Minute Caramel Sauce (page 306), if desired.

Refrigerate leftovers, covered, for up to 4 days.

BLISSFUL BLUEBERRY-CHIA STREUSEL BARS

Makes 9 bars | 1 hour +

Otherwise known as blueberry pie in bar form, these bars are a hit with pie lovers. A flavorful oat and pecan crust is baked to perfection and filled with a thick blueberry-chia jam before being topped with pecan streusel. I'm not going to come right out and say that these oat- and blueberry-laden dessert bars are breakfast appropriate, but I occasionally eat one for breakfast. Interpret as you see fit.

CRUST

1 tablespoon flaxseed meal (ground flaxseed)

3 tablespoons filtered water

2 cups old-fashioned rolled oats, divided

1/2 cup raw pecan halves

1/2 teaspoon ground cinnamon

1/4 teaspoon ground cardamom (optional)

1/8 teaspoon fine-grain sea salt

1/4 cup virgin coconut oil, melted

1/4 cup plus 1 tablespoon pure maple syrup

1 teaspoon pure vanilla extract

BLUEBERRY-CHIA FILLING

3 cups (18 ounces) fresh blueberries

3 tablespoons chia seeds

2–3 tablespoons pure maple syrup, depending on sweetness of the blueberries

STREUSEL TOPPING

1/2 cup raw pecan halves

1/4 cup coconut sugar

1 teaspoon ground cinnamon

For the Crust

Preheat the oven to 350°F. Line an 8 × 8-inch metal baking pan with parchment paper.

In a small bowl, whisk together the flaxseed meal and water. Set aside for 10 minutes to thicken.

Add 1 cup of the rolled oats to a food processor. Process for 4 minutes, or until a fine flour develops. Add the pecans and process for another 30 seconds, or until ground into a fine meal. Transfer to a large mixing bowl and whisk in the remaining 1 cup rolled oats, cinnamon, cardamom (if using), and sea salt. Add the flaxseed mixture, melted coconut oil, maple syrup, and vanilla and stir well to combine.

Scoop the crust mixture into the lined pan, and use a spatula to press and spread it into an even layer.

Bake for 25–30 minutes, or until light golden throughout the top with light golden-brown edges. Remove from the oven and transfer the pan to an oven-safe cooling rack. Cool completely.

For the Blueberry-Chia Filling

While the crust is baking, add the blueberries, chia seeds, and maple syrup to a medium saucepan over medium-low heat. Cover and simmer for 15 minutes, or until thick and bubbly, stirring occasionally. At first it will seem like there isn't enough liquid, but as the blueberries heat, they'll burst and release their juices.

Use the back of a fork to mash about half of the blueberries to thicken the filling. Chill in the refrigerator until ready to assemble.

(continued on next page)

For the Streusel Topping

Meanwhile, add the pecans, coconut sugar, and cinnamon to a food processor. Pulse 5–10 times to create a fine streusel.

To Assemble

Once the crust is almost completely cool, reheat the oven to 350°F.

Spread the filling over the crust. Sprinkle with the streusel and use the back of a spoon to evenly distribute. Bake for 15 minutes, or until the streusel is deep golden brown. Remove from the oven and cool completely.

Gently lift the bar out of the pan and slice into 9 squares.

Refrigerate leftovers, covered, for up to 4 days.

SWEET VANILLA CHICKPEA CAKE WITH
STRAWBERRY COMPOTE + COCONUT WHIP

Serves 10 | 1 hour +

This cake is a tribute to my grandma Shirley. When my cousins and I were just wee little ones, we loved spending the night at our grandma's house. We had several fun traditions: we painted ceramics, fed the ducks Wonder Bread in the local park, put on old T-shirts and repeatedly rolled down the hill in her backyard, and gathered around her tiny breakfast table to watch an angel food or vanilla cake puff up in the oven. That last tradition was always my favorite. Boxed origins aside, cake made alongside my grandma tasted better than any other. When angel food cake was in the oven, we could expect about five reminders from my grandma not to jump around. If our cake-induced excitement got the best of us and we moved too swiftly, she'd remind us that sudden movements could flatten a cake. I wasn't exactly sure what that meant at the time, but she seemed disturbed by the idea, so we did our best to keep still. Once the cake was released from the oven, we outfitted it in our favorite toppings: strawberries and whipped cream or canned vanilla frosting and sprinkles.

This time around, the ingredients step outside the box, but the flavors align with my childhood favorite. The batter, made with a combination of chickpea flour and oat flour, starts off fluffy and delicate like an angel food cake, yet bakes up buttery and rich like a classic vanilla cake. It's topped with strawberry compote and a generous dollop of coconut whipped cream, lending an irresistible strawberry-shortcake vibe. And yes, I tiptoe around the kitchen while this one is baking. Not because I have to but because I can't quite shake Grandma Shirley's no-jump rule.

SWEET VANILLA CHICKPEA CAKE

1 tablespoon flaxseed meal (ground flaxseed)

2 tablespoons filtered water

3/4 cup unsweetened almond milk, at room temperature*

2 teaspoons apple cider vinegar

3/4 cup unsweetened applesauce, at room temperature

1/2 cup virgin coconut oil, melted, plus more for greasing

1 tablespoon pure vanilla extract

1 cup coconut sugar

1 1/4 cups chickpea flour, sifted twice after measuring*

1/2 cup oat flour, sifted twice after measuring*

1 1/2 teaspoons aluminum-free baking powder

1/2 teaspoon baking soda

1/4 teaspoon fine-grain sea salt

For the Sweet Vanilla Chickpea Cake

Position a baking rack in the middle of the oven and preheat the oven to 350°F. Grease a 9-inch springform pan or 9-inch round cake pan with coconut oil.

In a small mixing bowl, whisk together the flaxseed meal and water. Set aside for 10 minutes to thicken.

In a large mixing bowl, whisk together the almond milk and apple cider vinegar. Let stand for 5 minutes to create a quick vegan buttermilk. Add the flaxseed mixture, applesauce, coconut oil, and vanilla extract. Using a handheld or stand mixer with the whisk attachment, whisk on medium-high for 45 seconds, or until incorporated.

Add the coconut sugar to a food processor and process for 2 minutes, or until it takes on a slightly finer texture. Transfer to a medium mixing bowl and whisk in the sifted chickpea flour and oat flour, baking powder, baking soda, and sea salt. Place within reach of the mixer.

Turn the mixer on low and slowly add the dry ingredients to the wet. Increase the speed to high and whisk for 2 minutes, or until the batter is thick and fluffy. Pour into the greased springform pan and use a spatula to gently smooth the surface.

(continued on next page)

STRAWBERRY COMPOTE

1 1/2 pounds fresh strawberries, hulled and sliced

3/4 cup filtered water

3 tablespoons pure maple syrup

TOPPING

1 recipe Coconut Whipped Cream (page 308)

Bake for 35–45 minutes, or until the cake springs back when gently pressed and a toothpick inserted into the center comes out clean. The edges will be a light golden brown. Remove from the oven and place on a wire cooling rack, pan and all. Let the cake cool completely.

For the Strawberry Compote

Make the strawberry compote while the cake is baking.

In a medium saucepan, combine the strawberries, water, and maple syrup over medium heat.

Bring to a boil, decrease the heat to low, and simmer, uncovered, for 20–25 minutes, or until the strawberries break down into a sauce, stirring every 5 minutes or so. In the last 5–10 minutes of simmering, use a large wooden spoon to gently smash the berries. The finished compote will have tender pieces of mashed strawberries surrounded by a ruby-tinged syrup. Remove from the heat. It will thicken as it cools.

For the Topping

Prepare the Coconut Whipped Cream and refrigerate until ready to serve.

To Serve

For looks, the cake is pictured fully assembled; however, I typically slice it into 10 pieces and serve each piece topped with a generous spoonful of compote and a dollop of whipped cream.

Refrigerate leftover compote and whipped cream for up to 3 days, and store the cake at room temperature.

No Nuts? No Problem | *To keep this cake nut-free, simply swap out the unsweetened almond milk for a nut-free plant-based milk, such as unsweetened soy milk or unsweetened rice milk.*

Measure Lightly and Precisely | *When measuring the chickpea and oat flours, use your measuring cup to lightly scoop out the flour. Then shake off the excess and gently level it off with a metal spatula. You want the measuring cup to be loosely packed with flour rather than jam-packed. Once measured, sift each flour twice.*

Serves 8–10 | 1 hour or less

Sweet and spiced and everything nice. It may sound cliché, but in this case, it's 100 percent true. Bosc pears are thinly sliced and fanned out over a layer of cinnamon-spiced coconut sugar. Then, a rich and nutty cardamom-pecan batter is poured over the top. The result is a dense, gooey, and puddinglike cake with the loveliest arrangement of pears strewn across its surface.

CARAMELIZED UPSIDE-DOWN PEARS

2 firm-ripe Bosc pears, peeled or unpeeled

1/3 cup coconut sugar

2 tablespoons virgin coconut oil, melted

1/2 teaspoon ground cinnamon

CARDAMOM PECAN CAKE

1 tablespoon flaxseed meal (ground flaxseed)

2 tablespoons filtered water

2/3 cup unsweetened almond milk, at room temperature

1 tablespoon apple cider vinegar

1/3 cup coconut sugar

1/4 cup pure maple syrup, at room temperature

1/4 cup virgin coconut oil, melted

1 tablespoon pure vanilla extract

3/4 cup raw pecan halves

1 1/4 cups oat flour

2 teaspoons aluminum-free baking powder

1 teaspoon ground cinnamon

1/2 teaspoon ground cardamom

1/4 teaspoon fine-grain sea salt

TOPPING

1 recipe 5-Minute Caramel Sauce (page 306)

For the Caramelized Upside-Down Pears

Preheat the oven to 350°F. Lightly grease the bottom and sides of an 8-inch springform pan. (Double-check your pan size—a 9-inch springform pan will not work for this recipe.) Place on a large, foil-lined baking tray to catch any drippings as the cake bakes.

Thinly slice the pears lengthwise into 1/8-inch-thick slices, discarding the seeds and cores. Set aside.

In a small mixing bowl, whisk together the coconut sugar, coconut oil, and cinnamon, and spread it evenly into the greased springform pan.

Arrange the sliced pears in a circular pattern on top of the coconut sugar mixture, overlapping their edges with the pointy ends facing inward. This layer will eventually be the top of the cake, so take your time with this step. Depending on the size of your pears, you might have a few leftover slices.

For the Cardamom Pecan Cake

In a small bowl, whisk together the flaxseed meal and water. Set aside for 5–10 minutes to thicken.

In a large mixing bowl, whisk together the almond milk and apple cider vinegar; let stand for 5 minutes to create a quick vegan buttermilk. Then, add the flaxseed mixture, coconut sugar, maple syrup, coconut oil, and vanilla. Using a handheld or stand mixer with the whisk attachment, whisk on medium speed for 45 seconds, or until the coconut sugar dissolves.

Add the pecans to a food processor and process for 30 seconds, or until ground into a fine meal. Add the oat flour, baking powder, cinnamon, cardamom, and sea salt, and pulse to incorporate. Place within reach of the mixer.

(continued on next page)

With the mixer on low, slowly add the pecan mixture to the almond milk mixture. Increase the speed to high and whisk for 2 minutes. Let the batter rest for 10 minutes to thicken. Then, pour into the springform pan, covering the pears.

Carefully transfer to the middle rack of the oven, and bake for 32–38 minutes, or until the top of the cake is subtly crackled, the edges have taken on a deep golden hue, and a toothpick inserted into the center comes out mostly clean with a few moist crumbs at the tip. Be careful not to overbake.

Transfer the pan to an oven-safe cooling rack, and allow the cake to cool slightly. This is a thinner, denser cake, so it will fall a bit.

Once the pan is cool enough to handle, release and remove the sides of the springform pan. Place a cake platter, face-side-down, on top of the cake. Get a firm grip on the bottom of the pan, and carefully flip the cake over onto the platter in one motion. Run a knife or metal spatula between the base of the pan and the pears to release.

To Serve

Prepare the 5-Minute Caramel Sauce

Slice the cake into wedges. Serve warm with a generous drizzle of the caramel.

PEANUT BUTTER COOKIES (TRIPLE REMIX)

Makes 14–16 cookies | 30 minutes or less

Running a food blog has taught me many things, but one of the best lessons has been this: A really good peanut butter cookie is a powerful thing. And if you offer up a peanut butter cookie recipe that's reliable, versatile, and damn tasty, you'll be repaid with dedicated affection and warm hearts. That's the best kind of payment, if you ask me.

I shared the original recipe, called "Soft + Tender Peanut Butter Cookies | Vegan and Gluten-Free" in 2013, and it's been the most popular recipe on my blog ever since, with rave reviews and praise from hundreds of vegans and non-vegans alike. The cookies are intensely peanut buttery and have an uncanny tenderness to them. People have remixed and revised the recipe in countless ways (e.g., adding dark chocolate chips, using a variety of sugars, and even using sunflower butter for a nut-free version), and the cookies roll with the punches time and time again. It's The Little Peanut Butter Cookie That Could.

The original recipe calls for brown sugar, and it will always be the nearest and dearest to my heart. For the book, I've also included a refined-sugar-free variation that uses coconut sugar, yielding cookies with only the tiniest bit of difference in terms of look, feel, and taste. Just for fun, I threw in another refined-sugar-free version that includes brown rice syrup for added density and a subtle chew. I love each version for a different reason, and I hope you will, too.

SOFT + TENDER ORIGINAL OR SOFT + TENDER REFINED-SUGAR-FREE COOKIES

1 cup brown sugar or coconut sugar*

1 cup natural peanut butter*

2 teaspoons pure vanilla extract

2/3 cup oat flour

1 teaspoon baking soda

1/8 teaspoon fine-grain sea salt

1/4 cup filtered water or unsweetened almond milk*

For the Soft + Tender Original or Soft + Tender Refined-Sugar-Free Cookies

Preheat the oven to 350°F. Line two large baking sheets with parchment paper.

In a large mixing bowl, beat together the brown sugar and peanut butter for 1 minute using a handheld mixer or stand mixer. Add the vanilla extract and beat for another 30 seconds.

In a medium mixing bowl, whisk together the oat flour, baking soda, and sea salt.

While beating the peanut butter mixture, slowly add the oat flour mixture and beat until a crumby dough forms. Add the water and continue to beat until just combined. Do not overmix.

Scoop out 1 1/2–2 tablespoons of dough, roll into a ball, and place on one of the lined baking sheets. Repeat with the remaining dough, leaving 2 inches of space between each cookie. Use a fork to press the dough down, forming crosshatch patterns.

Bake for 8–12 minutes, or until the cookies just barely start to turn golden on the edges. Allow the cookies to cool completely on the baking sheets before moving.

Store in an airtight container to maintain texture.

(continued on next page)

SOFT + CHEWY COOKIES

1 cup coconut sugar

1 cup natural peanut butter*

1/4 cup brown rice syrup

2 teaspoons pure vanilla extract

1 1/4 cups oat flour

3/4 teaspoon baking soda

1/2 teaspoon aluminum-free baking powder

1/8 teaspoon fine-grain sea salt

1/4 cup unsweetened almond milk*

For the Soft + Chewy Cookies

Preheat the oven to 350°F. Line two large baking sheets with parchment paper.

In a large mixing bowl, beat together the coconut sugar, peanut butter, brown rice syrup, and vanilla extract for 1 minute using a handheld mixer or stand mixer.

In a medium mixing bowl, whisk together the oat flour, baking soda, baking powder, and sea salt. With the mixer off, add the dry ingredients to the peanut butter mixture. Then pour the almond milk over the flour mixture and turn the mixer on low. Increase the speed to medium-low and beat for 30 seconds, or until just combined. The dough should pull together into large, moist mounds as it moves around the mixing bowl.

Scoop out 1 1/2–2 tablespoons of dough, roll into a ball, and place on one of the lined baking sheets. Repeat with the remaining dough, leaving 2 inches of space between each cookie. For puffy, rounded cookies, leave as is. For a more traditional look, use a fork to press the dough down, forming crosshatch patterns.

Bake for 9–12 minutes, or until the edges are just barely turning golden and the bottoms are deep golden, rotating the pans in the oven at the 5-minute mark to ensure both trays bake evenly. Let the cookies cool for 5 minutes on the baking sheets and then transfer to a cooling rack to cool completely.

Store in an airtight container to maintain texture.

No Refined Sugar? No Problem | *To keep these cookies refined-sugar-free, opt for coconut sugar.*

No Nuts? No Problem | *To keep these cookies nut-free, use sunflower butter instead of peanut butter and swap out the unsweetened almond milk for a nut-free plant-based milk, such as unsweetened soy milk or unsweetened rice milk.*

"AN ODE TO OHIO" PEANUT BUTTER COOKIE DOUGH + CARAMEL BUCKEYE BARS

Makes 25 bars | 45 minutes or less

O-H. Now your turn. I-O. Now that we're in the spirit, bring on the chocolate, peanut butter, and caramel. I attended undergrad at Miami University in Oxford, Ohio, and one of my earliest dining hall memories was my Ohio-born dorm mates screeching with joy at the sight of a platter of chocolate-covered peanut butter balls. I love the peanut butter/chocolate (PBC) combination as much as the next gal, but their excitement was hiked up a notch or two from the standard PBC love I had witnessed in the past. It wasn't until one of them referred to the balls as "buckeyes" that I inquired about the hype. They explained that the treats were delicious and conjured up warm memories of being home and watching Ohio State football games with family. Given that we were all in the throes of our first bout of homesickness at that point, their unbridled enthusiasm for the already-exciting treats made perfect sense. Throughout that first year at Miami, peanut butter buckeyes were offered in our dining hall in both ball *and* bar form. No matter their shape, they never failed to elicit a few overzealous squeals.

It turns out that we have Gail Tabor Lucas to thank for the hubbub. In 1964, she accidentally created a treat that resembled a buckeye nut when she failed to fully dip a peanut butter ball in chocolate, leaving a tiny round of the nutty interior exposed. The original treats require a pound of powdered sugar, a stick of butter, and a small scoop of shortening for the filling alone. Not that there's anything wrong with that, but it's completely possible to keep these treats just as decadent while leaning on minimally processed, plant-based ingredients. And just for kicks, I went ahead and added a layer of peanut butter caramel, because why not?

PEANUT BUTTER COOKIE DOUGH

1/2 cup old-fashioned rolled oats or raw buckwheat groats, plus more if needed

3/4 cup natural creamy peanut butter*

3 tablespoons pure maple syrup

1 teaspoon pure vanilla extract

1/4 teaspoon fine-grain sea salt

PEANUT BUTTER CARAMEL

1/3 cup natural peanut butter*

1/3 cup pure maple syrup

1/4 cup virgin coconut oil

1 1/2 teaspoons pure vanilla extract

1/8 teaspoon fine-grain sea salt

For the Peanut Butter Cookie Dough

Line either an 8 × 8-inch or a 9 × 9-inch glass or metal baking pan with parchment paper. If you have a square silicon pan, that works even better.

Add the rolled oats or buckwheat groats to a food processor, and process for 4 minutes, or until ground into a fine flour. Transfer to a small mixing bowl and add the peanut butter, maple syrup, vanilla, and sea salt; use a fork to stir and mash until all of the flour has been absorbed. It should be thick and hold its shape like a standard cookie dough. If it's runny or goopy, make a bit more flour and add another tablespoon or two as needed.

Transfer the dough to the lined pan and use the back of a spoon or a spatula to spread and press it evenly into the pan. Be patient with this step; you want a very even, compact layer of cookie dough.

Place the pan in the freezer to chill while you prepare the next layer.

For the Peanut Butter Caramel

In a small saucepan, whisk together the peanut butter, maple syrup, coconut oil, vanilla extract, and sea salt over medium-low heat until smooth and glossy.

(continued on next page)

CHOCOLATE LAYER

2/3 cup chopped vegan dark chocolate*

1–2 tablespoons virgin coconut oil, as needed to thin the chocolate*

Pour the caramel over the chilled cookie dough layer and tilt the pan back and forth to evenly coat.

Return the pan to the freezer for 20 minutes, or until the caramel layer is set. It's very important that the caramel is fully set before topping with the chocolate or the layers will run together.

For the Chocolate Layer

While the caramel sets, make the chocolate layer. Melt the dark chocolate and coconut oil in a double boiler or bain-marie over low heat until smooth and glossy, whisking occasionally.

Pour the chocolate over the chilled caramel layer and tilt the pan back and forth to evenly coat. Return the pan to the freezer for at least 10 minutes, or until set.

Carefully lift the bar out of the pan and use a sharp knife to slice into 25 squares. Store in the refrigerator or freezer.

No Nuts? No Problem | *To keep these treats nut-free, use sunflower butter instead of peanut butter.*

No Refined Sugar or Soy? No Problem | *To keep these treats refined-sugar-free and soy-free, swap out the dark chocolate and coconut oil in the chocolate layer for* Homemade Chocolate *(page 306).*

Serves 2 | 30 minutes or less

If you've got 20 minutes of time and a craving for something that'll satiate a sweet tooth in a pinch, then you've come to the right place in this book. This sundae comes together with minimal time and ingredients and hits the spot in the best of ways. Banana ice cream is layered with caramelized bananas to create a flavor reminiscent of bananas Foster but without all the hazardous flambéing. And if you want to really send your taste buds soaring, be sure to top with walnuts, caramel, and coconut whipped cream. Get caramelizing!

CARAMELIZED BANANAS

1 tablespoon virgin coconut oil, plus more if needed

2 ripe bananas, peeled and sliced into 1/2-inch-thick coins

3 tablespoons coconut sugar

BANANA ICE CREAM

3 ripe and speckled bananas, peeled, sliced, and frozen

1 teaspoon pure vanilla extract (optional)

2 teaspoon unsweetened almond milk, if needed*

OPTIONAL TOPPINGS

5-Minute Caramel Sauce (page 306)

Coconut Whipped Cream (page 308)

1/4 cup raw walnut pieces, roughly chopped*

For the Caramelized Bananas

Heat the coconut oil in a large, well-seasoned cast-iron skillet over medium-low heat.

Add the sliced bananas and coconut sugar to a medium mixing bowl and toss to coat.

Place the bananas in the skillet in a single layer, being careful not to over-crowd. Depending on the size of the pan, you may need to cook them in batches. Cook for 2 minutes, or until a caramelized layer develops. Use a spatula to gently flip the bananas and cook for another 2 minutes, or until caramelized.

Transfer to a small bowl and repeat, adding more coconut oil to the pan if needed.

For the Banana Ice Cream

Add the frozen bananas and vanilla (if using) to a food processor and pro-cess for 2–3 minutes, or until thick and creamy, stopping to scrape down the sides as needed. If absolutely necessary, add a tiny splash (no more than 1–2 tablespoons) unsweetened almond milk to encourage blending.

To Assemble

If using, prepare the 5-Minute Caramel Sauce and Coconut Whipped Cream.

Scoop or spoon the ice cream into 2 sundae glasses or bowls, layering and topping with the caramelized bananas. Add other toppings (if using) and serve immediately.

No Nuts? No Problem | *To keep this nut-free, simply swap out the unsweetened almond milk for a nut-free plant-based milk, such as unsweetened soy milk or unsweetened rice milk, and omit the chopped walnuts.*

HOMEMADE STAPLES

SPICY TOMATO JAM

4 cups grape or cherry tomatoes, halved

1/4 cup pure maple syrup

2 cloves garlic, minced

1 1/2 teaspoons ground cumin or to taste

1 teaspoon minced fresh ginger

1 teaspoon minced fresh red chile (optional)

1/2 teaspoon crushed red pepper flakes or to taste

1/4 teaspoon sea salt

In a medium saucepan, combine the halved tomatoes and maple syrup over medium-low heat. Cook for 5 minutes, or until the tomatoes begin to release their juices, stirring occasionally.

Add the garlic, cumin, ginger, red chile (if using), crushed red pepper flakes, and sea salt. Give the pan a good stir and bring to a rapid simmer. Decrease the heat to low, cover, and simmer for 30–35 minutes, stirring every 5–10 minutes.

Remove the lid and continue to simmer for 5–10 minutes to cook off some of the excess liquid. Remove from the heat and let cool. Transfer to an airtight jar and store in the refrigerator for up to 1 week.

Slice Your Tomatoes Like a Pro | *Quickly and easily halve the cherry tomatoes by placing 10–15 of them between two round plastic lids from food storage or takeout containers. The lids are shallow enough to hold the tomatoes in place while exposing their centers. Gently press down on the top lid to hold the tomatoes in place, and use a serrated knife to carefully slice between the two lids. Voilà! Halved cherry tomatoes in a matter of seconds.*

Makes 9 buns or 16 slider rolls | 1 hour +

1 1/4 cups peeled and small-cubed (1/3-inch cubes) Yukon gold potato (about 1 medium potato)

2 1/4 teaspoons active dry yeast (1 packet)

1/2 cup warm water (105°F–115°F)

1 teaspoon pure maple syrup

2 3/4–3 cups spelt flour, plus more for dusting*

1 tablespoon cold-pressed olive oil for the dough, plus more for greasing and brushing

3/4 teaspoon fine-grain sea salt

Sesame seeds (optional, for garnish)

Pour a bit of olive oil into the bottom of a large mixing bowl. Tip and turn the bowl back and forth to evenly coat the bottom and sides.

The potato needs to be measured precisely, so make sure you have exactly 1 1/4 cups of small-cubed potato. Steam the diced potatoes for 30 minutes, or until very tender. (Avoid steaming in the microwave, because it will dry out the potato rather than infusing it with moisture.) Transfer to a food processor and process for 30 seconds, or until completely smooth.

In a small spouted mixing bowl, gently whisk together the yeast, warm water, and maple syrup. Let stand for 5 minutes, or until foam develops on the surface.

Add the yeast mixture, 2 3/4 cups spelt flour, 1 tablespoon olive oil, and the sea salt to the food processor. Pulse 5 times, and then process for 15 seconds, or until the dough begins to roll into a loosely formed ball. The dough should be soft and sticky yet pulled together; if it's too loose or wet, add another 1/4 cup spelt flour and pulse to incorporate. Alternatively, if it's too dry, add more warm water, 1 tablespoon at a time.

Liberally dust a clean work surface with spelt flour. Pull the dough from the food processor and knead for 2–2 1/2 minutes (I set a timer), or until smooth and elastic, adding more spelt flour as needed. The dough is ready when it begins to hold its shape and springs back, slightly but not completely, when pressed. The gluten in spelt is delicate, so be careful not to overknead or you'll end up with dry, crumbly buns.

Shape the dough into a ball and place in the oiled bowl. Cover with a clean kitchen towel and let rise in a warm place for 1 hour, or until doubled in size.

Line a 9 × 9-inch glass or metal baking pan with parchment paper.

Punch down the dough and return to a clean, flour-dusted work surface.

To Make Buns: Gently form or roll the dough into a 9 × 9-inch square. Use a knife to score the surface, dividing it into 9 (3 × 3-inch) squares. Then, slice into 9 equal pieces. To Make Slider Rolls: Gently form or roll the dough into an 8 × 8-inch square. Use a knife to score the surface, dividing it into 16 (2 × 2-inch) squares. Then, slice into 16 equal pieces.

(continued on next page)

Gently roll each piece of dough into a ball and place in the prepared baking pan. They should be snug. Spelt has a looser gluten structure, which means it tends to spread outward rather than upward. Positioning the buns/rolls snugly next to each other helps them rise upward, making them taller and moister.

Lightly brush the tops of the buns/rolls with water, sprinkle with sesame seeds (if using), loosely cover the pan with parchment paper, and let the rolls rise in a warm place for 30 minutes, or until doubled in size. Meanwhile, preheat the oven to 375°F.

For the buns, bake for 12–16 minutes. For the slider rolls, bake for 10–14 minutes. They're ready when the tops are firm to the touch and very light golden in color. If you tap them, they'll have a slightly hollow sound.

Let cool in the pan. Break off as many buns/rolls as needed and leave the leftovers intact to maintain moisture. They can also be frozen for up to 1 month, thawed, and warmed in the oven at a low temperature.

Mind Your Spelt | *I recommend using VitaSpelt Whole Spelt Flour or Bob's Red Mill Whole Spelt Flour for best results.*

PUFFY POTATO PIZZA CRUST

Makes 1 pizza crust (serves 2) | 1 hour or less

2 3/4 cups peeled and small-cubed (1/3-inch cubes) Yukon gold or russet potatoes (about 2 medium potatoes)

1/2 tablespoon chia seeds

1 1/2 tablespoons filtered water

3/4 cup plus 2 tablespoons oat flour

2 tablespoons blanched almond flour*

1 1/2 teaspoons cold-pressed olive oil

1 1/2 teaspoons apple cider vinegar

3/4 teaspoon garlic powder

1/2 teaspoon dried basil

1/2 teaspoon dried oregano

1/2 teaspoon fine-grain sea salt

Pinch of crushed red pepper flakes (optional)

The potatoes need to be measured precisely, so make sure you have exactly 2 3/4 cups of small-cubed potatoes. Steam the potatoes in a steamer or steamer basket for 30 minutes, or until very tender. (Avoid steaming in the microwave, because it will dry out the potatoes rather than infusing them with moisture.)

When the potatoes have about 10 minutes left to steam, preheat the oven to 400°F. Line a large round pizza pan with parchment paper.

Meanwhile, in a small bowl, whisk together the chia seeds and water and set aside for 10 minutes to thicken.

Add the steamed potatoes to a food processor and process for 30 seconds, or until completely smooth, stopping to scrape down the sides as needed. The starches in the potato will yield a sticky, almost gooey consistency.

In a large mixing bowl, combine the puréed potatoes, chia mixture, oat flour, almond flour, olive oil, apple cider vinegar, garlic powder, basil, oregano, sea salt, and red pepper flakes (if using). Use a large wooden spoon to stir until well combined. The mixture should resemble a wet bread dough: thick, slightly stretchy, and difficult to stir.

Scoop the dough onto the lined pizza pan, and use a spatula to spread it out into a large 1/3-inch-thick circle or oval. This process takes a few minutes. If the dough is sticking, lightly grease the spatula with olive oil.

Bake for 20–25 minutes, or until the crust is set and the edges and top are golden. Remove from the oven. If the crust puffed up while baking, gently poke it with a toothpick and lightly press to deflate.

Add whatever toppings your heart desires. Bake for another 5–15 minutes, or until the toppings reach the desired doneness. Serve immediately. Refrigerate leftovers.

No Nuts? No Problem | *Use raw sunflower flour instead of almond flour. Make your own by processing raw shelled sunflower seeds in a food processor for 30–45 seconds, or until ground into a fine meal.*

Leftovers? | *This pizza crust reheats like a dream. Simply preheat the oven to 400°F. Place the pizza on a baking tray and bake for 8–12 minutes, or until the edges are crisp and golden.*

SWEET POTATO PIZZA CRUST

Makes 1 pizza crust (serves 2) | 1 hour or less

2 3/4 cups peeled and small-cubed (1/3-inch cubes) sweet potatoes (about 2 medium potatoes)

1/2 tablespoon chia seeds

1 1/2 tablespoons filtered water

1/2 cup plus 2 tablespoons oat flour

2 tablespoons almond meal or blanched almond flour*

1 1/2 teaspoons cold-pressed olive oil

1 1/2 teaspoons apple cider vinegar

3/4 teaspoon garlic powder

1/2 teaspoon dried basil

1/2 teaspoon dried oregano

1/2 teaspoon fine-grain sea salt

Pinch of crushed red pepper flakes (optional)

The potatoes need to be measured precisely, so make sure you have exactly 2 3/4 cups of small-cubed potatoes. Steam the potatoes in a steamer or steamer basket for 30 minutes, or until fork-tender. (Avoid steaming in the microwave, because it will dry out the potatoes rather than infusing them with moisture.)

When the potatoes have about 10 minutes left to steam, preheat the oven to 400°F. Line a large round pizza pan with parchment paper.

Meanwhile, in a small bowl, whisk together the chia seeds and water and let stand for 10 minutes to thicken.

Add the steamed sweet potatoes to a large mixing bowl and use a fork to thoroughly mash. Add the chia mixture, oat flour, almond meal, olive oil, apple cider vinegar, garlic powder, basil, oregano, sea salt, and red pepper flakes (if using). Use a large wooden spoon to stir until well combined. The mixture should resemble a wet quick-bread dough: thick and difficult to stir.

Scoop the dough onto the lined pizza pan and use a spatula to spread it out into a large 1/3-inch-thick circle or oval. This process takes a few minutes. If the dough is sticking, lightly grease the spatula with olive oil.

Bake for 20–25 minutes, or until the crust is set and the edges and top are golden. Remove from the oven. If the crust puffed up while baking, gently poke it with a toothpick and lightly press to deflate before adding toppings.

Add whatever toppings your heart desires. Bake for another 5–15 minutes, or until the toppings reach the desired doneness. Serve immediately. Refrigerate leftovers.

No Nuts? No Problem | *Use raw sunflower flour instead of almond flour. Make your own by processing raw shelled sunflower seeds in a food processor for 30–45 seconds, or until ground into a fine meal.*

Leftovers? | *This pizza crust reheats like a dream. Simply preheat the oven to 400°F. Place the pizza on a baking tray and bake for 8–12 minutes, or until warmed through with crisp edges.*

SUPERSEED PESTO

Makes 1 1/2 cups | 15 minutes or less

1 cup basil leaves

1/2 cup baby arugula

1/4 cup shelled hemp seeds

1/4 cup raw pepitas

2 tablespoons cold-pressed olive oil

1 tablespoon fresh lemon juice

1 clove garlic, peeled

1/4–1/2 teaspoon sea salt or to taste

Add all the ingredients to a food processor and process for 1–2 minutes, or until just shy of smooth, stopping to scrape down the sides as needed.

BALSAMIC REDUCTION

Makes 1/4 cup | 30 minutes or less

1/2 cup balsamic vinegar

Heat the balsamic vinegar in a small saucepan over medium-high heat. Bring to a boil, whisking constantly. Decrease the heat and simmer for 10–15 minutes, or until reduced and thick enough to coat the back of a spoon, whisking occasionally. Balsamic burns quickly and without warning, so keep an eye on it. Let cool and transfer to a small glass jar. Store in the refrigerator for up to 2 weeks.

Words to the Wise | *Use a back burner and an exhaust fan to vent the vinegar smell, and resist the urge to take a whiff of the simmering balsamic. Unless, of course, you enjoy a zingy nostril sting that'll give wasabi a run for its money.*

SHIITAKE BACON

Serves 4 | 45 minutes or less

12 ounces shiitake mushrooms, stemmed and very thinly sliced

3 tablespoons cold-pressed olive oil

3/4 teaspoon fine-grain sea salt

Freshly ground black pepper

Preheat the oven to 375°F. Line a large baking tray with parchment paper.

Add the shiitakes to the lined baking tray. Drizzle with the olive oil, sprinkle with the sea salt, and generously season with black pepper. Toss to coat and spread out into a single layer.

Bake for 20–30 minutes, or until the mushrooms are golden brown and crisp, using tongs to toss every 10 minutes. Remove from the oven and let cool slightly (they'll continue to crisp up as they cool).

SPEEDY TWO-MINUTE KETCHUP

Makes 1 1/4 cups | 15 minutes or less

1 (6-ounce) can tomato paste

1/4 cup filtered water

3 tablespoons apple cider vinegar

1 tablespoon balsamic vinegar

1 tablespoon pure maple syrup or more to taste

1 teaspoon onion powder

1/2 teaspoon garlic powder

1/2 teaspoon sea salt

1/8 teaspoon ground allspice (optional)

In a small mixing bowl, whisk together the tomato paste, water, apple cider vinegar, balsamic vinegar, maple syrup, onion powder, garlic powder, sea salt, and allspice (if using) until combined. Transfer to an airtight jar and store in the refrigerator for up to 1 week.

NUT // SEED PARMESAN CHEESE

Makes 1/2 cup | 15 minutes or less

1/4 cup raw shelled nuts or seeds*

1/4 cup nutritional yeast flakes

1/2 teaspoon fine-grain sea salt

Add all the ingredients to a food processor and process for 30 seconds, or until the texture resembles finely grated Parmesan cheese.

Transfer to an airtight container and store in the refrigerator for up to 1 month.

Mix It Up | *Any of the following raw nuts work great: cashews, almonds, Brazil nuts, macadamia nuts, and walnuts. Any of the following raw seeds work great: sunflower seeds, pepitas, and hemp seeds.*

No Nuts? No Problem | *To keep this nut-free, use seeds instead of nuts.*

HOMEMADE COCONUT BUTTER

Makes 1–2 cups | 15 minutes or less

4–6 cups unsweetened shredded coconut*

Add the shredded coconut to a heavy-duty food processor and process for 8–12 minutes, or until you have a smooth and glossy liquid, stopping to scrape down the sides several times. Transfer to an airtight jar and store in the refrigerator for up to 1 month. If needed, melt in a double-boiler over low heat before using.

Mind Your Coconut | *Make sure you purchase unsweetened, dehydrated shredded coconut and not dried, desiccated coconut. Desiccated coconut comes in grated, shredded, and flaked forms, mimicking the exact kind you need to make coconut butter, only it's been stripped of most of its moisture. Shredded coconut isn't always clearly labeled, so go by look; dehydrated coconut is a pure, bright white and tends to stick together in the bag when pressed, whereas dried or desiccated coconut is a bit duller, can be flecked with golden-brown hues, and is loose/confetti-like within the bag. If you've attempted to make homemade coconut butter but ultimately failed (my hand is raised), it was probably desiccated coconut that found its way into your food processor. Although it will break down into finer bits of coconut, it lacks the moisture needed to become a smooth coconut butter. Trust me when I say that you can process that stuff for days and never see the glossy glisten of coconut butter.*

Makes 2 cups | 15 minutes or less

1 (6-ounce) can tomato paste

6 1/2 tablespoons apple cider vinegar or to taste

1/4 cup coconut sugar

1/4 cup filtered water

3 tablespoons Bragg Liquid Aminos or tamari*

1–3 tablespoons seeded and minced chipotle peppers in adobo sauce, depending on desired level of spiciness

2 tablespoons pure maple syrup

2 tablespoons blackstrap molasses

1 teaspoon onion powder

1/4 teaspoon garlic powder

1/8 teaspoon ground allspice

Add all the ingredients to a medium saucepan and whisk together over low heat. Simmer for 5 minutes, whisking frequently. Remove from the heat, let cool slightly, and transfer to an airtight glass jar. Store in the refrigerator for up to 2 weeks.

No Soy? No Problem | *To keep this soy-free, swap out the Bragg Liquid Aminos or tamari for coconut aminos.*

CILANTRO-LIME CREMA

Makes 1 cup | 15 minutes or less

1/2 cup raw cashews*

1/2 cup filtered water

1/4 cup tightly packed stemmed cilantro

2 1/2 tablespoons fresh lime juice

1–2 cloves garlic, peeled

1/2 tablespoon apple cider vinegar

1/2 teaspoon sea salt or to taste

Add all the ingredients to a high-speed blender, and blend on high for 2 minutes, or until completely smooth. Transfer to an airtight jar. Store in the refrigerator for up to 3 days.

Be Kind to Your Blender | *If you're not using a high-speed blender (e.g., Vitamix or Blendtec), soak the cashews in water for 2 hours or boil them for 10 minutes to soften before blending.*

No Nuts? No Problem | *To keep this nut-free, swap out the raw cashews for shelled hemp seeds.*

SUNFLOWER // WALNUT TACO CRUMBLES

Makes 1 cup | 15 minutes or less

3/4 cup raw shelled sunflower seeds or raw walnuts*

1 tablespoon reduced-sodium tamari*

1 teaspoon apple cider vinegar

1 teaspoon chili powder

1 teaspoon smoked paprika

1/2 teaspoon ground cumin

1/2 teaspoon garlic powder

Add the sunflower seeds or walnuts, tamari, apple cider vinegar, chili powder, smoked paprika, cumin, and garlic powder to a food processor. Pulse several times and then process for 30 seconds, or until the texture resembles a fine crumble. Refrigerate in an airtight container for up to 1 week.

No Nuts? No Problem | *To keep this nut-free, use raw shelled sunflower seeds.*

No Soy? No Problem | *To keep this soy-free, swap out the reduced-sodium tamari for coconut aminos.*

CASHEW SOUR CREAM

Makes 1 1/2 cups | 15 minutes or less

1 cup raw cashews*

1/2–3/4 cup filtered water

1 1/2 tablespoons fresh lemon juice

1–2 teaspoons apple cider vinegar

1 teaspoon tahini

1/2 teaspoon sea salt

Add all the ingredients to a high-speed blender and blend on high for 2–3 minutes, or until completely smooth. Transfer to an airtight jar. Store in the refrigerator for up to 3 days.

Be Kind to Your Blender | *If you're not using a high-speed blender (e.g., Vitamix or Blendtec), soak the cashews in water for 2 hours or boil them for 10 minutes to soften before blending.*

TZATZIKI SAUCE

Makes about 1 cup | 15 minutes or less

1/2 cup raw cashews or shelled hemp seeds*

1/4–1/3 cup filtered water, as needed

1/4 cup peeled and roughly diced cucumber , plus 1/4 cup grated cucumber

1 tablespoon plus 2 teaspoons fresh lemon juice

1 clove garlic, peeled

2 teaspoons apple cider vinegar

1/4 teaspoon sea salt or to taste

Freshly ground black pepper

In a high-speed blender, combine the cashew or hemp seeds, water, diced cucumber, lemon juice, garlic, apple cider vinegar, sea salt, and black pepper to taste and blend on high for 2–3 minutes, or until completely smooth. Transfer to an airtight jar and stir in the grated cucumber. Taste and season with more sea salt and black pepper, if desired. Store in the refrigerator for up to 3 days.

Be Kind to Your Blender | *If you're not using a high-speed blender (e.g., Vitamix or Blendtec), soak the cashews in water for 2 hours or boil them for 10 minutes to soften before blending.*

No Nuts? No Problem | *To keep this nut-free, use shelled hemp seeds.*

LEMONY HUMMUS

Makes 1 1/2 cups | 15 minutes or less

1 (15-ounce) can chickpeas, drained and rinsed

2–3 tablespoons fresh lemon juice

1 tablespoon filtered water

1–2 tablespoons tahini or more as needed

1 clove garlic, peeled

1/4–1/2 teaspoon sea salt

Add all the ingredients to a food processor. Process for 4 minutes, or until smooth and creamy, stopping to scrape down the sides as needed. Transfer to a bowl. Store in the refrigerator, covered, for up to 3 days.

CASHEW // HEMP SEED SWISS CHEESE

Makes 1 1/3 cups | 15 minutes or less

1/2 cup raw cashews or shelled hemp seeds*

2/3 cup filtered water

1 tablespoon nutritional yeast flakes

1 tablespoon arrowroot starch

1 tablespoon apple cider vinegar

1 tablespoon tahini

1/2 teaspoon sea salt or to taste

Add all the ingredients to a high-speed blender. Blend on high for 2 minutes, or until completely smooth. Transfer to a small saucepan and whisk constantly over medium heat for 5 minutes, or until the mixture just becomes thick and slightly stretchy. Be careful not to overheat.

Be Kind to Your Blender | *If you're not using a high-speed blender (e.g., Vitamix or Blendtec), soak the cashews in water for 2 hours or boil them for 10 minutes to soften before blending.*

No Nuts? No Problem | *To keep this nut-free, use shelled hemp seeds.*

CASHEW // HEMP SEED MOZZARELLA CHEESE

Makes 1 1/3 cups | 15 minutes or less

1/2 cup raw cashews or shelled hemp seeds*

2/3 cup filtered water

1 tablespoon nutritional yeast flakes

1 tablespoon arrowroot starch

1 tablespoon apple cider vinegar

1/2 teaspoon sea salt or to taste

Add all the ingredients to a high-powered blender. Blend on high for 2 minutes, or until completely smooth. Transfer to a small saucepan and whisk constantly over medium heat for 5 minutes, or until it just becomes thick and slightly stretchy. Be careful not to overheat.

Be Kind to Your Blender | *If you're not using a high-speed blender (e.g., Vitamix or Blendtec), soak the cashews in water for 2 hours or boil them for 10 minutes to soften before blending.*

No Nuts? No Problem | *To keep this nut-free, use shelled hemp seeds.*

CASHEW // HEMP SEED CHEDDAR CHEESE

Makes 1 1/3 cups | 15 minutes or less

1/2 cup raw cashews or shelled hemp seeds*

2/3 cup filtered water

1/4 cup drained and roughly chopped jarred roasted red peppers

2 tablespoons nutritional yeast flakes

1 tablespoon plus 1 teaspoon arrowroot starch

1 tablespoon apple cider vinegar

1/2 teaspoon sea salt or to taste

Add all the ingredients to a high-powered blender. Blend on high for 2 minutes, or until completely smooth. Transfer to a small saucepan and whisk constantly over medium heat for 5 minutes, or until it just becomes thick and slightly stretchy. Be careful not to overheat.

Be Kind to Your Blender | *If you're not using a high-speed blender (e.g., Vitamix or Blendtec), soak the cashews in water for 2 hours or boil them for 10 minutes to soften before blending.*

No Nuts? No Problem | *To keep this nut-free, use shelled hemp seeds.*

HOMEMADE CHOCOLATE

Makes 2/3 cup | 15 minutes or less

1/3 cup cacao butter discs or roughly chopped chunks

1/4 cup cacao powder

2 tablespoons pure maple syrup

Melt the cacao butter in a double boiler or bain-marie over low heat until just melted. Be careful not to overheat or it will seize and take on a gritty texture. Remove from the heat and whisk in the cacao powder and maple syrup until smooth and glossy. Use as is or pour into a chocolate mold and freeze to set. Keep chilled in the refrigerator or freezer.

5-MINUTE CARAMEL SAUCE

Makes 1 1/4 cups | 15 minutes or less

1/2 cup pure maple syrup

1/2 cup creamy natural almond butter*

1/3 cup virgin coconut oil

2 teaspoons pure vanilla extract

1/4 teaspoon fine-grain sea salt

In a small saucepan, whisk together all the ingredients over medium-low heat until smooth and glossy (about 3–5 minutes). Remove from the heat and let cool slightly. As the caramel cools to room temperature, it thickens and takes on a perfect drizzle-worthy quality.

Enjoy over ice cream, apples, or straight from a spoon. Store in the refrigerator in an airtight jar or container for up to 1 month.

No Nuts? No Problem | *To keep this nut-free, swap out the almond butter for sunflower butter or tahini.*

Remix It | *Use whichever nut butter your heart desires to remix this sweet sauce. Think peanut butter, cashew butter, hazelnut butter, Brazil nut butter, etc.*

COCONUT WHIPPED CREAM

Makes 2 cups | 15 minutes or less

1 (14-ounce) can full-fat coconut milk, refrigerated for at least 8 hours

1 tablespoon pure maple syrup

Seeds from 1 vanilla bean (optional)

Chill a large metal mixing bowl in the freezer for 15 minutes.

Once the mixing bowl is chilled, remove the can of coconut milk from the refrigerator. Open the can and scoop only the solid white cream into the chilled bowl, avoiding the coconut water at the bottom of the can. (Discard the coconut water or reserve it for another use.)

Using a hand whisk or stand mixer with whisk attachments, whisk the coconut cream for 3 minutes or until fluffy. Add the maple syrup and vanilla bean seeds (if using) and whisk for another 1–2 minutes or until fluffy with stiff peaks.

Transfer to an airtight jar or container. Store in the refrigerator for up to 4 days. After chilling, use a hand whisk to re-whip to desired texture.

WITH GRATITUDE, HUGS + HIGH FIVES

To the loyal, generous, and talented people who each gave a piece of their heart to this book, thank you, thank you, thank you.

To each and every one of the devoted, kind, and encouraging Blissful Basil readers, thank you from the bottom of my heart. Without you, this book would be nothing more than a daydream. With you, it became a dream come true.

A huge thank-you to my wonderful literary agent, MacKenzie Fraser-Bub. You planted the cookbook seed and watered it with your empowering sense of optimism. Thank you for turning my long-held dream into a reality and for guiding me through every twist and turn along the way.

Endless gratitude and thanks to my publisher, Glenn Yeffeth, for this amazing opportunity. And to the BenBella team—Heather, Lindsay, Leah, Sarah, Jessika, Adrienne, and Alicia—thank you for bringing this book to life with your knowledge, creativity, and steadfast efforts. A gigantic thank-you and resounding high five to my gifted editor, Maria Hart, for giving such thorough care to each and every sentence in this book; you saw my vision and nurtured it to fruition. Thank you also to my copyeditor, Karen Levy, for noticing the small stuff and polishing the details.

To my devoted recipe testers—Emily Rose Aragona, Celeste Jackson, Mike Jackson, Sally Zollers, Kandy Melillo, Amy Baughman, Christeleny Berner, Sara Glaviano, Abby Mangold, T. Vincent Longfield, Lili Barelli, Jessica Daniels Burt, and Yeming Rankin—thank you for the hours you dedicated to transforming and fine-tuning these recipes. This book is more delicious because of you!

To my parents, all four of you, thank you for being my biggest cheerleaders. Mom, thank you for teaching me the value of self-care and gently nudging me in the direction of my dreams. Whether in life or in the kitchen, you've supported and believed in me no matter the undertaking and even when there has been reason to believe otherwise—like that time I took up baking and clumsily dumped five pounds of sugar onto your kitchen floor, for instance. To my dad, Dave, thank you for reminding me to stop and savor the little things—a delicious bunch of grapes, the chocolaty tip of an ice cream cone—and for teaching me the importance of working extra hard on the little details. From building beautiful homes to creating the perfect bowl of ice cream, your devotion to the details is inspiring. To my stepdad (aka "pops"), Mike, thank you for teaching me the value of investing in memories, for taking me under your wing in the kitchen, and for fully opening your heart to our family—life wouldn't be complete without you. To my stepmom, Deb, thank you for sharing your sunshiny optimism and nurturing kindness with everyone who surrounds you, no matter the circumstances; your good vibes are contagious. Oh yes, and thank you for creating insanely delicious vegan dishes on a whim.

To my siblings, thank you for your unconditional encouragement. To my brother Brad, thank you for being my trusted confidant and sounding board in life and throughout this process. You have the biggest, kindest heart of anyone I know, and I'm a better person because of you. To my sister, Morgan, thank you for your constant enthusiasm and heartfelt reminders that there was, in fact, a light at the end of the cookbook tunnel! To my littlest brother, David, thank you for your brilliant, sharp-as-a-tack business ideas and for entertaining the passion for physics I randomly discovered while procrastinating on book edits one night.

And with boundless, unending gratitude, thank you to my husband, Dan. Thank you for your unwavering support and patience, especially during the nine months when the kitchen was in shambles and date nights morphed into recipe-testing sessions. Thank you for being the ultimate taste tester and providing feedback for every recipe that made the cut (and selflessly sacrificing your taste buds for the ones that didn't). Thank you for writing "YOU'VE GOT THIS" in big, bold letters on the chalkboard in our kitchen when I most needed it. And thank you for transforming tears into laughter with your spirited sense of humor. Your compassion and playfulness infuse my days with warmth and possibility, and the world is a better place with you in it. I love you.

ABOUT THE AUTHOR

Ashley Melillo is the writer, photographer, and recipe-creator behind Blissful Basil (www.blissful-basil.com), a blog dedicated to unearthing the happiest side of life through wholesome, plant-based foods. A school psychologist by day and a vegan food blogger by night, Ashley is fascinated with the way that diet and lifestyle choices affect physical, cognitive, and emotional wellness. She incorporates a wide array of natural, health-enhancing ingredients into her recipes with the hope of guiding others on their path toward improved well-being all while enjoying delicious food (read: you can have your health and eat cake, too!). Ashley holds a Certificate in Plant-Based Nutrition and her recipes have been featured in *Women's Health*, *Redbook*, *The Huffington Post*, and *Shape*, among others. She lives in Chicago with her husband, Dan, and their orange tabby cat, Jack.

INDEX

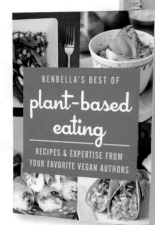